COLLABORATIVE GOVERNANCE

Traditional governance, even when it is functioning effectively and fairly, often produces clear winners and clear losers, leaving smoldering resentments that flare up whenever there is a shift in the balance of power. Over the past two and a half decades, a new style of governance has arisen to disrupt some of that winner-takes-all dynamic, offering parties a means to collectively navigate their interests in a highly focused and democratic way. *Collaborative Governance* is the first comprehensive practice-based textbook on the topic, presenting a solid grounding in relevant theory while also focusing on case studies, process design, and practical tools. Bringing together theory and tools from the fields of negotiation and mediation, as well as political science and public administration, this book introduces students and practitioners to the theory of collaborative governance in the context of practical applications.

Coverage includes:

- A connection of the practices of collaborative governance with the field's theoretical underpinnings;
- Tools for students and practitioners of collaborative governance—as well as public administrators and other possible participants in collaborative governance processes—to discern when collaborative governance is appropriate in politically complex, real-world settings;
- A roadmap for students, practitioners, and process participants to help them design—and effectively participate in—productive, efficient, and fair collaborative governance processes;
- An exploration of constitutional democracy and the ways in which collaborative governance can be used as a tool in building a more just, fair, and functional society.

Collaborative Governance is an ideal primary textbook in public administration, planning, and political science courses, as well as a jargon-free primer for professionals looking to learn more about the theory and practice of this important field.

Stephen Greenwood is the Director of Training and Academic Services at the National Policy Consensus Center in the Hatfield School of Government at Portland State University, recognized as one of the nation's most prolific university-based centers for advancing innovative, collaborative approaches for addressing public issues. In his current position, he has designed and led collaborative governance and leadership training both nationally and internationally. He is also the lead for Portland State University's online Graduate Certificate Program in Collaborative Governance and teaches the graduate-level class, "Foundations of Collaborative Governance."

Laurel Singer is the Executive Director of the National Policy Consensus Center in the Hatfield School of Government at Portland State University. Since joining NPCC in 2006, Laurel has served in several leadership roles, including directing NPCC's Oregon Consensus, Oregon Solutions, and training programs. For close to 30 years, Laurel has served as a champion for the use of collaborative decision-making and problem-solving. Her work as a private practice mediator for over 16 years focused on designing, convening, and facilitating collaborative process to address complex public policy across a wide range of issues. She is currently a founding faculty member in PSU's fully online graduate certificate in collaborative governance.

Wendy Willis is the founder and Director of Oregon's Kitchen Table, a statewide civic engagement program of the National Policy Consensus Center in the Hatfield School of Government at Portland State University. Wendy also serves as the Executive Director of the Deliberative Democracy Consortium, a global alliance of leading scholars and organizations working in the fields of deliberative democracy, public participation, and civic engagement. Wendy is also a widely published poet and essayist, writing frequently about American democracy and civic life. Her most recent book, *These are Strange Times, My Dear*, was released in 2019.

COLLABORATIVE GOVERNANCE

Principles, Processes, and Practical Tools

Stephen Greenwood, Laurel Singer, and Wendy Willis

Routledge
Taylor & Francis Group

NEW YORK AND LONDON

First published 2021
by Routledge
605 Third Avenue, New York, NY 10158

and by Routledge
2 Park Square, Milton Park, Abingdon, Oxon, OX14 4RN

Routledge is an imprint of the Taylor & Francis Group, an informa business

© 2021 Taylor & Francis

Library of Congress Cataloging-in-Publication Data
A catalog record for this title has been requested

ISBN: 978-0-367-77606-0 (hbk)
ISBN: 978-0-367-77601-5 (pbk)
ISBN: 978-1-003-17206-2 (ebk)

Typeset in Bembo
by KnowledgeWorks Global Ltd.

CONTENTS

FOREWORD

In 2014, I was appointed as Dean of the College of Urban and Public Affairs at Portland State University (PSU), OR. I came to PSU in large measure because of its long-term and nationally-recognized experience in and commitment to university-community engagement. The university's motto, "Let Knowledge Serve the City," was a powerful magnet.

A leading light in the College (and University) in efforts to utilize the knowledge, expertise, and capacity of the academy in partnership with community to create positive change is the National Policy Consensus Center. As a new dean, I quickly understood that this unit—comprised of leaders and staff with cumulative experience in community development, policy advocacy, and dispute resolution—was actively engaged in advancing collaborative solutions to challenging, sometimes "wicked" problems. I recognized that NPCC and its ancillary programs had learned powerful lessons for bringing people from diverse backgrounds and perspectives together. Through carefully crafted and mediated conversations, NPCC teams were able to empower community members, local governments and organizations and other relevant stakeholders to find their way, together, to solutions to the challenging problems.

The world we live in today faces an array of complex social, economic, and governance challenges. If these challenges are not resolved, opportunities are lost and harmful consequences are often sustained. On the other hand, collaborative solutions can change the trajectory, tap innovation, and generate positive change. Resolving these challenges—often in the face of deep division, partisanship and often injustice—can generate real and positive innovation.

Recognizing the talents of the NPCC team (along with that of colleagues in similar university centers focused on community collaboration), and the need for this work in greater society, I urged the team to share the knowledge—to disseminate strategies and models that were being activated to produce collaborative results. I made two suggestions: create a create a certificate program to advance professional development of those engaged in community problem solving and write a book or manual to guide those seeking to resolve complex, multi-disciplinary problems. My colleagues took me up on both. PSU now offers a graduate certificate in Collaborative Governance and the NPCC team has created this wonderful book.

Collaborative Governance: Principles, Processes, and Practical Tools provides a powerful guidebook to organizing efforts to create collaborative solutions. It commences with an exploration of the meanings and conceptions of this work—embracing terminology and perspectives that may be quite new to some. The book then outlines a myriad of processes and skills that can advance progress in collaborative decision-making. This guidebook is a must for those who want to join the cadre of people working to advance the lives and opportunities of our communities, large and small. The learning provided here empowers and inspires greater application of collaborative solution making.

Stephen Percy
President
Portland State University

ACKNOWLEDGMENTS

This book is based on the experiences of hundreds of people who have facilitated, participated in, and studied collaborative governance processes. Every day, we learn from our friends and colleagues at the National Policy Consensus Center, as well as from the creative and hard-working Oregonians who lead and participate in collaborative governance processes around the state. In addition, we have had the great good fortune to learn alongside some of the best mediators and facilitators in the country, many of whom are in private practice right here in Oregon. We also have tremendous academic partners and colleagues at Portland State University, including Dr. Craig Shinn, Dr. Connie Ozawa, Dr. Rick Morgan, Dr. Jennifer Allen, and our own Director of Research, Dr. Rebecca McLain.

We are also incredibly fortunate to benefit from supportive and creative leaders across the university, including Dr. Birol Yesilada, Director of the Mark O. Hatfield School of Government; Dr. Sy Adler, Dean of the College of Urban and Public Affairs; and Dr. Stephen Percy, President of Portland State University. All three of these extraordinary leaders have had faith in the project from the beginning.

We are also tremendously grateful to our colleagues who make up the University Network for Collaborative Governance. They always pick up the phone when we call.

We owe a debt to the groundbreaking work of those early leaders in the field, including Christine Carlson, Greg Wolf, and the board members of the Policy Consensus Initiative. We are also thankful for our students—the leaders of tomorrow—who always push our thinking forward.

We also wish to acknowledge the contribution of Dr. Richard Ingraham, whose ground-breaking teachings on group process have had a major influence on our work.

We offer thanks to Jonna Kangasoja of Akordi and Lasse Peltonen from the University of Eastern Finland for instigating creative thinking and being tremendous colleagues.

Many thanks to the whole staff at Routledge, especially Laura Stearns Varley and Katie Horsfall for seeing the potential of this book and offering keen thinking and encouragement at every step along the way.

Thank you to our families, who have tolerated late nights and long meetings, even on our days off.

We are boundlessly grateful to those colleagues who reviewed and commented on earlier drafts of this book. Mary Forst offered illuminating case examples and encouragement on early drafts of the chapters on assessment and design. And, in their generous and close readings of the manuscript, Sarah Giles brought a fine writer's eye and a passionate concern for the often under-represented members of our communities; Turner Odell brought deep expertise in assessments and unmatched attention to detail; and Cat McGinnis brought her intense focus and uncanny ability to sniff out where a word or a phrase or a citation was not quite right. This book is so much the better for their contributions to it.

Finally, Kristen Wright is in a category all her own. An essential member of our center's instructional team, she has contributed at every stage in the development and writing of this book. Her insights about the field, her just-right questions, and her thoughtful reviews have left a significant imprint on the final product. When it was needed, she pushed us to clarify an important concept or choose an incisive example to illustrate a point. This book is hers as much as anyone's, and we could not have done it without her.

INTRODUCTION

In 2010, the United States Fish and Wildlife Service (USFWS) determined that the Greater Western Sage-Grouse should be listed under the Endangered Species Act. The sage-grouse is a shy, ground-dwelling bird that can fly fast but not far. They are known for their elaborate mating rituals in which the males puff up their bright yellow throat sacks and engage in a strutting "dance" to attract the females. After mating, the hens nest on the ground, using sagebrush and tall grass for cover. Because of their need for both space and a very specific landscape, sage-grouse are particularly susceptible to habitat disruption, predators, and development. As a result of increased human presence, wildfire, and the spread of invasive species, by 2010, the Western United States had experienced a twenty percent loss in the sage-grouse population, with further losses predicted. Though warranted, the federal government did not immediately list the sage-grouse, because other, higher-priority species took precedence, and resources were limited. Shortly thereafter, a federal court gave USFWS approximately five years to make a final determination about whether or not to list the Western Sage-Grouse.

The decision whether or not to list the sage-grouse was a significant one. There are more than forty-three million acres of sagebrush habitat in the western United States, with eighteen millions of those acres in Oregon alone. That habitat spans public and private lands, is home to ranchers and other human residents, and is the location for iconic and heavily-used recreational sites. As a result, the decision to list the sage-grouse would have had far-reaching consequences for Central and Eastern Oregon, along with much of the rest of the Intermountain West.

Once the court set the timeline, the Governor of Oregon, in partnership with the Federal Bureau of Land Management, and the United States Natural Resource Conservation Service, convened a large cross-sector group to develop a collaborative approach to safeguard the sage-grouse and its habitat while also protecting the economic well-being of the region. The group coalesced as the Sage-Grouse Conservation Partnership (SageCon), which ultimately engaged hundreds of people and dozens of agencies and organizations in the effort to meet those dual goals.

Though the details are complex, the bottom line is relatively simple. The collaborative governance group met for over three years, simultaneously coordinating their work with eleven other Western states to develop the Greater Sage-Grouse Conservation Strategy, which resulted in a detailed plan and, significantly, in the USFWS declining to list the sage-grouse as an endangered species.

After the agreement was reached, Secretary of the Interior Sally Jewell praised the work of SageCon:

> This is truly a historic effort – one that represents extraordinary collaboration across the American West…. It demonstrates that the Endangered Species Act is an effective and flexible tool and a critical catalyst for conservation – ensuring that future generations can enjoy the diversity of wildlife that we do today. The epic conservation effort will benefit Westerners and hundreds of species that call this iconic landscape home, while giving states, businesses and communities the certainty they need to plan for sustainable economic development. (qtd. in "Historic")

We begin this book with that story because it contains everything. There are actors from all three *branches* of government—legislative, executive, and judicial—as well as all *levels* of government—federal, state, tribal, and local. There are ranchers and environmentalists and recreators. There are idiosyncratic birds. There are grazing cattle and off-road vehicles and wildfires and invasive juniper, all of which threaten sage-grouse habitat. There are legacy ranchers and relative newcomers to the West. There are decades-old disputes and budding friendships. There are obscure constitutional claims alongside a federal regulatory scheme that has wide-reaching power.

The end of the SageCon story has yet to be written. Changes in federal leadership along with constantly shifting dynamics create a fraught atmosphere for the parties who are still working to hold the agreement together and to fully execute on it. As individual parties come and go and as the incentives for collaboration shift—one way or another—the calculus changes. And yet, as of this writing, the SageCon group continues to meet and work to implement the details of the plan. The final outcome is far from certain and, in the end, it will likely be a mixed story of collaborative triumph and disappointment.

But even in that uncertainty—maybe because of that uncertainty—the story is an instructive one. In the midst of all that drama, turmoil, and complexity, the parties have always had a choice. They either could let traditional governance run its course, with the various interests rushing to press whatever levers of power they have access to, or they could collaborate. They chose the latter.

The sage-grouse collaborative and all it entails lays bare the complex environment in which the public's work is being conducted. Even when traditional governance is functioning effectively and fairly, there are often clear winners and clear losers, leaving smoldering resentments that flare up whenever there is a shift in the balance of power. Over the past two and a half decades, collaborative governance has arisen to disrupt some of that winner-takes-all dynamic and to offer parties a means to collectively navigate their interests in a highly focused and democratic way. Though the SageCon project was not the first complex, multi-year, high-stakes example of collaborative governance, it is one that dramatizes some of its most common instigators, the power of the approach, and some of the changeable forces that both promote and threaten its success.

The uncertainty of the future of SageCon is in many ways a sign of the times. As we finish this book, we are in the seventh month of a global pandemic— more than 200,000 Americans have died and millions more have become ill with COVID-19. The entire world has suffered tremendous loss of life and a downward economic spiral in a compound crisis unlike anything experienced in several generations. Meanwhile, the United States is in the midst of a movement that will no longer allow institutions—or any of us—to ignore the legacy of racism and white supremacy that have undermined the democratic legitimacy of the country since its founding. All the while, citizen mistrust of government is pervasive, American political life is as polarized as it has ever been, and every democratic institution from the presidency to the media to the electoral system is buckling under the stress of the moment. Many days, it seems as if the future of democracy itself is in question.

On several fronts, we are at a moment of reckoning. Two future scenarios seem equally possible—one in which institutions collapse into a chaotic and uncertain power-grab and another in which we begin to collectively rebuild a more just, resilient, and equitable society. Though the future is unknown, we believe that collective activity and joint action—including collaborative governance—could play an important role in seeding the latter, more promising version of the future. We believe that collaborative governance and other forms of collective activity can be useful tools in rebuilding a new generation of more just and democratic systems. We do not say this to suggest that collaborative governance is synonymous with activism and social movements. Rather, we believe that collaborative governance is complementary and additive to social movements. As the injustices of the current systems are fully exposed and disrupted, collaborative governance can and should provide a platform for a newly envisioned form of democratic self-governance. It can serve as a forum to reconcile emerging interests as they collide with existing institutions.

But we are keenly aware that we are releasing this book into a moving river. Traditional governance and public decision-making are changing rapidly, and undoubtedly, so will the practice of collaborative governance. In particular, we have spent the last few years wrestling with questions about how white supremacy and racism play out in our institutions, our communities, and our processes. We have modified our thinking and our practice substantially in recent years, and the results are promising. But our work in that regard is unfinished. We have a long way to go, and we are in a cycle of continuous learning about how to make our own practice of collaborative governance more just and responsive to the needs of communities that have often been left out of both traditional and collaborative governance. This book drops a pin in the place we find ourselves at this moment.

And yet, this book is already twenty years in the making. In many ways, the three of us follow the evolution of the field. Among us, there is a lawyer, a public administrator, and a mediator. Each of us worked in the traditional structures of our chosen fields—Wendy was a public defender. Stephen was a regional director for the department of environmental quality. Laurel started out as a mediator. And, in each instance, we found ourselves looking for a more holistic way to solve public problems. That search led each of us—via different paths—to the National Policy Consensus Center (NPCC) in the Mark O. Hatfield School of Government at Portland State University. Between the three of us, we have nearly sixty years of experience in the practice of collaborative governance, each of us with a slightly different practice area. In this book, we hope to bring those decades of experience together with collaborative governance theory and research.

And it is not just us. NPCC has a staff of approximately twenty and is the home of Oregon Consensus, which primarily works on agreement-seeking; Oregon Solutions, which is a platform for collective action; and Oregon's Kitchen Table, which works to engage everyday Oregonians in public decision-making. In addition, projects from all three programs have evolved into collaborative systems, which are longer-term and more structured collaborative governance arrangements.

Over the years, NPCC and its staff members and associates have managed and facilitated hundreds of collaborative governance projects in every county in Oregon. Last year alone, we worked on more than sixty projects. Though collaborative governance took root in the environmental and natural resource arenas first, we have been involved in projects touching on everything from early childhood education to housing to community development.

Although the three of us all situate ourselves squarely in the *practice* of collaborative governance, we are housed in a university, and we all have a deep interest in the theory and principles that underlie the practice. That interest led us to create the Collaborative Governance Certificate Program in the Hatfield School—a five-course graduate-level certificate offered to both professionals and current masters and doctoral students. It was in the context of that program that this book was born.

Though there are many important and helpful resources available for students interested in collaborative governance, we found a need for a comprehensive textbook that centers the practice of collaborative governance and yet still locates that practice within the theoretical and legal underpinnings of democratic governance. Throughout this book, we rely on the scholarship that has come before, and we also draw heavily on our own—and our colleagues'—experiences in the field.

In this book, we define and describe the practice of collaborative governance with four important purposes in mind: (1) to legitimately situate the aspirations of collaborative governance within a constitutional democracy and to establish collaborative governance as a significant tool in building a more just, fair, and functional society; (2) to connect the practices of collaborative governance with the field's theoretical underpinnings and to illustrate how the granular details of practice make the difference in maintaining procedural and substantive integrity; (3) to offer students and practitioners of collaborative governance— as well as public administrators and other possible participants in collaborative governance processes—the tools to discern when collaborative governance is appropriate in politically complex, real-world settings; and (4) to offer students, practitioners, and process participants a roadmap to help them design—or at least effectively participate in—productive, efficient, and fair collaborative governance processes.

This book is organized into three sections, followed by a conclusion. In the first section, we begin by setting out the context, philosophy, and theory in which collaborative governance operates. In chapter 1, we define collaborative governance by setting forth six definitional norms that distinguish collaborative governance from both traditional governance and from other types of collective decision-making and implementation. In chapter 2, we examine the constitutional and legal framework in which collaborative governance operates, and we specifically address some of the foundational critiques of collaborative governance. In chapter 3, we set out the three types of collaborative governance and how they are similar and different. In chapter 4, we explore some of the fundamental human and social dynamics that affect the decision whether to collaborate and then the quality of that collaboration.

In the second section, we focus on the details of collaborative governance processes from start to finish. In chapter 5, we introduce the assessment process, with a focus on determining whether a proposed project is appropriate for collaborative governance. Chapter 6 explores how to design and organize a collaborative governance process. Chapter 7 focuses on joint learning and the stages of deliberation and decision-making in a collaborative governance process. Chapter 8 examines the implementation of collaborative governance solutions and then the steps that follow the formal conclusion of a process, including evaluation and adaption.

In the third section, we explore some of the skills and practices that improve the effectiveness of collaborative governance processes. In chapter 9, we examine some common issues that arise in a collaborative governance process and introduce both theoretical frameworks and practical tools to help address those issues. Chapter 10 offers a primer on individual leadership skills to improve participants' and facilitators' ability to effectively participate in collaborative governance processes.

Finally, the conclusion looks forward to emerging issues in collaborative governance, with a particular focus on the questions left open in this book and in the field in general.

Reference

"Historic Conservation Campaign Protects Greater Sage-Grouse." *United States Department of the Interior*, 10 May 2017, www.doi.gov/pressreleases/historic-conservation-campaign-protects-greater-sage-grouse. Press release.

SECTION 1

Definitions, Context, and Dynamics

In this section, we define collaborative governance and put it in a historical, legal, and behavioral context. We examine how collaborative governance is similar to and different from traditional governance structures and how it can play a role in a more democratic society. We also explore some of the behavioral and group dynamics that frequently play out in collaborative governance processes.

In chapter 1, we define collaborative governance, distinguishing it from traditional governance and other forms of collaboration and grounding it in six definitional norms. In chapter 2, we examine collaborative governance in a constitutional context and consider some of the foundational critiques of collaborative governance. In chapter 3, we introduce the three typologies of collaborative governance and begin to explore how the differences and similarities among them might be significant in designing and executing processes on the ground. Finally, in chapter 4, we walk through some of the fundamental dynamics of collaboration and how they play out among the participants in collaborative governance processes.

This section is the most theoretical of the three in this book, drawing on a variety of disciplines and traditions to locate collaborative governance both in time and in aspiration. Even so, our purpose for exploring the theoretical underpinnings of the field is primarily to inform and enrich the practice of collaborative governance. In the end, it is the practice that defines and describes collaborative governance and also determines whether collaborative governance lives up to its democratic potential.

1

DEFINITIONS AND DESCRIPTIONS

Introduction

Because the field we have come to know as collaborative governance was born out of necessity and grounded in practice first, scholars are often playing catch-up, attempting to define the term in a way that is consistent with political and administrative theory that also rings true to practitioners working in communities. Though the practices we would now identify as the fundamentals of collaborative governance began to spread in the United States as early as the 1970s, the corresponding theory has only started to fully blossom over the past couple of decades.

Our interest here is in defining and describing collaborative governance in a way that: (1) highlights the relationship to and differences from traditional governance structures and practices; (2) sets it apart from forms of cooperation or joint action less tied to public purpose; and (3) roots it in practices that confer democratic legitimacy, more satisfying and fair experiences for stakeholders, and improved outcomes for communities.

In order to dramatize some of the choices at stake, we offer an example from our own work here in Oregon—the Tillamook Bay Flooding Reduction Project. Tillamook County is a northwestern Oregon coastal community named for a band of the Salish people who lived in the region. The city of Tillamook itself lies just to the west of the Coast Range, near the mouth of Tillamook Bay. The economy of the area is deeply dependent on dairy farming and the manufacture and marketing of dairy products such as milk, cheese, yogurt, and ice cream.

Five rivers descend through the Coast Range—which separates the ocean from the Willamette Valley—and then converge in Tillamook County just before they spill into the bay and then into the Pacific Ocean. Combine all that water with nearly 200 inches of rain per year, and flooding—sometimes catastrophic flooding—becomes a regular occurrence. Between 1996 and 2000, Tillamook County—with its population of 25,000 people—suffered $60 million in flood damage. Then, in December 2007, two typhoons met up over the central Pacific before they slammed into the Oregon Coast. Tillamook County was deluged with nearly seven inches of rain over two days, blocking access to the county from three sides and causing power outages that lasted for nearly a week in some communities. The county suffered $26 million in damages from that storm alone.

Over the years, a number of agencies deployed traditional flood management tactics. The U.S. Army Corps of Engineers, for example, constructed and maintained jetties and spillways as part of its mission to "deliver vital public and military engineering services ... and reduce risks from disasters" ("Mission"). But the cycle of storms and flooding continued, causing millions of dollars in damages and leaving the community increasingly frustrated with government's lack of effective response. In previous years, other federal agencies had tried to work with local stakeholders to address the problem in a more holistic way, but those unsuccessful efforts were seen by many local leaders as a federal intrusion on local autonomy and actually worsened working relationships.

As a result, in 2006, the governor of Oregon asked a state senator and a local county commissioner to convene a multi-sector collaborative governance group[1] to consider how better to mitigate flooding and its effects in the Tillamook Basin. He also invited our center (NPCC) to serve as a collaborative platform and provide facilitation staff. The goal of the group was "to develop and implement a plan to reduce flooding and the adverse impacts of flooding while incorporating environmental, social and economic values in the development of short- and long-term solutions" ("Tillamook"). The group included representatives from five federal agencies, seven state agencies, and several local governments, as well as team members from the nearby community college, the county farm bureau, several associations focused on environmental concerns, and representatives from the dairy industry.

As the group began meeting, there were many different opinions about how best to address flooding in the region. Though some team members openly expressed cynicism about the possibility of success, the collaborative governance group brainstormed almost twenty possible projects to reduce impacts of flooding in the region. Through an iterative year-long process in which the team worked together both in committees and as a full group, the team eventually agreed on nine projects to address flooding, which led to a $1 million appropriation from the Oregon Legislature to support their efforts. Once the collaborative governance group had agreed to the projects, they entered a second phase that focused on working together to implement them. Eight of the nine projects were eventually implemented, culminating most recently in a large-scale flood relief and habitat restoration project, which demonstrably reduced flooding impacts and restored thirteen miles of coho salmon habitat.

The experiences in Tillamook and other case examples set out in this book illustrate the breadth and depth of collaborative governance on the ground. Here we seek to explore that breadth and depth without struggling too much with definitional strictures. Others have done an excellent job of attempting to pin down working definitions in order to avoid some of the sloppiness and inconsistencies born out of a rapidly evolving field.

Chris Ansell and Allison Gash, in their groundbreaking 2008 article, "Collaborative Governance in Theory and Practice," defined collaborative governance somewhat narrowly, placing government in the center. Collaborative governance, as they defined it, is "a governing arrangement where one or more public agencies directly engage non-state stakeholders in a collective decision-making process that is formal, consensus-oriented, and deliberative and that aims to make or implement public policy or manage public programs or assets" (544).

More recently—and more broadly—Kirk Emerson and Tina Nabatchi defined collaborative governance to be "the processes and structures of public policy decision-making and management that engage people across the boundaries of public agencies, levels of government, and/or the public, private, and civic spheres to carry out a public purpose that could not otherwise be accomplished" (2).

Though we find both of those definitions theoretically and philosophically helpful, for our purposes, the most important definition of collaborative governance ultimately resides in how it is practiced. On the surface, collaborative governance often looks like a group of public-spirited individuals sitting around a table staring at a flip chart. As a result, it is sometimes difficult to distinguish collaborative governance from many other forms of cooperative human activity. Subtle distinctions are meaningful, and the quality of the design and deliberation make a big difference in whether the work of the group meets its promise as an innovative democratic practice or whether it bypasses accountability measures to jeopardize the group's legitimacy or whether it is just an ineffective and frustrating set of meetings with no clear purpose and fuzzy outcomes. Small decisions really matter.

Throughout this chapter and the ones that follow, we distinguish between three types of collaborative governance processes: (1) agreement seeking, (2) collective action, and (3) collaborative systems. While any given group may engage in multiple types of collaboration, there are certain characteristics of each type that are helpful in defining and describing—and distinguishing between—particular collaborative governance groups. We go into greater detail about the collaborative governance typologies in chapter 3, but we offer a brief description here to clarify some of the distinctions we make later in this chapter. First, *agreement-seeking* processes stem from what is sometimes known as multi-party dispute resolution. Although not all agreement-seeking collaborations involve high-conflict issues, those projects typically look and feel the most like multi-party consensus processes. Second, in *collective action* cases, the desired action or set of actions has more or less been agreed upon by the group, but no one agency or entity can implement the strategy on their own. The collaborative group is convened to determine both how the project will be implemented and what each stakeholder will contribute to the implementation. Finally, sometimes there is a need for a longer-term venue for collaborative problem solving. That group can be focused on agreement-seeking or collective action or both. We refer to these types of groups as "collaborative systems."

In this chapter, we take a prismatic approach to defining collaborative governance in an effort to avoid rigid definitions while also dramatizing some of the choice points that collaborative governance groups frequently face. First, we explain why we think it is important to distinguish between true collaborative governance and other less publicly oriented forms of collaboration. Second, we set forth the six definitional norms that are both aspirational and rooted in practice. Finally, we examine the role of the "collaborative platform" and take on the question of "neutrality," which has traditionally been considered a hallmark of legitimate collaborative governance but has the potential to replicate institutional racism and other injustices.

Why We Distinguish Collaborative Governance from Other Forms of Collaboration

We are fully aware that the dividing line between "collaborative governance" and other forms of collaboration is not always either clear or bright. Emerson and Nabatchi remind us that collaboration is "relatively easy to understand, being derived from Latin and literally meaning to co-labor or work together" (16). In the *Practical Guide to Collaborative Governance*, Christine Carlson defined collaboration as

> a catch-all term used to describe various processes that bring people together across sectors through various forms of public engagement to address policy issues. Such processes may also be known as *consensus building, conflict resolution, policy dialogue, and joint problem solving*, among other things. (6)

Collaborative governance is often utilized to resolve public policy differences, and looked to as an antidote for the stalemate and dysfunction of our current political climate. In other instances, collaborative governance has become an informal structure used to align and combine the authorities, resources, and actions of multiple organizations across sectors to implement solutions to public problems. It has become axiomatic that collaboration promises solutions that no individual organization or even sector could achieve on its own.

Because collaborative governance has been driven by the increased desire for improved public processes and outcomes, a good deal of the literature focuses on the necessity for and mechanics of effective, fair, and efficient collaboration. Though it is attractive to think of collaboration as a plug-and-play tool used to improve public outcomes, it is important to note that collaborative governance is an add-on, rather than a substitute for our legally established democratic processes, intended to make them work better. In addition, as detailed in the next chapter, in the context of a constitutional and representative democracy, collaborative governance should not be seen as a work-around, avoiding the messy inefficiencies of federalism, separation of powers, and anti-trust and anti-corruption laws.

In addition, we recognize that the word "collaboration" and its corollary, "collaborator," have some unsavory associations, particularly as they relate to World War II. For many, the very term "collaboration" suggests a connection to an occupying power in general and a treasonous cooperation with the Third Reich in particular. For still other organizations and individuals, particularly those whose work and identity are connected to dissent and protest against a particular government or set of policies, the notion of collaborating with a government that they find distasteful or immoral might be a nonstarter. As a result, in our work, we strive not to get too wedded to a particular set of terms. We understand that this terminology—as much as we struggle to define it precisely for ourselves—will require adaptations depending on the culture and circumstances of the particular context where it is being applied. In fact, there are many settings in which we do not refer to "collaborative governance" at all as we describe our work to community members because the term may either be fraught for the reasons set forth above or off-putting because it sounds overly bureaucratic and distant from the lived experiences of people and communities.

That said, we do hold ourselves to a high standard as we attempt to define the work. Collaborative governance, as we use the term, is not merely descriptive. It is also normative and aspirational. Collaborative governance—unlike other forms of collaboration—is both defined and constrained by rigorous practice and democratic norms. As a result, while "collaboration" can be defined rather broadly and functionally, it is important to precisely consider what we mean by "governance."

In its simplest form, governance merely refers to how a group collectively makes and implements decisions. Emerson and Nabatchi define it as "how actors use processes and make decisions to exercise authority and control, grant power, take action, and ensure performance—all of which are guided by sets of principles, norms, roles, and procedures around which actors converge" (15). In that sense, governance could refer to any group of individuals who have adopted some formal decision-making process—a church, a company, a co-op, a nonprofit, or even a family, presumably.

And yet, we do not consider that type of purely private decision-making to fall into the realm of collaborative governance, even if the actors come from a wide variety of institutions. For us, the distinguishing characteristic is that a collaborative governance process results in public benefit, which can include the resolution of a public dispute, the cooperative generation of public policy, or the coordinated effort to pool resources, authority, and/or expertise in order to implement a public project that is otherwise unlikely to come to pass.

Looked at that way, collaborative governance is not just an efficient way to work around government dysfunction, but is in fact profoundly democratic. Daniel Kemmis and Matthew McKinney write about collaborative governance as an emergent form of democracy and distinguish "collaborative democracy" from representative democracy, direct democracy, and even deliberative democracy (8, 9). As they and others argue, ordinary citizens[2] have often been held at a distance from administrative decision-making as bureaucracies have become more specialized, professionalized, and powerful. Collaborative governance, Kemmis and McKinney argue, returns to the basic democratic principle that those people most affected by the outcome of a decision must have meaningful input into the decision and its implementation (3). And Carmen Sirianni argues that "shared governance between elections" is essential to a renewed sense of citizens' efficacy in the public sphere and to a more robust democratic culture (ix).

Definitional Norms

That view of grassroots, inclusive, democratic decision-making aligns with our sense of collaborative governance. Neither collaboration alone nor improved government efficiency elevates a cooperative project to collaborative governance or "collaborative democracy," as Kemmis and McKinney refer to it (8). As a definitional matter, collaborative governance is bound by the norms and practices of a constitutional democracy, and those norms and practices both affect the experience of stakeholders and engender legitimacy in the broader community. In other words, the particularities of practice define whether a process falls under the rubric of collaborative governance or not. We believe that there are six norms to consider in determining whether a process meets the definition of collaborative governance: (1) public purpose, (2) cross-boundary participation, (3) representativeness, (4) inclusiveness and belonging, (5) shared authority and power-balancing, and (6) deliberativeness.

Public Purpose

Collaborative governance, in the sense that we use it, is intended to fulfill a public purpose. Though, as discussed earlier, collaboration is used to meet a variety of private needs, it is the public purpose that moves ordinary collaboration toward collaborative governance.

From very early on in the collaborative governance literature, scholars and practitioners have argued that traditional, siloed government agencies are increasingly incapable of dealing with the complex set of issues that have become known as "wicked problems." The "wicked problems" frame was first used in the early 1970s to describe problems that are intricate, interconnected, and have no clear boundaries or ready solutions.

As more and more of the problems that governments struggle with are wicked problems, the potential interventions have also become increasingly complex. Emerson and Nabatchi described it like this: "Because wicked problems ignore the boundaries that shape our public sphere, the responses to these problems must transcend these boundaries, including governmental, sectoral, jurisdictional, geographic, and even conceptual demarcations" (7). In short, the fact that wicked problems cannot be addressed by a single organization acting alone creates the conditions for collaborative governance.

Though wicked problems are not public issues by definition, the vast majority of complex, large-scale, and difficult-to-solve issues fall within the public sphere—climate change, generational poverty, mass migration, public lands disputes, pandemics—and collaborative governance, at least in the sense that we use it, is a means by which to address or at least better manage some of those complex public issues.

Cross-boundary Participation

One of the hallmarks of collaborative governance is that it crosses jurisdictional boundaries and involves multiple sectors. Some scholars and practitioners suggest that true collaborative governance *requires* participation from all three sectors—public, private, and civic. Although we do not draw such a bright line, we do note that collaborative governance most often involves two or more levels of government (federal, state, local, or tribal), typically involves multiple jurisdictions within the same level of government, and almost always engages at least two different sectors.

Often that broad-based participation is a matter of practicality. With regard to agreement-seeking processes, it is often necessary to include representatives from all three sectors in order to reach a decision that can satisfy a wide variety of interests and withstand litigation or political pressure or both. Similarly, in the context of collective action, if an issue is too complex for a single government entity to address on its own, it often requires resources, ideas, and political capital from multiple jurisdictions and multiple sectors. Take, for example, the Tillamook flooding project described earlier in this chapter, where the parties engaged in both agreement-seeking and collective action. In that case, the causes of flooding were too complex and there were too many divergent interests for the Army Corps of Engineers—or any other single agency—to address the issues alone. Instead, it took a team of twenty-three stakeholders, representing a diverse and divergent set of interests, to collectively decide on specific strategies to improve flood mitigation and management in the region. And then, those same stakeholders pooled their resources—and attracted additional ones—to engage in collective action and implement the projects upon which they had agreed.

Representativeness

The legitimacy of a collaborative governance process is almost entirely dependent on the integrity of its representativeness. Iris Marion Young argues that the promise of democracy itself is met only when "all members of a society in principle have the opportunity to try to influence public policy to serve or protect their interests" (17). She contends that every member of a society should have input into the "decisions and policies [that] condition a person's options for action" (23). And yet, Young recognizes that it would be impracticable—or "absurd," as she puts it—to include every single person affected in every single decision, no matter how trivial the interest (23). As a result, democracy itself relies on representativeness.

As in other aspects of a constitutional democracy, collaborative governance relies on representatives to carry the interests and values of particular individuals and communities to the broader group. Organizations outside government— particularly civic, grassroots, and advocacy organizations—often represent the interests of citizens whose voice otherwise might not be heard in the process. But the authenticity and legitimacy of that representativeness must be reinforced at each point in the process.

Young suggests that community members have a sense that they are authentically represented when: (1) the representative or representatives look after their interests; (2) the principles, values, and priorities that they believe should guide decision-making are voiced in the process; and (3) the representative or representatives share—or at least express—the experiences of their social group (134). Collaborative governance processes should attend to all three factors.

The legitimacy and accountability created by representativeness do not end with the composition of the group, however. If there is an understanding that an individual or an organization in the collaborative group represents a particular constituency, it is essential that those representatives continue to touch bases with that constituency in order to assure that their interests are being represented in the process. We sometimes refer to this as "the table behind the table" to mean that the collaborative governance group must not forget about those whose interests are essential to the process but who are represented by other individuals or organizations in the collaborative governance group. In addition, the collaborative governance group or subset of it may need to use the tools of civic engagement and public participation to better understand the interests—even the diffuse interests—of communities who may not be fully represented in the process.

Inclusiveness and Belonging

Representativeness alone, however, is not enough. In order for collaborative governance to fulfill its democratic promise, everyone at the table must be able to participate at their highest level, and that requires that the process be rigorously and persistently inclusive. Indeed, a persistent sense of *exclusion* from highly specialized bureaucratic decision-making is in part what propelled citizens and communities to seek other forms of policy-making, including collaborative governance. But because collaborative governance is in some sense a self-generating system, it is critical that the collaborative governance group and the agencies that sponsor it attend to inclusion at every step in the process.

Moreover, because collaborative governance is necessarily connected to institutions and their relationships to one another, collaborative governance processes run the risk of replicating structural racism and other long-term injustices baked into those institutions. Without attention and care to the dynamics of the group and the intentional disruption of systemic exclusion, collaborative governance cannot live up to its promise as a democratic innovation.

That said, however, there is tremendous potential to improve democratic access and procedural and substantive equity if the collaborative governance group commits itself to inclusion and belonging for everyone involved. There are several ways in which inclusion and belonging may be practiced in a collaborative governance group. Of primary importance is that the process eliminate the barriers and burdens for communities that traditionally have been excluded from public decision-making. For example, in producing the background materials for projects, we often work with translators in multiple languages and a plain-language translator in English to ensure that the materials are accessible to everyone. Representatives of agencies or advocacy groups will sometimes push back, arguing that some nuance or another is lost when technical vocabulary is eliminated. The upside, however, far outweighs the downside of losing technical details. Everyone begins the process with a shared understanding of the issues that the group is facing and is ready to bring a full panoply of resources to resolve the shared problem. On the contrary, if the issue is framed in the internal—and sometimes highly technical—language of the agencies, many participants already feel excluded before the process begins. But if everyday speech and shared understanding is the central value of the group, they begin to speak to one another in language that honors multiple ways of knowing and clarity rather than in a detached, technocratic language that serves to maintain the separation between agencies and "civilians."

A sense of belonging is both a close cousin to and a byproduct of persistent inclusion. If everyone—particularly those from historically underrepresented communities—feel as if they truly belong in and to the collaborative governance group, the group is much more functional and much more democratic. As john a. powell and Stephen Menedian put it, "The most important good we distribute to each other in society is membership. The right to belong is prior to all other distributive decisions since it is members who make those decisions" (32). They describe what they call "belongingness" as "an unwavering commitment to not simply tolerating and respecting difference but to ensuring that all people are welcome and feel that they belong in the society" (32).

In an example from our work, we worked on a housing project intended to provide multi-generational living spaces in a Native American community. About a third of the participants were Native American, many of them representing community-based organizations. The other two-thirds of the participants mostly represented government entities, and the majority of them were white. At the first team meeting, the participants spent about fifteen minutes introducing themselves, focusing on name, job title, and organization. The meeting followed the agenda and went fine, but the government representatives spoke much more and offered many more ideas about how best to complete the project than the Native American participants did. In preparing for the next meeting, one of the Native American participants suggested that the group follow the practice of introducing themselves by way of their ancestors and family lineage rather than introduce themselves in relation to their jobs and organizations. At the second meeting, the whole group followed that practice. The introductions took longer than the first ones did, but the conversation that followed was much more robust and balanced than the first one had been. Of course, that is not to suggest that introductions or other potentially symbolic forms of inclusion will solve long-term racialized misallocation of society's resources, but it is the start of what Iris Marion Young calls "internal" inclusion, the kind of inclusion and belonging that extends beyond just inviting historically underrepresented groups to a preset table and then proceeding as usual (55).

In short, a commitment to inclusion and belonging asks the collaborative governance group to pay close attention to every aspect of the process and to be willing to amend it in order to include everyone in the group. Here, for us, a big dose of humility is in order. While inclusion and belonging *is* a definitional norm and *is* the aspiration for each process in which we are involved, we undoubtedly have fallen short in the past and almost certainly will fall short in the future. In fact, living up to the aspirations of a more inclusive and democratic practice is one of the most important challenges we and other practitioners in the field face.

Shared Decision-making and Power-balancing

One of the central dilemmas of collaborative governance is, ultimately, where decision-making authority lies. Because collaborative governance is not explicitly constitutionally authorized and is rarely statutorily mandated, the power of a collaborative governance group to act most often must be derived from one or more of the stakeholders—typically one of the government agencies. And because that power sharing is typically informal and voluntary, there is almost always the possibility that the power will be snatched back to its originating agency, creating instability and sometimes mistrust between the participants in a collaborative governance group.

With regard to legally conferred power, there is a complex and delicate balance as government agencies strive to ensure that they fulfill their mandates while still binding themselves to the will of the group. Government entities cannot abdicate their legal obligations and yet, as Ansell and Gash put it, "we believe that collaborative governance is never merely consultative" (546). The potential for more creative, more effective, and more democratically arrived-at decisions is dependent upon the collaborative governance group having real influence over the decision or project at hand. As a result, as set forth in detail in the next chapter, the public participants in a collaborative governance process have a special role in managing that tension that is at the heart of collaborative governance.

Once the issue of decision-making authority is on the table, questions of power become explicit, and the group must consider where power lies both with regard to the group and outside institutions and within the group itself. Though it would be a diversion for us to dive into a survey of the extensive literature on power, the three laws of power that Eric Liu identifies in *You're More Powerful than You Think*, are helpful in considering the dynamics a collaborative governance group is facing:

- First, power *concentrates*. That is, it feeds on itself and compounds (as does powerlessness);
- Second, power *justifies itself*. People invent stories to legitimize the power they have (or lack);
- Third, power is *infinite*. There is no inherent limit on the amount of power people can create (26).

The first two laws of power make it clear just how much a collaborative governance group is asking when it expects an agency or other entity to share power with the group. But the third law creates a safety valve for inclusive and representative collaborative governance groups. This is where the makeup of the group really matters. Hannah Arendt, in her 1958 book *The Human Condition*, argues that power can multiply in what she calls "the space of appearance," in which people gather and transparently share their interests. In that space, power is generated by the discourse and the action itself. As she puts it, "[p]ower springs up between men when they act together and vanishes the moment they disperse" (200). That power requires, however, what she calls "the condition of plurality;" in other words, it is the interaction among the diversity of interests that generates new power (201).

In the same way that collaborative governance expands the substantive possibilities to address complex problems, an inclusive and representative collaborative governance group also expands the possibilities for community and citizen-centered power within a collaborative process.

Nonetheless, it is incumbent upon collaborative governance groups and those who are facilitating them to be cognizant of power imbalances within the group itself. As mentioned above, institutions may—indeed, will—carry structural inequities into a collaborative process with them, and in order for collaborative governance to fulfill its promise as a legitimate democratic practice, collaborative leaders must attend to those power imbalances so that all stakeholders can meaningfully participate. Again, the mechanics of such power balancing are situational, nuanced, and dynamic and will be discussed in more detail in section two. But for the purposes of a normative definition of collaborative governance, suffice it to say that the group must attend to power imbalances, including those rooted in oppression or disadvantage based on race, culture, religion, class, wealth, disability, geography, gender identity, sexual orientation, immigration status, education level, language, and differing communication styles, among others.

Deliberativeness

Deliberativeness is one of the key elements that distinguishes collaborative governance from other forms of participatory democracy. If practiced well, what will emerge is not simply an amalgamation of previously formed opinions, but an altogether new option that is forged by the deliberative process. The process both increases the number of possibilities for a substantive solution and changes the participants themselves.

Over the years, it has been hotly debated whether collaborative governance must be "consensus-based" or "consensus-seeking" in order to be legitimately collaborative. At the most basic level, the contested question is whether a vote amongst stakeholders is ever appropriate in a collaborative governance process. There are inherent reasons why consensus decision-making is often used in collaborative governance (see chapter 4), but we leave the details of the consensus question for a later discussion (see chapter 7). That said, we do believe that collaborative governance is necessarily and by definition deliberative.

Jane Mansbridge defines deliberation as "mutual communication that involves weighing and reflecting on preferences, values and interests regarding matters of common concern" (27). As Carmen Sirianni contends, deliberation is central to creating a democratic culture in a collaborative governance group:

> Policy design should enable citizens to engage in reasoned dialogue, evaluate evidence, weigh options, and consider costs, benefits, and possible trade-offs. Rather than simply ratify expressed preferences and preexisting perspectives in some aggregative formula intended to yield the greatest good for the greatest number, policy design should encourage citizens to reflect upon their own self-interests in a mutual search for common interests, shared values, and pragmatic solutions—though there is no guarantee that these will emerge. (50)

Chapter 7 focuses on the detailed conditions and dynamics of deliberation, but for the purposes of defining collaborative governance, deliberation has five essential characteristics:

1. It seeks information relevant to the issue;
2. It reveals individual stakeholder preferences;
3. It seeks overlapping concerns and interests;
4. It is concerned with trade-offs;
5. It asks stakeholders to consider what they can live with, even if a particular solution is not their first choice.

Table 1.1 illustrates some of the differences between conversation, dialogue, and deliberation.

Daniel Kemmis summarizes the skills essential to deliberation and what he calls collaborative democracy: "The skills required for solving those kinds of problems turn out to include: learning to listen carefully, speaking authentically and truthfully, and staying open to surprising solutions" (*Can Collaboration Help*). Those skills are central to deliberation and the interests that must be surfaced, compared, and reconciled if stakeholders are to reach solutions that serve the needs of all the stakeholders and those they represent.

There are most certainly other principles, practices, and skills that increase the effectiveness of a collaborative governance group (see chapter 10). The characteristics listed above, however, are definitional and are central to collaborative governance earning and maintaining democratic legitimacy.

TABLE 1.1 Distinctions between conversation, dialogue, and deliberation

Features	Conversation	Dialogue	Deliberation
Intent	Intends to connect	Intends to understand	Intends to make decisions (which often requires connection and/or understanding)
Focus	No specific focus	Focus on listening	Focus on overlapping interests (which also requires listening)
Structure	Loose structure	Structured toward sharing	Structured toward common ground
Pace	Moves at the pace of the discussants	Slows down for understanding	Slows down for clarification and understanding
Engagement	Engages pleasure, often in the form of affirmation	Engages different points of view	Engages trade-offs (which often includes different points of view)
Values	Values connection	Values understanding	Values change (which may require connection and/or understanding)

The Role of Collaborative Platforms

Though much of what we now consider to be collaborative governance evolved from the sometimes urgent need for cross-boundary decision-making in communities, it would be daunting for organically formed collaborative governance groups to establish and sustain the definitional norms listed above as well as the design elements and best practices detailed in later chapters. In fact, when you scratch the surface of most successful collaborative governance projects, underneath, there is a "collaborative platform" that creates a foundation upon which collaborative governance groups can function both democratically and effectively.

We borrow the term "collaborative platform" from a 2017 article by Chris Ansell and Alison Gash in which they argue that the concept of "platforms" as it is used in the tech world is useful to describe the catalytic function of organizations that support multiple collaborative projects. As they put it, "Collaborative platforms fill a particular niche in the world of governance: they specialize in facilitating, enabling, and to some degree regulating, 'many to many' collaborative relationships" ("Collaborative Platforms" 17). Consistent with our experience, Ansell and Gash rightfully point out that there are certain organizations that serve as hubs for multiple collaborative efforts and that some of those organizations focus at least as much on the principles and practice of collaborative governance as they do on the underlying subject matter of the project or projects.

Ansell and Gash define a collaborative platform to be "an organization or program with dedicated competences, institutions and resources for facilitating the creation, adaptation and success of multiple or ongoing collaborative projects or networks" ("Collaborative Platforms" 19–20). And while our experience is not entirely consistent with all the characteristics that Ansell and Gash attribute to collaborative platforms, we find the concept to be useful in describing an essential function in the field.

For the purposes of our work, there are two types of relevant collaborative platforms: (1) an organization or collaborative governance group focused on a particular issue, set of projects, or substantive content area that spins off multiple collaborative projects over time; or (2) an organization or institution that specializes in collaboration itself and assists and supports multiple collaborative governance groups across content areas and types of projects. The first category is typically comprised of agencies, which generate collaborative governance processes intended to improve outcomes in their subject-matter areas, such as early childhood education collaboratives created by a state department of education or air quality collaboratives supported by a state department of environmental quality. That category of collaborative platform may overlap with what we call collaborative systems (as described in chapter 3) and what Emerson and Nabatchi call collaborative regimes. Our work, which crosses subject-matter and jurisdictional boundaries, falls squarely in the second category.

As described above, the details of how collaborative governance is practiced are essential to both its legitimacy and its effectiveness. To use another metaphor, a collaborative platform creates a container in which a collaborative governance group can establish and maintain norms and keep the process moving toward a mutually beneficial outcome. If each collaborative governance group was required to reestablish the overarching norms and principles of collaborative governance at the outset of every project or process, not only would there be more risk to the integrity of the process, but it would also drain the energy of the group into resolving process questions rather than addressing the substantive issue at hand.

Let's return to the Tillamook example for a moment. In that case, there was a high potential for conflict and both technical and political complexities that had prevented individual agencies from satisfactorily managing flooding in the county. The governor turned to the National Policy Consensus Center—the university-based center where we work—to convene and manage the collaborative governance group. A facilitator was assigned who both staffed the project and provided process expertise and coaching throughout. The facilitator scheduled the meetings, worked with the team to establish the agenda, distributed notes, and otherwise ensured that the team was able to focus on the substance of the issue. But even more importantly, the facilitator—and the center itself—served as a platform for the process. The facilitator did not have a position on the outcome of the process, but worked with the collaborative governance group to ensure that the project served a public purpose and was cross-boundary, representative, inclusive, power-sharing, and deliberative.

Here, we digress for a moment into what we think of as "the neutrality problem." Because many of the early principles of collaborative governance were derived from the field of dispute resolution, a central tenet of early collaborative governance literature was "neutrality." In fact, for many years, we referred to our university-based center as a "neutral forum." What we meant by that was that we did not have a position on the outcome of any particular collaborative governance process and that it was our job to maintain the integrity of the process, while it was the job of the stakeholders to advocate for their preferred solutions.

Neutrality, however, is deeply problematic when it is considered in the context of structural racism and other institutional oppressions. To remain "neutral" in the face of those biased systems creates the very real possibility—and perhaps even the probability—that the injustices and unfair power imbalances inherent in institutions will be replicated inside the collaborative governance group itself. It also undermines the core definitional norm that power should be considered and balanced amongst the stakeholders in a collaborative governance process.

The field of collaborative governance continues to wrestle with the question of neutrality. Some practitioners use the terms "impartial" or "multi-partial," which offer the possibility that they are agnostic to the outcome but still have an eye toward corrosive power differentials. Still others use consensus-seeking processes to ensure that each participant in a collaborative governance group has the opportunity to interrupt bias or unfairness when he or she or they see it. There are no easy answers to this dilemma, and we continue to grapple with how best to frame the issue and how to equitably address the underlying problem.

We find the idea of the collaborative platform to be helpful, however. A collaborative platform serves the needs and interests of all of the parties, and is intended to support the parties in achieving their shared goals. In addition, a collaborative platform, grounded in the democratic definitional norms set forth above, creates a greater possibility of a shared culture in which representativeness, inclusion and belonging, and power-sharing govern both the composition of the project team and the process itself, alleviating some of the needs to assert the concept of neutrality.

Conclusion

These definitions and descriptions are not intended to be rigid or even primarily theoretical. Rather, they are intended to be flexible, reflective of practice, and normative. They are intended to help practitioners and public managers recognize opportunities for collaborative governance to improve both the outcomes of their work and the resiliency of democracy at all levels of governance.

Notes

1 Throughout this book, we refer to a team of people engaged in collaborative governance as a "collaborative governance group," a "collaborative governance table," or occasionally as a "project team."
2 We use the word "citizen" in the most inclusive sense. We use it to refer to the identity that individuals take on when they live and work in the public sphere, regardless of country of origin or legal status. Because citizenship is both descriptive and normative, we hope to spur an aspirational usage of the word, rather than a cramped one that is based on a technical—and oftentimes xenophobic—reading of who is in and who is out of a particular jurisdiction.

References

Ansell, Chris, and Alison Gash. "Collaborative Governance in Theory and Practice." *Journal of Public Administration Research and Theory*, vol. 18, no. 4, 2007, pp. 543–571.

Ansell, Chris, and Alison Gash. "Collaborative Platforms as a Governance Strategy." *Journal of Public Administration Research and Theory*, vol. 28, no. 1, July 2017, pp. 16–32.

Arendt, Hannah. *The Human Condition.* 2nd ed., U of Chicago P, 2018.

Carlson, Christine. *A Practical Guide to Collaborative Governance.* Policy Consensus Initiative, 2007.

Emerson, Kirk, and Tina Nabatchi. *Collaborative Governance Regimes.* Georgetown UP, 2015.

Kemmis, Daniel. *Can Collaboration Help Us Heal Our Democracy?* Leading Voices in Collaborative Governance. *National Policy Consensus Center*, September 2016. Video.

Kemmis, Daniel, and Matthew McKinney. "Collaboration as an Emerging Form of Democracy." *National Civic Review*, vol. 100, no. 2, 2011, pp. 2–12.

Liu, Eric. *You're More Powerful than You Think—A Citizen's Guide to Making Change Happen.* The Perseus Books Group, 2017.

Mansbridge, Jane. "A Minimalist Definition of Deliberation." *Deliberation and Development: Rethinking the Role of Voice and Collective Action in Unequal Societies*, edited by Patrick Heller and Vijayendra Rao, World Bank Group, 2015, pp. 27–50.

"Mission & Vision." *US Army Corps of Engineers Headquarters Website*, www.usace.army.mil/About/Mission-and-Vision.

powell, john a., and Stephen Menedian. "The Problem With Othering: Toward Inclusiveness and Belonging." *Othering & Belonging*, vol. 1, 2016, pp. 14–39.

powell, john a., et al. "Targeted Universalism: Policy & Practice." *Othering & Belonging Institute*, 8 May 2019, belonging.berkeley.edu/targeteduniversalism.

Rittel, Horst W. J., and Melvin M. Webber. "Dilemmas in a General Theory of Planning." *Policy Sciences*, vol. 4, 1973, pp. 155–169.

Sirianni, Carmen. *Investing in Democracy: Engaging Citizens in Collaborative Governance.* Brookings Institution Press, 2009.

"Tillamook Basin Flooding Reduction." Oregon Solutions, orsolutions.org/osproject/Tillamook.

Young, Iris Marion. *Inclusion and Democracy.* Oxford UP, 2000.

2

COLLABORATIVE GOVERNANCE IN A CONSTITUTIONAL CONTEXT

Introduction

As collaborative governance has taken root in theory and practice, it has become the subject of both enthusiastic expectations and increased scrutiny. Because we do not believe that collaborative governance is a flash-in-the-pan or the latest efficiency fad, but rather is an integrated and legitimate process for public decision-making and collective action, we know we must locate it within the fabric of American democratic systems and as such, within a constitutional context.

In addition to important theoretical questions involving constitutional legitimacy, there are practical considerations, as well. Because collaborative governance is both institutionally and functionally cross-cutting, collaborative governance processes are enmeshed in an intricate web of authorizing charters, democratic accountability, and competing decision-making cultures. As Lisa Amsler put it, collaborative governance "encompasses public voice: the public and stakeholders working together across the policy continuum. It includes policymaking in the legislative branch upstream. Within the executive branch, it includes the quasi-legislative arena upstream, implementation and management midstream, and quasi-judicial downstream" (702). As a result, collaborative governance intersects with the United States Constitution, as well as with state constitutions, city charters, and federal, state, and local statutes, not to mention regulations at all levels of government.

There is also an important set of critiques that require our attention. Some of them stem from the particulars of individual projects, but some are rooted in more fundamental questions about the constitutional and legal legitimacy of collaborative governance. There are two particular critiques that we believe require thoughtful consideration: (1) collaborative governance is the new "smoked filled room," undermining both federalism and separation of powers by forging new ways for governments to work across jurisdictions and branches of government, all of which creates the potential for new forms of influence peddling, subversion of checks and balances, and aggregation of power; and (2) collaborative governance bestows power on unelected stakeholders in the private and civic spheres, granting them undue influence on public decision-making and resource allocation. In the United States, at least, those two criticisms go straight to the heart of our form of government and the foundational documents that established it.

Here we must apologize to our readers who are not residents of the United States. For those practicing collaborative governance outside the United States, the foundational documents, as well as the cultural sources of collective democratic values, will be unique to the context in which they are working. That said, we hope this exploration of the United States Constitution will serve as a model for exploring how collaborative governance fits into a broader governance system.

In this chapter, we explore the tensions inherent in our constitutional system and how those tensions converge and are at least partially managed in the practice of collaborative governance. This is not a simple undertaking, and we run directly into the philosophical conflicts embedded in the Constitution itself, as well the complexities created by multiple levels of government responding to critical needs and a rapidly changing societal context. First, we begin with an overview of the values at stake in the United States Constitution, particularly the roots of divided government and what they mean for the practice of both traditional and collaborative governance. Second, we explore how collaborative governance can serve as a safety valve to mitigate against some of the worst potential side effects of divided government and how some form of collaborative governance is necessarily embedded in the constitutional system. Finally, we examine the practice of collaborative governance and how the details of that practice can bolster—rather than undermine—constitutional and democratic values.

A Backdrop of Divided Government

In the United States, the Constitution is our most significant statement of shared democratic values, and those values have been incorporated and adapted into other foundational documents such as state constitutions and city charters, as well as into our collective sense of how a democracy should function. Daniel Kemmis, one of the early advocates for collaborative governance, put it this way, "A constitution is more than a legal document. It is the single most expressive act by which separate, individual people *constitute* themselves as *a people*" (4). And though there has been near-constant disagreement since the nation's founding about some very fundamental issues, it is a unique feature of American democracy that questions of constitutionality are often front and center in the public debate about everything from public lands to public education. As Doug Morgan, Richard Green, Craig Shinn, and Kent Robinson put it in their groundbreaking book on public administration, "It is common practice for citizens to assert arguments about the constitutionality of a proposed policy as a reason to favor or oppose its passage" (73).

We go into some detail about constitutional values in this chapter because the tendency to turn to the Constitution also extends into debates about the multiple ways in which Americans work together to create public goods, including collaborative governance. Vera Vogelsang-Coombs contends that there are four constitutional pillars to the American system of government: "(1) representative governance, (2) competent governance with executive capacity, (3) the protection of minority rights, and (4) engaged citizens involved in democratic governance that respects the different civic traditions of diverse geographic communities" (81).[1] Not surprisingly, those four values sometimes conflict with one another, creating a clash of interests and generating dozens of arguments about what the Constitution "means" for the purposes of good governance.

Rather than choosing winners and losers among those values or even "balancing" them in the toothless way that we often hear such things described, the drafters of the Constitution, "designed a constitutional system that would hold conflicting principles in irresolvable tensions, thus forcing public servants at all levels (even street level) to cope with them in the ongoing administration of justice" (Morgan et al. 5).

On one hand, there are justifiable expectations from the citizenry that the government operate effectively and efficiently. On the other, the American government is designed to prevent the consolidation of power that could result in tyranny, significant government overreach, or the undue influence of powerful interests. The resulting checks and balances often slow down the adoption or implementation of policies, even policies with which large majorities agree. So, while efficiency and effectiveness are pillars of good governance, *maximum* efficiency and effectiveness have been sacrificed in favor of other values.

The founders recognized that interest groups would form in order to compete for their preferred policies, but they did not want any of those interests to become so strong that they swamped other interests, particularly minority interests. The hope for the federalist system was that a unified executive combined with an otherwise fragmented government would have sufficient power to maintain order but not enough to stifle individual ingenuity.

There were two major strategies employed to prevent interest groups from gaining too much political power and wreaking havoc on the system. The first strategy was structural, creating what we refer to as the "separation of powers": "The designers of our Constitution integrated such precautions through checks and balances that would force separate, superintending branches and levels of government to negotiate for control over the administrative machinery of government" (Morgan et al. 5).

The second strategy was demographic and geographic. In *Federalist 10*, Madison argued that keeping people separated from one another over a broad territory would prevent active and potentially nefarious factions from becoming too powerful (Hamilton et al. 51). That philosophical stance—alongside a healthy fear of consolidated federal power—led to a myriad of governing structures at the state and local level, culminating in the Tenth Amendment, which reserves all rights not specifically enumerated in the Constitution to the states.

We ground ourselves in these values not because we think this is the venue to explore the many permutations of federal constitutional theory, but rather because the United States Constitution is one of the few—if not the only— ratified statements of our collective democratic values. As Newbold and Rosenbloom put it, we—and here we mean elected officials, public managers, and citizens alike—are called to grapple with the Constitution as an expression of our shared "regime values" (7).

And so, it is against that intricate backdrop of divided government and dispersed power that the contemporary administrative state emerged, followed by collaborative governance.

Collaborative Governance is Baked into the Constitutional System

One critique of collaborative governance is that it can be used to subvert the protections of divided government. At first blush, that argument has some appeal. After all, it does seem as if one of the dominant constitutional goals is the fragmentation of governance functions in order to avoid a consolidation of power and all of its nefarious consequences. But there are other values at stake and there is substantial evidence that the system allows for—and perhaps even requires—collaborative governance.

First, the deliberative practices at the heart of collaborative governance are essential to managing the tensions embedded in our system of government. From the very outset of the republic, and even more so in recent years, Americans have had to navigate the complexities of divided government, pluralism, and conflicting values. Thirty years ago—in a much lesser technologically connected context than the one we find ourselves in today—Robert Zinke argued that our interconnectedness and the resulting exposure to the "pluralities of people, traditions, customs, and languages that inhabit the nations" make it impossible for a unified substantive tradition to serve the needs of the entire country, let alone the entire world (25). Rather, it is the dialogue among those multiplicities that defines our national identity as a constitutional democracy. As Zinke puts it, the American republic is a "rhetorical republic" (14).

Collaborative governance—along with some of its sister fields of dialogue and deliberation, deliberative democracy, and others—provides a platform for those ongoing conversations that is structured, relational, and focused on shared solutions. As set forth in the previous chapter, deliberation defines collaborative governance, placing our work in the center of the "rhetorical republic." In addition, by locating ourselves and our work within the deliberative legacy of the Constitution, it largely frees us from the debate about the morals of the founders themselves. In embracing the deliberative nature of the Constitution and the resulting ongoing conversation about core American principles, we need not focus on the intent of individual founders at all. Rather, we are free to debate the questions surrounding constitutional values past, present, and future without feeling as if we must either defend or ignore practices like slavery or colonialism or genocide in order to retain the democratic values that have been passed down from prior generations or to forge new versions of those values that serve the needs of current and future generations.

Second, there are practical reasons why some version of collaborative governance was envisaged in the Constitution. Lisa Bingham and Rosemary O'Leary argue that collaboration is not just passively allowed by the Constitution, but it was explicitly baked in from the beginning. Relying on *Federalist 51*, they argue that "collaboration was not simply a happy by-product of innovating a new nation; it was a conscious design for promoting the articulation and reconciliation of diverse interests as a means of avoiding the tyranny of the majority in voting" (Bingham and O'Leary S80). The core of their argument is that the dual federalist goals of divided government and executive efficiency anticipated and required collaboration across branches and levels of government.

In *Federalist 51*, Madison wrote: "In the extended republic of the United States, and among the great variety of interests, parties, and sects which it embraces, a coalition of a majority of the whole society could seldom take place on any other principles than those of justice and the general good ..." (267).

Bingham and O'Leary conclude that the authors of the *Federalist Papers* and the framers of the Constitution believed that collective decision-making and joint action, like that at issue in collaborative governance, would be possible only when there was a broad and deep consensus. As they put it,

> The authors of the *Federalist Papers* here are proclaiming the virtues not of majority rule, but rather rule by consensus. They argue for the division of society and government into smaller and smaller parts and interests such that it is harder for them to combine. If it is harder for them to combine, they will do so only when there is overwhelming agreement. (Bingham and O'Leary S81)

Forebearers of what we now call collaborative governance have been part of the democratic fabric from very early on in the United States. As Zinke points out, the

Constitution requires joint action—or at least "interactive communication"—between the House and Senate and between both legislative branches and the executive branch of government (50). The House and Senate must negotiate to reconcile differing versions of legislation. The president is required to seek "advice and consent" of the Senate for certain appointments. Even the judiciary finds itself in a "continuing colloquy" with the legislative and executive branches to determine the constitutionality of particular pieces of legislation (51).

That spirit of joint decision-making and collective action also—and perhaps especially—took hold at the local level. As far back as the 1830s, when Alexis de Tocqueville visited the United States, he found Americans working together to achieve shared community goals. Tocqueville introduced the mediating concept of self-interest "rightly understood" (384), which has become one of the most influential ideas in public administration generally (Morgan et al. 80) and in collaborative governance specifically (see chapter 4). Behind it is the idea that working with others to uncover overlapping interests is actually more beneficial to each individual interest than it would be to simply jockey for advantage and then rely on raw power to take it.

The associational activity and collective action described by Tocqueville was a precursor to the more formalized collaborative governance being practiced today, and it played a similar role in creating opportunities for otherwise fragmented government entities to work in concert with organizations and individuals representing a broad range of interests. Decision-making across formal and informal boundaries and collective action have been part of American democratic culture from very early on, and they help blunt some of the potentially frustrating inefficiencies of divided government.

As a result, the critique that collaborative governance is a sneaky subversion of federalism and the separation of powers does not extend beyond its surface appeal. In fact, deliberation and collaboration are values deeply embedded both in the American constitutional system and in collaborative governance. Examined with those values in mind, collaborative governance is not a stealthy attempt to work around democratic norms but rather is an additional venue in which those norms can be put into practice.

The Practice of Collaborative Governance in a Constitutional Democracy

As always, the devil is in the details. And though collaborative governance has a solid foundation in constitutional values, it is *how* collaborative governance is practiced that ultimately confers its legitimacy. As mentioned above, one of the other primary criticisms of collaborative governance is that it could be used to subvert federalism and separation of powers, creating an opportunity for powerful or organized interests to capture the attention and resources of a collaborative group. In addition, some critics suggest that unelected, unaccountable participants in collaborative governance processes might have undue influence on public decision-making and the expenditure of public resources.

Once again, practices on the ground matter, and those practices are the means by which collaborative governance groups establish and maintain their democratic legitimacy. There are four pillars of practice that help establish and maintain legitimacy and accountability: (1) constitutional and legal stewardship, (2) multi-axial representativeness, (3) transparency, and (4) democratic capacity building and shared responsibility.

Constitutional and Legal Stewardship

Because collaborative governance groups necessarily cut across legal and jurisdictional boundaries, the public sector members of each group have a particular role in establishing and maintaining the legal and constitutional sideboards of any collaborative governance process. It is up to those government representatives to be clear about the source and limits of their authority both within the group and within their own agency. It has become a tenet of contemporary public administration that public agencies and the managers that serve in them have an important role in "conserving constitutional values and embedding them in management practices" (Newbold 14). When considering the role of local governments, Vera Vogelsang-Coombs wrote: "Local officials must understand their role as constitutional stewards in order to perform their deliberative governance roles effectively. This means that they must learn to preserve and balance the tension laden conditions of a thriving constitutional polity" (82). Clearly the same is true for state and federal officials. And because the purpose of any collaborative governance process is—by definition—public, there is an ongoing obligation for the public sector participants to serve as constitutional and legal stewards to the collaborative governance process. A collaborative governance process cannot be used to thwart either rights or responsibilities, and each participant is required to play his or her or their part in maintaining firm boundaries.

This is not to suggest, however, that public sector members of collaborative governance groups use their stewardship role to thwart the progress of the group or to shield themselves from full participation. Occasionally, in our experience, representatives of government agencies will assert their legal obligations in a way that stalls the group's ability to reach decisions or take meaningful action. They will claim that they are somehow prohibited from doing one thing or another that would support the group's work. Sometimes there is truly a legal snag. Sometimes, however, after further inquiry, it becomes clear that they are not legally prohibited from fully participating but that they are retracting because the process and the potential outcomes feel different from business as usual. That is a natural fear reaction, but it is incumbent on those public sector representatives to clearly distinguish between constitutional and legal limits on their authority and habits and practices that are constraining their ability to work in a different, more creative way.

The staff members of collaborative platforms also have a role to play in constitutional and legal stewardship. It is not necessarily realistic to expect that all government officials will have thought through the complexities of how the laws of multiple jurisdictions, as well as the United States Constitution, apply to the practice of collaborative governance. But because collaborative platforms are organizations that support multiple collaborative governance processes, the staff members of those organizations are likely to have at least some sense of the issues that might arise, and as a result, they can support the collaborative group in seeking counsel about any legal or constitutional questions that might arise. And while they are not in a position to give legal advice, staff members of the collaborative platform may also be able to help public sector representatives ask the right questions to untangle true legal limitations from habits that are impeding the progress of the group.

To guide their work, public sector members of collaborative governance groups, along with the staff of collaborative platforms, might ask themselves the following questions:

- What are the goals and proposed actions of the collaborative group?
- Is there specific constitutional authority for the proposed actions?
- If so, what?
- If not, is there implied authority?
- Is there statutory authority?
- Are there constitutional or other legal prohibitions that might affect the actions of the group?
- Are there procedural requirements that the group should be considering as it does its work?
- Is an identified barrier actually a legal barrier or is it a barrier created by habit?
- Does the group need more information or legal advice to proceed?

Multi-axial Representativeness

As mentioned above, we occasionally hear the critique that collaborative governance processes bestow power on a group of unelected organizations and individuals who make decisions and expend public resources outside the authority and accountability bestowed by elections. In particular, we have encountered individuals and organizations who are already deeply concerned about government overreach, and they find the addition of unelected representatives to a decision-making process to be profoundly alarming. While we take that potential risk very seriously, in practice, one of the most effective inoculations against a claim of illegitimacy and overreach is to ensure that the collaborative group is broadly and deeply representative (see chapters 1 and 6). In fact, three of the four constitutional values identified by Vera Vogelsang-Coombs are implicated by representativeness in a collaborative process: representative governance, the protection of minority rights, and the engagement of a broad and diverse citizenry (81).

Collaborative governance, if practiced well, offers an alternative to the constricted sense of representation that is based entirely on elections. In fact, collaborative governance groups have the potential to be *more* accountable to more communities than election-based representative government. This is not to suggest that collaborative governance is a replacement for the traditional system, but rather that by bolstering and enriching representativeness in collaborative processes, collaborative groups can increase participation in important public efforts, particularly among historically underrepresented communities.

We find the work of Nadia Urbinati and Mark Warren to be particularly instructive in considering some of the questions surrounding representativeness. As they point out, the central feature of traditional, electoral representativeness is based on geography:

> Beginning with the formation of the modern state, territorial residence became the fundamental condition for political representation—a condition more inclusive than status- and corporate-based representation. Indeed, territory has had an important historical relationship to political equality that carried over into modern times. (389)

Consequently, elected representation is an important, though limited, sense of representation. Individuals are affected by public decision-making in many cross-cutting ways that are never fully considered in geographic representation, such as "religion, ethnicity, nationalism, professional identity, recreation, gender identity, and many social movements" (Urbinati and Warren 390). In addition, many constituencies are not fully represented in the electoral system because of interlocking factors like age, legal status, disenfranchisement, and voter suppression.

Occasionally in our projects, staff members of elected officials or even of public agencies will resist expanding the membership of a collaborative governance group, claiming that they represent "the people" because they are appearing on behalf of a duly elected government. In one project we were involved with, a city staff person who worked for one of the regulatory departments initially advocated against including a broad range of community-based organizations on a project team, arguing that she and other city employees rightfully represented the public interest. In the end, we worked with her to recognize that many members of the community saw the city as a stakeholder representing its own interests in that particular project, making it difficult or impossible for city staff to represent the broad range of opinions and interests that existed in the public at large.

As articulated in the preceding chapter, modern collaborative governance arose in large part because of the increasing complexity of public issues. As the issues become more complex, so do the demands of representativeness. Embracing a more intersectional and nuanced sense of representation is a necessary part of collaborative governance practice.

Moreover, it has become clear that, in the United States, individuals' fates are often tied to their zip codes with regard to safety, education, public health, access to green spaces and healthy food, and on and on. In addition, some of the most pernicious forms of institutional and structural racism have been codified through residential segregation, using tools like red-lining and restrictive covenants. As a result, tying representation *only* to geographic residence may well reinforce those disparities and injustices.

Once again, we find the pathway to a more inclusive sense of representativeness in the practice itself. As Urbinati and Warren put it, "fair representation requires some relationship of trust between individuals and representatives, based on shared experiences, perspectives, and interests" (394). To simplify a bit, and to bring Iris Marion Young's thinking to bear on the realities of collaborative governance in practice, robust representativeness has three prongs: (1) authority to represent a particular group, (2) behavior consistent with the interests of the represented group in the course of the collaborative governance process itself, and (3) accountability to the represented group (134; Urbinati and Warren 394–95).

Authority

First, of the three prongs of representativeness, authority is the thorniest in the context of collaborative governance. The authority analysis for government participants is relatively straightforward because they are authorized by elections at various levels. But, as Urbinati and Warren point out, in community-based processes, there is a proliferation of "self-authorizing" representatives (403).

Many of the non-governmental participants in collaborative governance processes are self-authorizing in the sense that they represent nonprofits or associations that rely on individuals to voluntarily step forward to help achieve the mission of the organization. On one hand, these participants play a very important role in rounding out the representativeness of a collaborative group. However, self-authorizing representatives are, well, self-authorizing, so it is incumbent on the collaborative group to be attentive to the source of the authority claimed by a particular participant and especially to the other two markers of representativeness—representative behavior during the course of the collaborative process and accountability to the represented group. Nonetheless, policing the representative authority of other members of the collaborative group might well be both outside the expertise of group members and be a source of tension that could ultimately inhibit the group's ability to achieve its substantive goals.

Again, a collaborative platform could play an important role in helping the group determine who has the authority to represent a particular interest, particularly in the assessment phase. As set forth in chapter 5, a well-designed and thorough assessment—with an eye toward inclusiveness and belonging—can help identify both the interests at stake and participants who can legitimately and effectively represent groups potentially affected by the outcome of the process.

Behavior Consistent with the Interests of the Represented Group

With regard to representativeness during the course of the process itself, it is important for the collaborative group to ensure that the interests of represented groups are being raised and discussed regularly in the process. Often this can be achieved through a series of well-timed questions from either participants or the facilitator for the group. Any collaborative governance group should check in regularly to ensure that the interests of the "table behind the table" are being surfaced and thoroughly considered as the group conducts its work.

There also may come a time in a process when the collaborative governance group might also need to consult with the broader community or some subset of the most affected communities. As George Fredrickson put it, in the context of public administration, "the more difficult task ... is accounting for the well-being and interests of the inchoate public" (410). In order to ensure that the collaborative group represents all affected interests, particularly diffuse interests, it will likely need to engage a broader public at one or more points using the tools of civic engagement and public participation (see chapter 7).

Accountability

Accountability likely is the easiest prong of representativeness to consider in a collaborative process. In the case of the public sector, accountability is imposed most directly through elections, but it is also exercised through feedback—sometimes vociferous feedback—from the public. In the current era, similar interaction is easily sought and received between self-authorized representatives and the groups they purport to represent. Membership organizations can hold internal deliberations and/or vote about how they want their interests represented in a collaborative process. And other identity and interest groups can express their pleasure—or more likely displeasure if accountability is at issue—through a variety of means, including online and through formal and informal media outlets.

This is also another place where the collaborative platform staff might play a helpful role. Again, if it is unclear whether particular team members are effectively representing the interests at stake, the facilitator can ask questions to determine the extent to which team members are staying in touch with the communities they purport to represent.

Focused attention on representativeness is an effective antidote to the critique that collaborative governance is a Trojan horse for unelected and unaccountable stakeholders who might use a process to press for their own advantage. In fact, if practiced well, collaborative governance can offer more robust democratic accountability than that afforded by elections alone.

Transparency

All of this, of course, depends on represented groups and other affected parties knowing what is happening during a collaborative process. Transparency has become one of the primary means by which democratic norms are enforced. In 1913, Supreme Court Justice Louis Brandeis colorfully wrote that "sunlight is said to be the best of disinfectants" (ch. 5). Similarly, in signing what he called the "Open Government Initiative," President Obama asserted that "openness will strengthen our democracy and promote efficiency and effectiveness in Government" (United States Executive Office 4685–4686).

Because public sector participants are central to collaborative governance processes and because the processes themselves often involve a public benefit, government transparency laws from multiple levels often apply to processes. Of course, the representatives from those government entities are responsible for meeting their own professional and legal obligations, but it is important for both the collaborative group and the staff of the collaborative platform to recognize that transparency is a good in and of itself that may enhance the legitimacy of the process. As a result, legal standards that apply to particular participants may well be a floor rather than a ceiling for communicating with the public. If the proceedings are transparent to the broader public and to the affected communities, it is much more likely that the collaborative governance process will meet the necessary legal standards and will more fully represent the needs of the communities affected by the process.[2]

Democratic Skill Building and Shared Responsibility

Though much of what we have discussed in this chapter relies upon the collaborative platform and the public sector participants to monitor and steward their legal obligations, the practice of collaborative governance is much more likely to be constitutionally and democratically sound if the collaborative group itself develops what Vera Vogelsang-Coombs calls a "democratic group dynamic" (91). As Stephanie Newbold put it in the context of public administration, "leaders must have the knowledge, skills, and abilities to create an organizational culture that recognizes the central role of the law and democratic-constitutional norms and values in public service" (20).

In practice, democratic group dynamics and democratic skill-building have tremendous overlap with the definitional norms set forth in chapter 1. If the collaborative governance process meets the definitional norms of public purpose, cross-boundary participation, representativeness, inclusiveness and belonging, shared authority and power balancing, and deliberativeness, it is much more likely to spread the responsibility for constitutional and democratic awareness across the collaborative governance group.

In addition to those definitional norms, participants in collaborative governance groups are obliged to take individual responsibility for ensuring that the collaborative governance process does not just serve their particular interests but that it is compatible with underlying constitutional values (Fredrickson 409). That may go so far as keeping a constitutional perspective when boundaries between the public interest and private interest start to blur or when the separation of powers becomes compromised (Newbold 15). It may also extend to ensuring that all the affected interests are well-represented when making public decisions or considering collective action.

In that sense, we recognize that collaborative governance processes require more from government agencies, civil society participants, private-sector representatives, and the public itself than most of the well-established processes embedded in traditional governance. By asking citizens across a variety of interests and roles to meet face-to-face to problem-solve in service of the public good, the responsibility for both addressing important public issues *and* protecting democratic values belongs to everyone involved.

Conclusion

Collaborative governance processes function within an elaborate constitutional and legal ecosystem. As a result, participants, conveners, facilitators, and staff members of collaborative platforms are required to attend to the democratic legitimacy of the process. That said, however, the suggestion that collaborative governance is a means to evade federalism or is a platform to allow unaccountable individuals to insinuate themselves into public decision-making is not born out either philosophically or practically. In fact, the values of collaborative governance are in full alignment with the deliberative and collaborative norms embedded in the United States Constitution. And, if practiced well, collaborative governance provides a space for even more robust democratic engagement.

Notes

1 In summarizing the four values at play in the United States Constitution, Vogelsong-Coombs draws heavily on the work of Morgan and his co-authors.
2 There are the rare occasions, especially in agreement-seeking cases, where some or all of the process is confidential. Those cases are few and far between and are driven by very particular intersections of the interests of the parties and the law.

References

Amsler, Lisa Blomgren. "Collaborative Governance: Integrating Management, Politics, and Law." *Public Administration Review*, vol. 76, no. 5, 2016, pp. 700–711.

Bingham, Lisa Blomgren, and Rosemary O'Leary. "Federalist No. 51: Is the Past Relevant to Today's Collaborative Public Management?" *Public Administration Review*, vol. 71, 2011, pp. S78–S82.

Booher, David E. "Collaborative Governance Practices and Democracy." *National Civic Review*, vol. 93, no. 4, 2004, pp. 32–46.

Brandeis, Louis Dembitz. *Other People's Money, and How the Bankers Use It*. Project Gutenberg, 1914, http://www.gutenberg.org/files/57819/57819-h/57819-h.htm.

Diamond, Martin, et al. *The Founding of the Democratic Republic: An Introduction to American National Government*. F. E. Peacock, 1981.

Frederickson, H. George. "Toward a Theory of the Public for Public Administration." *Administration & Society*, vol. 22, no. 4, 1991, pp. 395–417.

Freeman, Jody. "Collaborative Governance in the Administrative State." *UCLA Law Review*, vol. 45, no. 1, Oct. 1997, pp. 1–43.

Gutmann, Amy, and Dennis Thompson. "Deliberative Democracy Beyond Process." *Debating Deliberative Democracy*, Blackwell Publishing, 2003, p. 31.52.

Hamilton, Alexander et al. *The Federalist Papers*. Yale University Press, 2009.

Levine, Charles. "Citizenship and Service Delivery: The Promise of Coproduction." *Public Administration Review*, vol. 44, 1984, pp. 178–187.

Levinson, Sanford. *Our Undemocratic Constitution: Where the Constitution Goes Wrong (and How We the People Can Correct It)*. Oxford UP, 2006.

Kemmis, Daniel. *Community and the Politics of Place*. U Oklahoma P, 1992.

Morgan, Douglas F., et al. *Foundations of Public Service*. Routledge, 2012.

Morgan, Douglas F. "The Public Interest." *Handbook of Administrative Ethics*, 2nd ed., Routledge, 2019, pp. 151–180.

Newbold, Stephanie. "Why a Constitutional Approach Matters for Advancing New Public Governance." *New Public Governance: A Regime-Centered Perspective*, Routledge, 2015, pp. 13–22.

Newbold, Stephanie P., and David H. Rosenbloom. "Providing the Foundation for 21st Century Governance." *The Constitutional School of American Public Administration*, edited by Stephanie P. Newbold and David H. Rosenbloom. Routledge, Taylor & Francis Group, 2016, pp. 3–7.

Rosenbloom, David H., and Mei Jen Hung. "Administrative Law and Culture for the U.S. Collaborative Governance State." *Journal of Dispute Resolution*, vol. 2009, no. 2, 2009, pp. 1–16.

Rosenbloom, David H. "Public Administration and the Erosion of the Rule of Law in the United States." *Journal of Chinese Governance*, vol. 4, no. 1, Feb. 2019, pp. 1–14.

United States, Executive Office of the President [Barack Obama]. Executive Order E9-1777: Transparency and Open Government: Memorandum for the Heads of Executive Departments and Agencies. 21 Jan. 2009. *Federal Register*, vol. 74, no. 4685, pp. 4685–4686.

Urbinati, Nadia, and Mark E. Warren. "The Concept of Representation in Contemporary Democratic Theory." *Annual Review of Political Science*, vol. 11, no. 1, 2008, pp. 387–412.

Tocqueville, Alexis de, et al. *Democracy in America*. Saunders and Otley, 1835.

Vogelsang-Coombs, Vera. "The American Constitutional Legacy and the Deliberative Democracy Environment of New Public Governance." *New Public Governance: A Regime-Centered Perspective*, Routledge, 2015, p. 79.100.

Young, Iris Marion. *Inclusion and Democracy*. Oxford UP, 2000.

Zinke, Robert C. "American Constitutionalism in the Interconnected World: Administrative Responsibilities in a Rhetorical Republic." *Dialogue*, vol. 12, no. 2, 1990, pp. 12–59.

3

TYPOLOGIES

Introduction

At base, collaborative governance is a structured form of group problem solving, and in many—if not most—instances, the principles, practices, and tools described in this book apply across the various types of collaborative governance processes. For example, questions of inclusion and representativeness are as relevant in an agreement-seeking process as they are in a process intended to bring about collective action. And those questions apply equally—if not more—to collaborative systems. Throughout this book, we usually write about collaborative governance generally.

Nonetheless, there are times when the type of collaborative governance process does affect how it should be conceived, designed, and implemented. Sometimes the needs of the group or the structure of the meetings will be driven by the type of problem the group is collectively trying to solve. Sometimes there will be more conflict. Sometimes there will be less. Sometimes the group needs more formal structure; sometimes the group needs maximum flexibility. We find that these differing needs often line up along typology lines, so we offer those distinctions here and, where relevant, at other points in the book.

Though there are many ways to differentiate between collaborative governance processes, for the purposes of this book, we look to the type of work the group is undertaking. Again, these distinctions are driven by practice. There are deep explorations of collaborative governance types available, one of the most comprehensive of which is the analysis of collaborative governance regime typologies set out by Emerson and Nabatchi (162–167).

Using a practice-based lens, there are two major types of collaborative governance processes: agreement-seeking, in which the participants are endeavoring to arrive at a shared decision; and collective action, in which the participants are endeavoring to achieve a shared goal by aggregating their resources. Although we draw a distinction between agreement-seeking and collective action processes, the line between them can be somewhat fluid. Some groups must make decisions in order to undertake collective action. Other groups must act collectively in order to move on to the next decision. And yet, we do find that there are distinctions between the group types and that too often collaborative governance theory and practice meanders between the two without discerning what kind of work is at issue and what type of process is needed to accomplish it.

In addition, we often include a third type, which we refer to as collaborative systems. Collaborative systems can involve agreement-seeking, collective action, or both, but we treat those processes separately here because they are longer-term, less project-driven, and typically require a more formal governance structure.

In this chapter, we offer a brief description of each of the three types. Throughout the rest of the book, we distinguish between them where necessary, and we do not when the topic at hand applies across all collaborative governance types.

Agreement-seeking

At base, agreement-seeking groups are convened to make a collective decision or set of decisions. The work of the group is to surface the various interests and perspectives, and then to align those interests to find a window of agreement. The group's task differs somewhat from that of a single policy analyst for a public agency, whose primary focus is often determining the most efficient or cost-effective strategy for attaining a public goal. While efficiency and cost-effectiveness can be important considerations in a collaborative agreement-seeking process, the primary reason for convening that process is to ensure that the chosen policy is supported by various stakeholder groups, including those that could otherwise impede either its adoption or implementation.

Collaborative agreement-seeking derives in part from what is sometimes called multi-party dispute resolution and is grounded primarily in negotiation theory, utilizing the principled negotiation theory advocated by Fisher and Ury, Susskind and Cruikshank, and others. One of the central tenets of principled negotiation theory is to focus on the interests of the participants rather than the positions (Fisher and Ury). Interests are complex as they can be substantive, relational, or process-related. Interests also vary based on the specific circumstances of individual stakeholders. Moreover, each participant inevitably has multiple interests, some of which may be contradictory. Finally, seemingly contradictory positions among parties can actually be based on similar underlying interests.

As an example, our center was invited to help with a conflict at a large public university over the decision to replace unarmed campus security guards with an armed campus police force. Because of historical and ongoing police violence against Black people and people of color around the country, many Black students and students of color (in addition to many white members of the campus community) strongly opposed introducing armed police to campus. By contrast, some other students favored—or at least did not oppose—arming campus police so that those sworn officers could enter off-campus buildings where students were living and intervene in cases such as those involving sexual and domestic violence. In addition, several members of the board of trustees favored the addition of armed campus police officers, arguing that those officers could respond quickly in the event of a mass shooting or other emergency on campus. The debates were bruising and contentious, but it became clear that beneath the superficial simplicity of the yes-no question, should we introduce armed police officers on campus?, the common interest was safety. For some students and members of the board of trustees, the presence of additional police officers offered a sense of *more* safety and for others—particularly Black students—the addition of more weapons in the hands of the police made them feel distinctly less safe. Though the campus community did not undertake a full-blown collaborative governance process to make a decision nor was the issue settled with any finality, surfacing the interests changed the nature of the dialogue, particularly among students.

In order for an agreement-seeking process to fulfill its potential, it is important that all sides acknowledge the legitimacy of others' interests and then work together to develop a shared solution. Agreement-seeking requires a series of reciprocal actions to meet others' interests, and ultimately support for the solution. Though the parties may still see themselves as adversaries, collaboration involves a sense of partnership, the purpose of which is to reconcile their interests, and in so doing, generate solutions for mutual benefit. As a result, collaborative agreement-seeking is simply not appropriate for all public policy disputes. If some or most of those factors are not present, collaborative agreement-seeking has little or no chance of success.

That said, differences in interests and differences in the degree to which various parties value or prioritize their interests actually provide opportunities for agreement. A few years ago, we facilitated a project involving a conflict between the commercial fishing industry and the recreational fishing industry in Oregon. Each season, there were a finite number of salmon available for harvest, and each side staked out a position that would give them more (and the other group less) of that harvest. For every additional fish allocated to one group, there would be one less allocated to the other—a classic win-lose proposition. It was all about the numbers. However, when the two groups began to identify their underlying interests, it became clear that the commercial industry wanted to harvest their allocation in the shortest period of time. In addition to the numbers, the commercial fisheries were also interested in efficiency, reducing labor and fuel costs, and wrapping up the season without unnecessary expenditures. Charter operators and guides—those whose living depends upon taking tourists out for an enjoyable day of salmon fishing—were interested in the total number of fish available, but they were also interested in the length of the season and the number of days they could take paying customers out on the river. The conversation was not just about the number of fish anymore, but also about the length of the respective seasons, opening up the *possibility* that the parties could find a mutually satisfying solution.

In most instances, including the one above, each participant has more than one interest. The fact that some of one party's interests conflict with those of another party doesn't mean that *all* of their interests conflict. In another instance, we led the facilitation team for an agreement-seeking process to develop a wildlife management plan for the Malheur National Wildlife Refuge in far Eastern Oregon. There were long-term and high-profile conflicts between ranchers and environmental groups about grazing rights and other natural resource issues, creating a volatile situation for local communities, the federal land manager, and the tribes. Many of the participants entered the project mired in suspicion about one another and dubious about the prospects for the project's success. But, relatively quickly, they discovered that they shared at least one common interest— reducing the invasive carp in Malheur Lake. It was upon this initial common interest that the parties built what ultimately became a successful agreement on the larger wildlife management plan.

In agreement-seeking processes, each party has: (1) an interest they are trying to serve; (2) the potential to negatively (or positively) affect the interests of others; and (3) a desire to reach an agreement with other parties that is preferable to, or at least more durable than, what they might achieve outside the collaborative governance process. As discussed in chapters 4 and 7, it is the interrelationship of those factors that drive success—or failure—in an agreement-seeking process.

As is clear from the examples above, agreement-seeking processes are most often consensus-based. In other words, in seeking to reconcile conflicting interests, collaborative governance groups seek to reach decisions that everyone in the group can at least tolerate.

Consensus-based processes are sometimes criticized because they can create pressure to reach consensus in order to avert more severe conflict or to appease powerful group members. There is also sometimes the countervailing sense that a disgruntled individual has the power to capriciously derail a consensus emerging among the rest of the group. Chapter 4 offers strategies to deal with both of those dynamics. It is worth noting here that a consensus-based process also has the potential to protect minority interests from being swamped by majority rule. There are times when minority interests, particularly those of communities of color and other historically underrepresented communities may benefit from stopping an outcome that disproportionately serves a more powerful majority. In that sense, a consensus-based process, as opposed to a process based strictly on voting, may serve to disrupt the potential unfairness of strict majority-rule. Consensus-seeking also has the potential to be a potent tool in destabilizing power dynamics that consistently disadvantage communities of color and other historically underrepresented communities.

We will go into more detail about the intricacies of collaborative decision-making in chapter 7, but it is important to note that some of the biggest challenges that collaborative governance groups using agreement-seeking approaches face include: (1) zero-sum thinking and positional bargaining, (2) disparities in power between participants, (3) asymmetric commitments to the process, and (4) trust issues that lead to non-collaborative behavior and diminish the perceived value of certain offers.

Collective Action

Collaborative governance groups devoted to collective action are more focused on the aggregation of resources, actions, and authorities, and less on the dynamics of decision-making. In a collective action project, there is almost always some general agreement among the parties about the overall goal or objective of the process. In the parlance of economists, the goal of collective action is to co-create a public good. The problem that the group seeks to address is that no individual institution has the authority, expertise, or resources to accomplish the task by itself.

While consensus-building is based largely on negotiation theory, the intellectual foundations of collective action derive primarily from public goods theory in economics, including the work of economists such as Mancur Olsen and Elinor Ostrom. The goal or objective of a collective action process is less about finding agreement among disparate interests than about accomplishing more by aligning resources and actions.

Moreover, the solution to the problem depends upon the type of collective action needed. Collective action processes typically fall into one of three categories: fixed goal, incremental improvement, or coordinated interdependent actions.

Fixed Goal

A collective action process with a fixed goal focuses on a public good that has a requisite size and design requirement—the resources needed are already fixed, and the question is how to reach the goal. An example of this is a collective effort to raise funds for a facility, such as a school or a park. The goal is known, and the strategy is simply a matter of determining who is going to contribute and how much.

Incremental Improvement

In an incremental improvement project, there is usually some initiating action. Rather than a fixed target, however, the objective of collaboration is to see how much bigger, better, faster, or cheaper the project can be as parties incrementally add their contributions. One project facilitated began with the United States Army Corps of Engineers connecting abandoned gravel pits to the Willamette River in order to create side channels for migrating salmon to use on their trip upriver. Creation of the channels would have happened with or without the collaborative governance process. But the project created an opportunity to build other amenities as part of the larger effort. In the end, a group of about twenty organizations added respectively: construction materials and labor to build a wildlife viewing platform, volunteer labor to monitor fish counts, volunteer labor to construct a recreational trail, a parking lot for visitors, and more. There was no fixed goal beyond the side channels, but each contribution complemented the next and improved the outcome.

Coordinated Interdependent Actions

Sometimes a successful project requires coordination of several interdependent actions. Regulatory approval might be required before initiating an action, and that action may enable someone else's subsequent investment in the project. We worked on a project requiring coordinated interdependent actions a few years ago when members of a neighborhood group identified a vacant piece of property that they wanted to develop into an off-road bicycle park. The land had at one time housed a jail, and when the jail was torn down, the state department of transportation took over the property to store equipment for highway repair. The city agreed to own and operate the land if the department of transportation would transfer it at a reasonable price, and the neighbors would raise the funds to cover the cost of development. There were three interlocking pieces to the project, and if any one of them had not happened, the project would not have gone forward. In the end, the state transferred the land for a reasonable price, the community raised the money to build the park, and the city now owns and operates an off-road bicycle park in an area of town with a shortage of parks and other green space.

The ultimate expression of collective action is the combination of complementary resources or actions that produce a synergistic effect. The interdependence between the parties in a collective action process is that they each have something unique to contribute to the solution. It may be expertise, money, regulatory authority, political capital, or other resources or actions, but everyone has both something to offer and something they seek from others in order to improve the project. This is not to suggest that participants must pay to play in a collective action project. Rather, the theory of collective action is intertwined with asset-based community development and is rooted in the idea that communities have often organized for a long time to meet their own needs (Sirianni 45). Collaborative governance processes that are focused on collective action are designed to combine governmental and other institutional resources with the important assets that communities have already gathered, developed, and nurtured.

As explored in the next section, some of the biggest challenges that collaborative governance groups focused on collective action face include: (1) the problem of free-riders, (2) accountability and control, and (3) the risk-reward problem (Who takes the risk? Who gets the credit?).

Collaborative Systems

In broad terms, we refer to the third type of collaborative governance processes as collaborative systems. The defining features of collaborative systems are: (1) they involve ongoing work that extends beyond a single decision or project, and (2) they fulfill the need for ongoing relationships and repeated interactions between the parties over time. Some collaborative systems are initially formed as a short-term collaborative governance group focused on either agreement-seeking or collective action. As the group progresses, the participants discover additional decisions or projects that would benefit from a collaborative approach, so they band together to create a more long-term system. Other collaborative systems are created by a formal authority such as a state legislature or an administrative agency, and the process must be designed to meet the formal requirements.

Our version of collaborative systems is similar to Emerson's and Nabatchi's notion of "collaborative governance regimes." As they define it, a collaborative governance regime is "a system for public decision making in which cross-boundary collaboration represents the prevailing pattern of behavior and activity" (10). The authors go on to provide a comprehensive overview of how collaborative governance regimes function, with a particular emphasis on how they are initiated and the implications of those beginnings for the collaborative governance regimes.

For our purposes, we draw a distinction between collaborative systems and the other types of collaborative governance processes for two reasons:

First, collaborative governance systems are more likely to be a hybrid of the other two types of collaborative governance processes. In other words, it is more typical for a collaborative governance system to undertake both agreement-seeking and collective action over its lifespan. Watershed councils are some of the most enduring collaborative systems in Oregon. There are fifty-nine community-based watershed councils, funded by state government and charged with developing and implementing a watershed action plan (Oregon Revised Statutes, sec. 540.910). Each watershed council is made up of residents, landowners, environmental organizations, scientists, government representatives, and other relevant stakeholders. The purpose of each council is to address watershed health "from ridgetop to ridgetop." Together, the participants first use a collaborative agreement-seeking model to develop a watershed plan and then use collective action principles to implement that plan, often engaging many community members beyond those on the council, including school groups and other volunteer organizations. They complete the cycle by monitoring watershed conditions and adjusting the plan and the implementation accordingly.

Second, we distinguish between collaborative systems and the other two types of collaborative governance groups because collaborative systems can sometimes require a more formal decision-making structure or even a new legal entity. The biggest challenge in a collaborative system is loss of focus and integrated action. Once the initial decision is made or project is complete, the group may want to continue to meet, but the purpose of the group can drift. Once a group drifts from a clear purpose, meetings can become a tedious round of information-sharing rather than a robust forum for ongoing collaboration. In addition, there is a secondary risk that the collaborative system can become so habituated and ossified that it becomes another bureaucratic layer that lacks the trademark nimbleness and responsiveness of collaborative governance.

In order to reduce the risks of a collaborative system becoming either unfocused or ossified, it is important that participants revisit their interdependence and the values driving their collaboration. It is also helpful to create a structure that touches on the following components:

- The group's purpose;
- The appropriate entity type;
- The powers and duties of the group;
- The form and function of a governing body for the group;
- The structure, purpose, and rules for any committees;
- The method for making decisions and for resolving disputes (Johnson et al. 5).

Though many of the components are similar to the components of an ordinary, shorter-term collaborative governance process, it is important for the participants in a collaborative system to revisit earlier decisions regarding how they do their work and either reaffirm them or alter them to better suit a collaborative system.

As part of that review process, it is essential for participants in a collaborative system to determine what type of entity the group will become. If the collaborative system is a continuation of a group that meets regularly to discuss issues and occasionally act together, that system can probably function as a loosely structured committee or task force. If, however, more external accountability is required or the group needs an ongoing fundraising mechanism, the group may need to draft an intergovernmental partnership or even form a nonprofit organization or intergovernmental agency. In general, the more complex the decision-making and the more necessary external accountability is, the more formal the structure will need to be (Johnson et al. 13–19).

Once the entity is formed, the participants can better determine how the collaborative system should be structured and how it will do its work. For example, if the group forms a nonprofit corporation, there will be formal governance requirements that will not be required of a less formal coalition or committee of participants. By attending to structural issues first, the participants in a collaborative system can mitigate the tendency toward either drift or ossification.

There is one final distinction regarding collaborative systems. Because collaborative systems often have no set endpoint, it is important for the group to periodically evaluate their work and the efficacy of their framework. As Emerson and Nabatchi noted, collaborative regimes have "life cycles" that require adaptation and perhaps eventual disbandment (19). The collaborative governance group should stay attentive to that life cycle. Upon review, it may be that either the purpose of the group has evolved or the group has outgrown its original structure. The group should then go through another process to determine the right entity type and resulting governing system. The group should also stay alert to the possibility that a collaborative system may have served its purpose and run its course.

Conclusion

A deep dive into the intricacies of each of these collaborative governance types could span an entire book. But for our purposes here, we see these types as interlocking categories of practice grounded in theory, and throughout the following chapters, we continue to illustrate how and when the practice of collaborative governance might differ depending on the type of process at hand.

References

Emerson, Kirk, and Tina Nabatchi. *Collaborative Governance Regimes.* Georgetown UP, 2015.
Fisher, Roger, and William Ury. *Getting to Yes: Negotiating an Agreement Without Giving In.* Arrow, 1991.

Johnson, Jim, et al. *Building a Collaborative Governance Framework: A Five-Step Process.* National Policy Consensus Center, Portland State University, 2020.

Olson, Mancur. *The Logic of Collective Action Public Goods and the Theory of Groups.* Harvard UP, 2012.

Ostrom, Elinor. *Governing the Commons: The Evolution of Institutions for Collective Action.* Cambridge UP, 1990.

Sirianni, Carmen. *Investing in Democracy: Engaging Citizens in Collaborative Governance.* Brookings Institution Press, 2009.

Susskind, Lawrence, and Jeffrey L. Cruikshank. *Breaking the Impasse: Consensual Approaches to Resolving Public Disputes.* Basic Books, 1989.

4

FUNDAMENTAL DYNAMICS OF COLLABORATION

Introduction

Though we have spent the first three chapters examining the context in which collaborative governance operates, collaboration is, in the end, a human activity.[1] There are certain common dynamics at play in every collaborative process, which will in large part determine whether the process is likely to live up to the potential of collaborative governance. In essence, there are certain common behaviors that will trigger other behaviors, which will send a collaborative governance process into either a virtuous cycle that will lead to better outcomes and better experiences for the participants or a vicious one that leaves the participants no better off than when they started, and sometimes worse off.

This chapter elaborates on those dynamics and provides a foundation for understanding the strategies and actions that help make collaborations more successful. First, we examine the role self-interest plays, and why "moving northeast" is the fundamental objective of all collaborations. Second, we delve into the voluntary nature of collaboration and how that affects choice-making in collaborative processes. Third, we examine the nature of interdependence and how it affects the parties. Finally, we examine why trust is so important to collaborative relationships, and the role it plays in helping collaboration succeed.

Moving Northeast

We believe that the key to a successful collaboration in almost any setting is the principle of "moving northeast," a term borrowed from Howard Raiffa, one of the founders of the Harvard Negotiation Project. Raiffa used the concept to describe how parties might reap additional gains after an agreement has been reached (141), but we have adapted the term to describe the fundamental objective of collaboration itself. In order to fully understand the importance of moving northeast, it is important to explore the role of interests in collaborative governance processes.

The Role of Interests

Every party, whether an individual or an institution, has a set of interests that might loosely be described as overall goals. A consumer advocacy group, for example, might have a set of interests that includes better quality products, cheaper prices for those products, and more safety controls in the manufacturing of those products. Every party to a collaborative process brings its own set of interests, whether overtly stated or not. As Mancur Olsen points out, it is the self-interests of the parties, and the intersection of those interests that bring the collaborative group together in the first place (5). That is why they are there.

Research in the field of social value orientation by Pletzer (and others) has shown that persons who are more "pro-social" (that is, concerned about collective outcomes) exhibit greater cooperation than persons whose values are "pro-self" (76). Fair enough. However, some may construe these findings to mean that successful collaboration requires a kind of consciousness-raising, such that participants need to become more altruistic and seek to benefit the group rather than their own interests. We believe this call to rise above one's self-interest may well lead participants down a path that can raise questions about their own legitimacy at the table and, ultimately, lead to inferior outcomes in the collaboration itself. If someone representing a public or nonprofit agency in a collaborative process were to tell their agency director that, in a fit of altruistic spirit, they had offered a higher financial contribution than instructed, they would be unlikely to elicit a favorable reaction. Each organization or constituency needs to keep its own interests in mind as it enters into a collaborative process.

In addition, parties that do not advocate for their own interests in a collaborative process are likely to court suspicion and mistrust from the other parties. (What's going on here? What's their *real* agenda? What else are they not telling us?) It can also raise questions about whether a participant is a legitimate spokesperson for his or her or their organization or constituency. Perhaps most important, it is that friction, the bumping together of the different (and sometimes conflicting) interests, that brings forth the creative problem-solving that can truly make collaborative solutions more than just the sum of their parts. Without the synergy that can happen when parties seek solutions that incorporate everyone's interests, the potential for a greater outcome is abdicated.

Far from being unacceptable, entering into a collaborative process with the aim of furthering one's interests, and being clear about those interests, is usually *essential* for a productive outcome.

Furthering Multiple Interests

The reader may ask, how then does a collaborative group focus on collective goals, and not devolve into a bunch of self-interested squabbling? The answer lies in a few critical qualifying conditions.

The participants in a successful collaborative process, while advocating for their own interests, must simultaneously recognize the legitimacy of other parties doing the same. The work of a collaborative group is to consider the interests of all parties and to map where those interests overlap. The objective is to find mutual benefit, what we describe as moving northeast.

The term moving northeast comes from thinking about a problem graphically and geographically. A party attempting to further their interests is on a continuum trying to move as far in one direction as possible as they try to fulfill their interests.

In a directly *competitive* relationship, there are two parties whose interests compel them to move as far as possible in opposite directions (see Figure 4.1). The relationship is, thus, zero-sum, as one party moves forward on the continuum, the other necessarily moves back. Consequently, in a competitive relationship, one party's gain is the other's loss and vice versa. That is simply the nature of competition. It is quite common in agreement-seeking collaborations for the parties to come into the collaboration with a history of competing, and consequently with this win-lose mindset.

A *collaborative* relationship, on the other hand, even among former adversaries, looks quite different. The parties' interests are not necessarily the same, but they are not seen as diametrically opposed. This relationship may be illustrated by an x-y axis (see Figure 4.2). One party tries to move as far as possible toward their interests in one direction. The other party heads off in another direction toward their interests. The parties' interests may be divergent, but they are diametrically opposed. In contrast to the competition scenario, one party's gain does not necessarily require the other's loss. The dot at point A, B shows where the parties' *collective* interests line up based on their current progress along their continuum of interests. Where, then, should they look for a collaborative solution?

The only direction on the graph that a collaborative solution can be found is "northeast" (shown by the shaded box in Figure 4.3) because it is the only direction that provides for mutual benefit. It is the only direction that allows both parties to move further along their interest lines. This leads us to an important insight regarding the difference between competition and collaboration: while

Party 1   Party 2

FIGURE 4.1 Competitive relationships

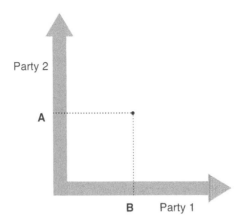

FIGURE 4.2 Divergent interests

in competition you can only win if the other side loses, when in collaboration you can only win (that is, further your interests) if the other party also wins. It is a profoundly different approach to the negotiation process.

Let's consider for a moment the alternative to moving northeast. Why would one party work collaboratively with another to get a result that is less than if they hadn't collaborated at all? Moving into that northeast box is the only logical goal when collaborating with others. We should note that this does not mean both parties must necessarily move in equal measure. The collaborative solution can potentially be in any portion of the shaded box. Exactly where in the box becomes a matter of fairness, which we discuss in a later chapter. This principle of moving northeast has critical implications for the kind of behavior that leads to success in collaborative groups. It means that, in order to further

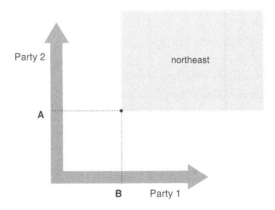

FIGURE 4.3 Collaboration: moving northeast

his or her or their interests, each party needs to pay attention to ensuring that the other parties advance their interests as well. And this means first understanding their interests and considering them when proposing solutions or agreements.

It is important to note here that, while Figure 4.3 represents a two-party relationship, collaborative governance usually involves multi-party relationships, sometimes involving twenty-five or more separate parties. We use the two-party model for clarity and simplicity, but the principles of moving northeast are the same. It is also worth noting that the principle of moving northeast does not necessarily require each party to improve upon today's conditions. When we talk about the current condition, we take into consideration a party's future prospects and the tolerance for the risk of poor outcomes. If, for example, one or more parties face a potential downward turn in their fortunes (such as a change in regulation, or a potential loss in the courts), they might compare a collaborative solution to that less-favorable expected future.

Although the need to look northeast for collaborative solutions may appear obvious, we find that it is not universally practiced. Many groups who profess to be collaborating are, in fact, still competing. Each party is still trying to out-maneuver the other, to recruit supporters among the others at the table, and—quite simply—to prevail. David W. and Robert T. Johnson call these "pseudo-groups" (23). When parties have an acrimonious history, each understandably approaches the relationship as zero-sum, rather than win-win, and often has a vocal constituency that reinforces that view. Consequently, they become as focused on making sure the other parties lose as they are on gaining a positive outcome for themselves. With a competitive history, it is logical to assume that both sides have, at one time or another, sought to take advantage of the other's vulnerability, which means that each party feels aggrieved by the other party's past behavior. They understandably enter a collaborative process in a protective or even retributive mode and then wonder why progress in the collaborative process is slow.

Real collaboration is joint problem-solving, and the essential problem is finding a way to move northeast. It requires honoring the legitimacy of others' interests and moving beyond the question of who's right and who's wrong to the question of how to reconcile competing or incompatible goals. In a true collaboration, each party works hard to find that space where all sides feel the outcome has been worth their time and effort. This is a fundamentally different approach than trying to get the other side to capitulate. "The key to doing well," says Robert Axelrod, "lies not in overcoming others, but in eliciting their cooperation" (8). The central question goes from: Why won't you give just a little more? to how can we make this proposal work for you?

We don't wish to portray this task as an easy one. When groups have widely disparate interests, finding northeast (win-win solutions) can sometimes be extremely challenging and requires very creative problem-solving. But that is the real, and ultimately rewarding, work of collaboration.

Some may be uncomfortable with this overtly transactional framing of collaboration. Isn't there a role for altruism? Shouldn't we all be working for the common good? Perhaps, but actions or decisions that serve the larger community frequently benefit one's long-term self-interests as well. As we discussed in Chapter 2, this is what Tocqueville conceived of as self-interest rightly understood (384).

In addition, efforts to serve the common good create social capital, resulting in reciprocal (collaborative) actions from others. That reciprocity may occur sometime after the initial act. Barn-raising has these very roots. If I help you build your barn today, when it comes time to rebuild my barn (perhaps years from now), you and others in the community are more apt to help me.

Another way that altruistic behavior becomes a form of enlightened self-interest is through the many indirect connections and relationships that bind parties together. A local business may contribute to the building of a neighborhood park because its employees may use that park, and young families might be more attracted to the community, which is good for business. Martin Nowak cites a fascinating study by Nicholas Christakis and James Fowler that reinforces this point. It shows that when one person is happy, the probability of a friend living within one mile being happy rises 25 percent and the probability that his or her or their immediate neighbors are happy rises 34 percent. It doesn't stop there. The probability of a friends' friends being happy rises nearly 10 percent, and the probability that *their* friends will be happy, people they will likely never see or know, rises 6 percent (243). The interconnections between people are many and often unseen.

All Collaboration is Voluntary

Embedded in the objective of moving northeast is the essential notion that collaboration involves a relationship with others. As Ostrom and Walker note, successful collaboration has an exchange at its heart. It is a joint enterprise in which the participants exchange a benefit to another party for a different benefit to themselves (6). And here's a critical point that affects all collaborative dynamics. The decision to confer that benefit is a *voluntary* one. No one can make anyone else collaborate.

Collaborative processes are sometimes mandated by legislatures or other decision-making bodies. The issue here is not whether the process can be mandated. It can be. The issue is how the parties will behave once they arrive at the table. Emerson and Nabatchi specifically distinguish between collaborative regimes that are voluntary and those that are mandated, and they find that mandated collaborative regimes are generally less successful than those that are voluntary (152).

In other words, you can lead a stakeholder to the table, but you can't make her collaborate.

The decision to cooperate with others or not, is the central subject of game theory and social dilemma research.[2] A social dilemma is a situation in which each member of a group has a self-interest separate from the interests of the larger group to which they belong. In this situation, there is an inherent short-term temptation for each individual to pursue that self-interest at the expense of the group. If everyone pursues this more selfish, noncooperative course of action, however, everyone is worse off than if they had cooperated. Social dilemmas exist in a wide range of contexts, large and small, including the workplace, the home, neighborhoods, and virtually every collaborative governance process. College roommates experience a social dilemma when someone needs to tackle the pile of dirty dishes after a party. Everyone wants them done and will benefit once they are, but each hopes one of the others will take on the task.

This kind of social dilemma is famously represented in game theory by what is known as the "prisoners' dilemma" developed by the Rand Corporation in the early 1950s to help analyze strategies for preventing nuclear war. In any single interaction, there is always a temptation and a short-term advantage to act selfishly. Paradoxically, however, if all parties act on that incentive, they all achieve a worse outcome than if they had all behaved cooperatively. More importantly, when the interactions are repeated over time, the short-term incentive to act selfishly quickly reveals itself to be a downward spiral. This is because acting selfishly motivates other parties to act selfishly in return, if only to protect themselves. Even parties initially inclined to cooperate will soon shift to not cooperating. The lessons from game theory can help us better understand the following implications of the voluntary nature of collaboration:

- Whether one chooses to act cooperatively with others depends upon how one predicts others will act. And those predictions will be largely based upon their past actions. Those who act on the temptation to take short-term advantage can count on creating distrust and, therefore, encountering noncooperation from others in future interactions;
- Acting on one's short-term self-interest in social dilemmas, therefore, comes at the expense of one's own self-interest in the long run;
- In repeated interactions, such as those in collaborative governance, it is in one's self-interest to *start* by cooperating (creating an atmosphere of trust), and then to see what happens. If the other parties cooperate, the research strongly suggests, one should keep cooperating because all will benefit. If others act uncooperatively and take advantage, however, one should stop cooperating;
- Interestingly, game theory also suggests that parties should be somewhat forgiving. People make mistakes. Perhaps that college roommate was late

coming home and forgot it was his turn to do the dishes. One might step in and do the dishes for him, so they are clean the next morning. In fact, to do so may elicit reciprocal cooperation when the roles are reversed. But it is *not* best to keep trusting or cooperating when there is repeated uncooperative behavior. If that roommate forgets his turn every week, stepping in (that is, cooperating) only reinforces that behavior.

The decision about whether or not to cooperate is not consigned to theoretical games. The incentive to take advantage of others' cooperation in the short term is what makes nuclear disarmament discussions between nations so tricky. If two nations both agree to disarm, and one cooperates and disarms first, the other nation is tempted to then exploit their advantage and keep their arms.

In virtually all collaborative governance processes, every party faces that temptation to take advantage of the other's cooperation. A recent example involved a manufacturing firm in the Pacific Northwest that faced a proposal for strict state legislation that would have forced them to control noxious air emissions at great cost to the company. Community and environmental advocates agreed to withdraw the proposed legislation in exchange for the company's commitment to engage in a collaborative process to identify emissions and implement necessary control measures. Once the legislation was off the table, however, the manufacturer essentially stopped cooperating and did little to reduce its emissions. The understandable response by the community advocates was then to halt their own cooperation.

This voluntary nature of collaboration follows from the horizontal nature of collaborative relationships. In bureaucratic organizations, there are normally vertical relationships of reporting and accountability. When a supervisor assigns an employee work, they are not collaborating. The employee is directly accountable to perform the work and report back, with implied consequences if they do not complete their assignment. Traditional organizational charts essentially diagram these vertical reporting relationships (see Figure 4.4).

In collaborative processes, however, the governance among autonomous organizations relies on informal social structures. This is in stark contrast to

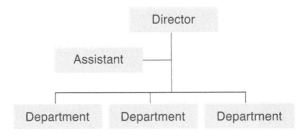

FIGURE 4.4 Vertical (hierarchical relationships)

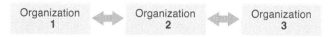

FIGURE 4.5 Voluntary cooperative relationships

structures of control and accountability that exist within most organizations. The relationships in collaborations are not vertical but horizontal (see Figure 4.5). There is no direct reporting relationship, and each party is counting upon other parties to voluntarily cooperate.

Simply put, because they do not report to one another, parties in a collaborative process choose whether or not to act cooperatively. The voluntary nature of collaborative behavior has some far-reaching implications. It means that even if parties come to the table, they will not necessarily cooperate. They may instead be looking to take advantage of other parties' collaborative behavior. Moreover, each party's assessment of whether to cooperate can vary over time as circumstances change. This means that everyone, whether consciously or not, is constantly keeping an eye on the others, looking for indications of whether they are cooperating. Perhaps the most important implication of this fact is that one must act collaboratively in order to attract collaborative behavior from the other parties.

Some may argue that some parties do not have a choice about whether or not to act cooperatively because their options are limited, and other parties at the table have more power. Even in these cases, we would argue that they are still choosing to cooperate based upon their assessment of the alternatives, rather than cooperating because someone directed or mandated them to do so. It is simply that their alternatives to collaboration are not very attractive.

All of this begs the question: If collaboration is always voluntary and involves time, expense, and risk, why collaborate at all? Why not go it alone, or utilize non-collaborative alternatives such as litigation? The reason to collaborate, as we will explain below, is interdependence among the parties.

Interdependence: The Basis for Collaboration

Interdependence is the reason parties come together in the first place, and it is the glue that keeps them together. Without interdependence, there really is no need or advantage for people to work with others. This point was emphasized as early as 1949 by Morton Deutch in his theory of cooperation and competition. Even when interests among group members may differ, "the essence of a group is the interdependence among members...which results in the group being a 'dynamic whole'...group members have to know that they swim or sink together" (25). Interdependence characterizes a relationship wherein the outcome for each party is dependent upon the actions of others.

Some of the early theoretical work on interdependence was done by H. H. Kelly and John W. Thibaut, who developed a structure for analyzing the interdependence in any given situation. That work identified several key elements:

- *Level of dependence among the parties*. Dependence, and interdependence, are not binary conditions, but are best understood as existing along a continuum from low interdependence to high interdependence;
- *Basis of dependence*. Each party brings contributions and needs to the process. The quality of the dependence among the parties will differ based on the interplay of those contributions and needs;
- *Mutuality of dependence*. Dependence among parties is not always symmetrical. Some parties need others' help in furthering their interests more than the others. This asymmetry can lead to differences in power;
- *Alignment of interests*. Some interdependence is based upon mutual interests between parties, and some is based upon conflicting interests. In both cases, there is interdependence (each party can influence the outcome of the other), but the degree to which interests are in conflict can have a significant effect on the dynamic of the collaboration;
- *Temporal structure*. Whether the interdependence involves a one-time interaction or longer-term relationship will have a significant influence on how cooperative parties are, and how they view their interdependence;
- *Information*. Perhaps more than the level of interdependence, the parties' *awareness* of their interdependence will play a critical role in how they behave. (Van Lange and Balliet 71).

It is important to note that interdependence does not require parties to have the same goals. Ansell and Gash note that even antagonistic stakeholders can successfully collaborate if they are also highly dependent on each other (553). In one of our cases, affordable housing advocates and other stakeholders were entrenched in long-standing disagreements about the amount and source of funding for affordable housing in Oregon. Those disagreements played out over several sessions of the state legislature, resulting in no substantial progress. Finally, the chair of the senate housing committee told the parties that she would not advance any legislation that did not have the support of all the stakeholders. As a result, affordable housing advocates, bankers, home builders, realtors, and representatives of community development services, came together in a collaborative governance process that resulted in a shared legislative agenda that included funding levels for affordable housing, a document-recording fee to increase funding, and an agreed-upon stance on a real estate transfer tax and on mandatory inclusionary zoning. In that case, the parties were made interdependent by a powerful legislator, each of them needing the other to come to the table so that they had some say in the final legislation and so they could make some progress toward their goals.

In an interdependent system, individuals have the ability to help each other through their actions and choices, but they also have the ability to hurt each other by preventing one another from reaching their goals. Take, for example, an environmental advocacy group and an industry group, each trying to maximize their interests related to pollution policies. The industry group may feel that one of its options is to seek resolution from a legislative body. On the other hand, if they go to the legislative body with a compromise solution that is supported by the environmental group, it would likely help their chances that the legislature would pass it. And it also might prevent a lawsuit from the environmental group that could delay or stop implementation, costing them potentially millions of dollars. From the environmental group's perspective, an agreement with the industry group might get them a better environmental result more quickly. And it might save them litigation costs and the uncertainty of a court ruling in the process. Indeed, it is this interdependence that motivates the parties to sit down and try to work out an agreement in the first place.

Project teams are often more interdependent than they realize, and as Van Lange and Balliet point out, the level of their awareness affects the nature of their collaboration (71). Understanding the particularities of the parties' interdependence can inform and improve collaborative outcomes. Moreover, interdependence plays out slightly differently in collective action projects than it does in agreement-seeking projects, and it is particularly important to collaborative systems.

Agreement-seeking

In agreement-seeking processes, the parties most often want different things, but each can get a better result through the other's cooperation. This is because each party faces a risk that the other parties might prevent them from satisfying their interests by blocking or delaying policy decisions, failing to take certain actions, or by taking action without the benefit of their perspective.

A good example is the interdependence of farmers, ranchers, fishers, environmental groups, and community interests participating in watershed councils as discussed in chapter 3. While there may be some shared goals and values, the parties also bring different, and sometimes conflicting, interests to the table as well as unique perspectives and knowledge on the question of how to best manage watersheds. Along with these differences are the means to affect outcomes for the other side. Environmental advocacy groups can take court action that might stop (or require) certain actions. Farmers and ranchers can affect the health of the watershed through their individual and collective choices. Each party's ability to affect the outcome for the others makes the parties interdependent.

It is this interdependence—the need for some resource or some action that others can offer—that brings people to the table. And, as Jones and her co-authors explain, the higher the task complexity, the greater the interdependence (921).

In contrast to the popularly cited trend of individuals and ideological groups becoming more isolated and autonomous because of technology and other societal trends, Shinn and Morgan argue that the need for collaboration and collaborative governance has actually expanded in recent years, precisely because of the greater interdependence brought about by what they call an increasingly "power-shared world" (4). Stanley McCrystal, a former United States Army General, believes the growing complexity of problems and governing structures in our society create greater interdependence, and thus a greater need for collaboration and communication (54).

As mentioned above, Van Lange and Balliet noted that the awareness of interdependence is a crucial factor for collaboration. We often do not find that awareness present at the beginning of our processes. Many of the parties come to the table with only the vaguest idea of what they need from others, having thought even less about what others might need from them. A number of years ago, in preparation for a major collaborative governance process to determine a local water supply strategy, we asked one of the principal environmental organizations what they were hoping to get from the other parties to further their particular interests. The representative stared blankly for a moment, unsure what we were asking. They were so accustomed to being in a responsive, protective mode, that they had not thought through what they might want to actually get out of the collaboration to further their own interests. The irrigators and other business organizations, while able to articulate what they wanted, had not stopped to consider what the environmental groups might be looking for from them.

In our experience, the interdependence of the parties, and more specifically their awareness of their interdependence, is essential to the success of any collaborative process. When individuals become aware that their goals and well-being are intertwined with the goals and well-being of others, they are willing to do the hard work of finding solutions that are acceptable to all. And when you know you will interact over time, on multiple issues, research shows there is increased sensitivity to interdependence, leading to increased collaboration (Axelrod; Ostrom; Balliet; Van Lange).

Collective Action

When engaged in collaboration for collective action, the parties are generally seeking the same public good, but they need each other's help to create it. Each party needs the complementary assets of others, be it money, skills, political connections, or other assets.

A transportation project in central Oregon provides an example of this interdependence. The Oregon Department of Transportation had the capital funding for new buses to serve a cluster of rural communities. The local council of governments had the administrative capacity to run the system. Several communities had buses to contribute to the system. One larger city had a shop in which to store and repair buses. And several social service agencies had funding to invest in service for their special-needs clients, which helped cover some of the operating costs. Each party was dependent upon the resources or capacities of the others to reach their common goal. By acting on that interdependence, they now have a successful, operational bus system.

Sometimes what is needed, rather than complementary assets, is coordination of actions or authorities. An example of this comes from a project intended to improve forest management in the Fremont-Winema National Forest area near the town of Lakeview, Oregon. The town had suffered economically following the reduction in logging in the nearby national forest, caused in part by environmental advocates' opposition to the previous policy of old-growth logging. Meanwhile, the forests themselves were in an unhealthy condition because of decades-long fire suppression practices. A forest products company offered to build a small-diameter mill (that would process smaller trees), which promised to create eighty-five new jobs in the community. However, in order for this investment to be made, the company required a relatively long-term commitment from the United States Forest Service for a certain level of stewardship cutting (tree-thinning) in federal forests. And in order to make that commitment, the Forest Service needed an agreement from environmental groups not to challenge these stewardship projects in court. The environmental advocates agreed based on the mill owner's promise that the mill would be relatively small, with a modest long-term capacity. The key parties were dependent upon each other to make the project successful. In the end, all three parties made the commitments needed, and two years later there was a new mill operating in Lakeview, Oregon.

Collaborative Systems

The interdependence between stakeholder groups plays an even more prominent role in the formation and continuation of ongoing collaborative systems, as opposed to collaborative projects. The very reason stakeholders choose to form an ongoing collaborative, such as an intergovernmental council, is because they recognize that they will have multiple issues or problems over time that they will need to tackle together.

This interdependence can take many forms. An intergovernmental council may form to address issues that transcend geographic boundaries, and require a coordinated effort. They work together because a problem in one jurisdiction can affect the other jurisdictions. Alternatively, service providers in a given geographic area with a mutual interest in addressing a particular policy domain, may come together in a collaborative system because of a need to share information and align or coordinate their resources to better effect. Such is the case with the education collaboratives and local public-safety coordinating councils with whom we have worked. Yet another form of interdependence is represented by collaboratives whose primary focus is to bring together stakeholder groups with *conflicting* interests, such as forest collaboratives or watershed councils. In each of these cases, it is the interdependence of the parties that brings them, and holds them, together.

Trust: The Social Capital of Collaboration

We now turn our attention to the primary tool in countering the short-term incentive to take advantage of others' cooperation: trust. Let's start by returning to one of the key lessons learned from game theory, that trust between the parties is highly dependent on how those parties have acted previously. If one party begins a working relationship by cooperating, others are much more likely to trust that cooperative behavior will continue, and they will, therefore, reciprocate that cooperation. The opposite is also true. If someone starts by taking advantage of others' cooperation, they are less likely to be trusted going forward.

Defining Trust

In a relationship between parties, trust is the belief that if one party cooperates, others will not try to take advantage of that cooperation. Trust necessarily involves a degree of uncertainty about the others' behavior. To trust is to accept some vulnerability (Dasgupta 51). If the outcome were certain, if one party somehow knew that every other party was going to cooperate, there would be no need for trust.

Collaborative relationships, we have noted previously, involve transactions or exchanges between parties. Those exchanges often involve actions or commitments today in exchange for promises of actions or commitments at a later date, which means there is always some element of uncertainty and risk involved. At a baseball game, Roland McKean reminds us, either the peanut vendor or the fan with the money has to give first (29). One must trust the other. If the promises of future action are not credible, that is, if they are not trusted, they become meaningless or severely discounted. And the degree of trust will largely determine the ease or difficulty of the transaction.

An example may help illustrate the concept. Each party in a collaborative relationship, in trying to further their interests, offers something of value to another party (actions, resources, and so forth). If a party is not fully trusted to follow through with a promise, however, the value of that offer will be discounted. In a collaboration involving water policy, irrigators may offer to improve watershed conditions on ten miles of a stream in exchange for an environmental group supporting an increase in water for irrigation. If the environmental group fully trusts that the irrigators will make good on their commitment, they might accept the deal, concluding it would result in a net benefit for the environment. However, if the environmental group does not fully trust that the irrigators will actually make good on their promise of future action, for example, if they believe there is only a 20 percent chance the improvements will actually be made, they may discount the offer accordingly and reject the deal. In our experience, these probabilities are rarely actually calculated with such precision. In general terms, however, this is the type of thinking that goes on when one party considers another's offer.

Trust is consequently a form of social capital, for if others perceive that you will follow through on your commitments or promises of future actions, it becomes a form of credit. One party can expand the range of possible collaborative agreements when other parties believe they can trust the first party not to take advantage of their cooperation. And, as Nowak and Highfield point out, this social capital is not limited to those who have had previous experiences with one another. A collaborative reputation, what Nowak and Highfield call "indirect reciprocity," can enable parties to "spend" that social capital even between parties who have not previously interacted (25).

We distinguish here between two types of trust:

- *Dispositional trust* is related to someone's personal traits. Through their history and reputation, they have demonstrated that they are, by their nature, either trustworthy or not;
- *Situational trust*, means, independent from someone's personality, they can be trusted, or not, because of the circumstances involved. It may be that a person who is otherwise trustworthy does not speak for or control the actions of other parties who could negatively impact a deal. Or, it may be that someone who is not otherwise trustworthy may be constrained by contingencies or other consequences to actually cooperate.

It is also important to note here that distrust can be based upon historical harm. Even if the parties have not personally interacted in other settings or even if they have never heard of one another, some historical harm is so significant or pervasive that the parties start from a stance of distrust. For example, we have been involved in several projects involving school systems. In some of those processes, Black parents and other parents of color have shared stories about their own negative experiences with school systems, including racial targeting, unjust disciplinary action, and disregard and neglect. In some of those cases, though their children may be enrolled in an entirely different school system from the one they attended, Black parents and parents of color viewed invitations to collaborate with their children's schools with suspicion and distrust.

Collaboration Without Trust

What does collaboration look like without trust? Robert E. McCarthy describes an atmosphere of fear, a tension that you can feel in the room. People around the table are guarded and cautious, the real issues are avoided, and the monitoring and transaction costs go up significantly (26). We have found that collaborating without trust is a little bit like trying to buy a house with no money in the bank and a terrible credit rating.

We've previously described trust as accepting some risk, some vulnerability. Without trust, there is little risk-taking and very little vulnerability expressed or exposed. The parties stick to their positions, and consequently, almost nothing happens to change the status quo or to enable exploration of creative solutions or exchanges. When there is little trust among parties in a collaborative governance group, nobody wants to be the first to initiate a cooperative approach because they suspect that others will take advantage of them. Parties do not want to waste their time on fruitless efforts. So, everyone waits to see if someone else will cooperate first. It can be a long wait. Perhaps most importantly, without trust, everyone acts accordingly, which is to say each party exhibits defensive, competitive behaviors that may be understandable, given that history, but only reinforce the atmosphere of distrust. And the downward spiral continues.

Building an Atmosphere of Trust

So, what to do? How does one begin to build a climate of trust among parties so that a collaboration can be productive and move northeast?

Game theory and the prisoners' dilemma game can again be instructive in this regard, as researchers have simulated hundreds of thousands of iterations of the game to determine the optimum strategy for solving the dilemma. The key answer, as Axelrod has noted, is to always begin by cooperating (that is, trusting). This approach is the most likely to elicit reciprocal trust and cooperation. And never be the first to act selfishly for short-term advantage. Conversely, if one begins the interactions by taking short-term advantage, the effect is to immediately start the downward spiral of distrust.

The good news is that trust and reciprocity together can create a virtuous cycle of trust, reciprocity, and cooperation that builds on itself. The research has demonstrated time and again that trust can build incrementally and, as it does, the willingness to cooperate expands to accommodate ever-greater levels of risk (Ansell and Gash 561).

Begin by explicitly acknowledging the goal of mutual benefit, writes Robert McCarthy: "The conscious decision by two people or groups to understand and take seriously the interests of others is the foundation of trust. Now it is possible to explore how the interests of multiple parties can be satisfied" (26). The first step is what we call "collaborative listening," the simple act of listening with an intent to understand others' interests. It is also helpful to acknowledge or even advocate for the interests of others, as a way of demonstrating one's commitment to finding mutual benefit. A forest collaborative we were advising was nearing a decision on the management of a section of the forest that had been the subject of significant disagreement, and one of the key parties was going to be absent at an upcoming meeting, providing an opportunity for the environmental groups to engineer a decision to their own advantage. Instead, they recommended that the group suspend their decision until the timber industry's input could be heard. Not surprisingly, when the absent member found out about this, it had a measurable impact on the trust level in their relationship.

Another way to promote trust, which may seem counter-intuitive, is disagreement, a topic we expand on in chapter 10. To express conflict or disagreement, but do so in a way that acknowledges the different interests (and the desire for mutual benefit), is an act of vulnerability, an act that says, "I believe that this is a safe place to voice my concerns." To not voice a disagreement, when you have one, is to actually raise doubts about your own trustworthiness, and about the entire collaboration.

There are other ways of demonstrating a commitment to mutual benefit and trust-building. The simple act of sharing information can engender trust and information-sharing in return. Offering something of value to another party, even if it is small, offers opportunities for reciprocity. Sometimes actively working on a project together, something real, can help build relationships by giving the parties a chance to rely on each other, and then to make good on that reliance. Finally, acknowledging past harms or mistakes and offering some form of amends can be a powerful step in restoring trust.

The Secret Sauce: Reciprocity

Perhaps the biggest single tool for building trust is reciprocity. Reciprocity is repaying cooperation with cooperation, the very basis of the barn-raising tradition. The concept is, of course, far older than that. *Quid pro quo*, the ancient Romans used to say—something for something.

Reciprocity breeds reciprocity and creates an upward spiral of collaboration. Each party has received information that the other party will not take advantage of their cooperation, which further increases their confidence in cooperation for the next interaction. Repeated reciprocal actions of this nature can create a climate of trust and reciprocity within a group, which opens up wider possibilities for collaborative agreements and actions. In a climate of reciprocity, people are more willing to accept longer payback times and greater uncertainties about outcomes, expanding the universe of potential exchanges.

If we return to our x-y axis showing the northeast quadrant in which collaborative solutions will be found (see Figure 4.3). The shaded box illustrates the universe of potential solutions.

But collaborative groups do not operate in a theoretical universe. While the entire large shaded box may constitute *all* possible solutions, a group operating with a low degree of trust will have those options constrained, limited to the smaller shaded box in Figure 4.6. It is important to note here that certain solutions that would otherwise be mutually beneficial are off the table because without a climate of reciprocity, those options are seen as too risky.

With a group climate and pattern of reciprocity, however, that range of options begins to expand (see Figure 4.7). Options that include a little more risk and require more trust are now back on the table, providing more opportunity for the group to move even further northeast, for greater mutual benefit.

This principle holds true both for agreement-seeking and collective action projects, as well as for collaborative systems. The research of Kurzban and Descioli found that many who participate in a collaborative process contribute in greater amounts when they are able to observe that others have already made a contribution to the public good (141).

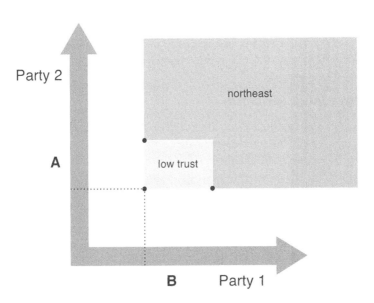

FIGURE 4.6 Solutions when trust is low

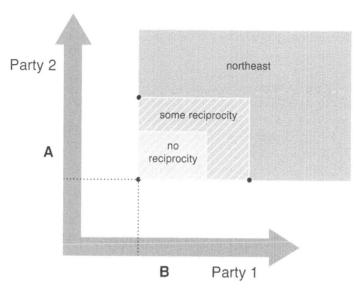

FIGURE 4.7 Universe of solutions when reciprocity exists

Caveats

Up to this point, we have spoken of trust as a positive thing, essential to productive collaboration and something to be cultivated. However, there are some caveats to this line of reasoning.

First, while trust is helpful to collaboration, one should not practice blind trust. That is, a party should not continue acting cooperatively while other parties repeatedly exploit that cooperation for their own benefit (and to others' detriment). Our students will sometimes argue that blind trust is taking the high road or doing the right thing. We ask in reply, what is right or moral about reinforcing exploitative behavior? Elinor Ostrom did pioneering work in showing that the effectiveness of reciprocity in building trust is dependent upon the willingness of the parties to reciprocate negatively when called upon, that is, "to use retribution to some degree" to punish uncooperative behavior (10).

Negative reciprocity can be valuable because it is not uncommon in multi-party settings to have what some describe as a bad apple, a party who acts non-collaboratively, selfishly taking advantage of others' cooperation. There is a non-trivial portion of the population—Pletzer has labeled them "pro-self"—who will act this way, and they can have a significant impact on collaborative groups. Research has shown that cooperative behavior in a group setting can go from 50 percent to 20 percent with the addition of a single bad apple (Kerr 604). Dealing with uncooperative behavior from these bad apples directly and quickly is important in order to preserve a group norm of cooperation.

Second, in a variation of which-came-first-the-chicken-or-the-egg, Gambetta challenges the accepted paradigm that trust is a prerequisite of collaboration. Often, he argues, trust is an outcome of collaboration (225). We agree, to a point. We have seen groups with major trust issues work together on a small collaborative project, with a result being much higher levels of trust. Even in these cases, however, there needs to be at least some minimal trust to get the parties together. Even when there is no dispositional (personal) trust of the other parties, trust in the process, or trust in the conditions or contingencies of the collaboration, can enable parties to collaborate.

Finally, there may be conditions when trust simply can't be built, including when the distrust between parties arises directly out of a historical harm based on racism or some other oppression. It may be that there is too great a trust gap to ask the harmed parties to collaborate with the parties who caused harm until some other kind of restorative work has been done outside the collaborative governance process.

These caveats notwithstanding, trust creates the social capital that enables the exchanges that are the substance of collaboration. The absence of trust makes those exchanges less valued and more difficult, and the transactions and monitoring costs much higher. Moreover, as we have seen, distrust leads to behaviors that only reinforce that distrust. Halting or reversing that vicious spiral, when parties have an adversarial history, can be one of collaboration's biggest challenges.

Earning and Losing Trust

Trust and distrust are not symmetrical opposites (Gambetta 234). Trust is something earned, or won, over time. Parties come to learn, through repeated interactions, that they can trust someone. However, distrust can manifest in an instant, with one betrayal, even after years of repeated trustworthy behavior.

Once lost, trust can take a long time to restore, even in the best of circumstances. And, interactions between parties where trust has been lost are rarely the best of circumstances. So, how does one attempt to rebuild trust once it has been lost? Can parties work together once that trust has been breached? The answer, fortunately, is yes. Robert Axelrod writes, "Cooperation based on reciprocity can develop even between antagonists" (3). We will talk more about how to do this in section 2, but here we offer some theory to underscore the point.

When there is a lack of trust, the parties are in protective mode, and they are trying to avoid the risks of the other parties taking advantage of any cooperation on their part. The overall strategy, therefore, is to understand and then reduce those risks.

When a party says to another, "we just don't trust you," it can stop the conversation. It essentially is translated as: "Any offer you put on the table will be rejected because we don't trust you to follow through. So, there's really no point in talking further." It doesn't give either party much to work on and doesn't help to produce agreement. It also serves to absolve the accuser of any responsibility for the hard work of finding mutual beneficial solutions.

What we say to participants in collaborative governance groups who tell others, "I don't trust you," is that it implies that if they *did* trust the other party, they would be willing to act in a more cooperative way. "I don't trust you" is an incomplete and unhelpful sentence, but if it were completed, it could give both parties something to work on—demonstrations or contingencies, perhaps—and provide a roadmap to moving through the impasse. When parties do not trust each other, we sometimes ask them to think through their answers to at least some of the following sentences:

> I need to trust that you will (or will not) _____ before I am willing to _____.
> If I do _____, I do not trust you to _____.
> If I trusted you to _____, then I would be willing to _____.

Being able to articulate, with some specificity, what assurances one party needs in order to trust the other party can then aid in the development of contingencies or other conditions essential for clarifying expectations when parties have a bad history with each other. These contingencies (for example, if, after three years, less than ten miles of riverbank is restored or riparian vegetation upgraded, the additional water rights will be rescinded) can reduce the risks that any parties face when they accept promises of future action.

A final word here about repairing or rebuilding trust when there is an adversarial history: without contingencies or some similar conditions, to trust the other side would be a form of wishful thinking. To expect such a party to suddenly trust the other party under these circumstances is simply not realistic or even rational. To shift the dynamic from competitive to collaborative, from selfish behavior to cooperative, each party will rightly seek to minimize their risks as much as possible. That is why we suggest, as a starting point, baby steps—small pilot projects where the consequences of failure are low.

Conclusion

These fundamental dynamics of collaboration, while important in themselves, build upon and reinforce one another to define and shape collaborative processes. It is the interdependence between the parties that motivates them to voluntarily collaborate with others. It is that voluntary nature of collaboration—the choice to cooperate with others or not—that elevates the importance of trust and reciprocity. And all of it is in service to addressing the interests of the parties in moving northeast.

Notes

1 Throughout this chapter, we discuss the dynamics of collaboration. Though we do not always distinguish between collaborative governance and other types of collaboration, our interest is in the dynamics at play in collaborative governance processes.
2 We often use the terms "collaborate" and "cooperate" interchangeably. Although some authors in the field of public participation make a technical distinction between these two terms, we believe that distinction can be both confusing and misleading. We draw instead on the literature and research of game theory and social dilemmas, which use the term "cooperate" in a more general sense to describe mutually supportive behavior.

References

Ansell, Chris, and Alison Gash. "Collaborative Governance in Theory and Practice." *Journal of Public Administration Research and Theory*, vol. 18, no. 4, Oct. 2008, pp. 543–571.

Axelrod, Robert. *The Evolution of Cooperation*. New York Basic Books, 1984.

Balliet, Daniel, and Paul A M Van Lange. "Trust, Conflict, and Cooperation: A Meta-Analysis." *Psychological Bulletin*, vol. 139, no. 5, 2013, pp. 109–112.

Dasgupta, Partha. "Trust as a Commodity." *Trust: Making and Breaking Cooperative Relations*, edited by Partha Dasgupta, U of Oxford, 2000, pp. 49–72.

Deutch, Morton. *The Resolution of Conflict*. Yale UP, 1973.

Emerson, Kirk, and Tina Nabatchi. *Collaborative Governance Regimes*. Georgetown UP, 2015.

Gambetta, Diego. "Can We Trust Trust?" *Trust: Making and Breaking Cooperative Relations*, edited by Diego Gambetta, U of Oxford, 2000, pp. 213–237.

Johnson, David W., and Robert T. Johnson. "Cooperative Learning and Social Interdependence Theory." *Theory and Research on Small Groups*. edited by Scott Tindale et al. Plenum Press, 1998.

Jones, Candace, et al. "A General Theory of Network Governance: Exchange Conditions and Social Mechanisms." *The Academy of Management Review*, vol. 22, no. 4, 1997, pp. 911–945.

Kelly, H. H., and John W. Thibaut. *Interpersonal Relations: A Theory of Interdependence*. John Wiley and Sons, 1978.

Kerr, Norbert L., et al. "'How Many Bad Apples Does It Take to Spoil the Whole Barrel?': Social Exclusion and Toleration for Bad Apples." *Journal of Experimental Social Psychology*, vol. 45, no. 4, 2009, pp. 603–13.

Kurzban, Peter, and Peter Descioli. "Reciprocity in Groups: Information-Seeking in a Public Goods Game." *European Journal of Social Psychology*, vol. 38, 2008, pp. 139–158.

McCarthy, Robert E. *Navigating With Trust: Transform Your Organization With Energy, Direction and Joint Effort*. Rock Bench Publishing, 2012.

McCrystal, Stanley, et al. *Team of Teams: New Rules of Engagement for a Complex World*. Penguin, 2014.

McKean, Roland N. "Economics of Trust, Altruism, and Corporate Responsibility." *Altruism, Morality, and Economic Theory*, edited by Edmund Phelps. Russel Sage Foundation, 1975.

Nowak, Martin, and Roger Highfield. *Super Cooperators: Altruism, Evolution, and Why We Need Each Other to Succeed*. Free Press, 2012.

Olson, Mancur. *The Logic of Collective Action: Public Goods and the Theory of Groups*. Harvard University Press, 1968.

Ostrom, Elinor. "A Behavioral Approach to the Rational Choice Theory of Collective Action: Presidential Address, American Political Science 1997." *American Political Review*, vol. 92, no. 1, Mar. 1998, pp. 1–22.

Ostrom, Elinor, and James Walker, editors. *Trust and Reciprocity: Interdisciplinary Lessons for Experimental Research*. Russell Sage Foundation, 2003.

Pletzer, Jan Luca, et al. "Social Value Orientation, Expectations, and Cooperation in Social Dilemmas: A Meta-Analysis." *European Journal of Personality*, vol. 32, no. 1, 2018, pp. 62–83.

Raiffa, Howard, et al. *Negotiation Analysis: The Science and Art of Collaborative Decision Making*. Belknap Press, 2003.

Shinn, Craig, and Douglas Morgan. "Symposium: Community Capacity, Social Trust and Public Administration." *Administrative Theory and Praxis*, edited by Henry Kass, Vol. 21, no. 1, Mar. 1999.

Tocqueville, Alexis de, et al. *Democracy in America*. Saunders and Otley, 1835.

Van Lange, Paul A. M., et al. "The Psychology of Social Dilemmas: A Review." *Organizational Behavior and Human Decision Process*, vol. 120, 2013, pp. 125–141.

Van Lange, P.A.M., and Balliet Daniel, "Interdependence Theory." *APA Handbook of Personality and Social Psychology*, edited by Mikulincer and Shaver, American Psychological Association, 2015.

SECTION 2

Framework and Process

The last section introduced the defining norms, constitutional context, typologies, and dynamics that underpin the field of collaborative governance. This section applies those principles and dynamics to the practice of working with multi-sector groups to address public issues.

A number of authors have provided outstanding examples of the progressive steps of an agreement-seeking process for resolving public issues ranging from Carlson's three stages of a collaborative process (18) to Carpenter and Kennedy's multiple-step model for public dispute management (67). In our center, the practice of collaborative governance is guided by a framework, illustrated in the figure below, which is a synthesis of these models. The framework consists of four primary phases: (1) assessment, (2) design and organization, (3) deliberation and decision making, and (4) implementation and adaptation. Each phase is characterized by a guiding question that speaks to the overarching purpose of that phase, along with the key activities needed to fulfill that purpose. This framework is effective across the diverse span of agreement-seeking, collective action, and building of collaborative systems to address public issues in virtually every sector, from transportation and natural resources to education and health. This framework offers a structure for guiding a collaborative governance process from conception to implementation. At the same time, the framework can be adapted to each particular situation, allowing for creativity and the use of novel methods for group work at various points. Using a common framework across a range of projects has the added benefit of fostering the ability of leaders, practitioners, and participants to share experiences, explore comparisons, and build learning across these diverse applications.

Although the framework is organized into distinct phases, it operates less as a linear progression and more as an upward spiral; as a group works together and develops more in-depth understanding of an issue during the deliberation phase, for example, they may revisit key tasks of an earlier stage to reframe their initial focus or engage new members who can bring expertise related to this revised focus. In that sense, the framework should be viewed not as a rigid set of steps for a group to march through. Rather, the framework can offer milestones a collaborative group can use to track its progress, to suggest next steps when the

Assessment

Guiding Question:
Can a collaborative governance approach help the situation at hand?

Key Indicators to Explore:
Common purpose and a workable scope
Sufficient information
Identifiable interests and legitimate representation
Incentives for participation
Sufficient trust
Adequate resources and time
Opportune legal and political context
Adequate balance of power between parties
Enabling legal authorities

Design and Organization

Guiding Question:
How is the group best organized to achieve its desired outcomes?

Key Elements to Design and Organize:
Framing the common purpose and values
Identifying key roles and responsibilities
Clarifying the processes for decision-making and conflict resolution
Building the form to support the function
Creating working agreements

Deliberation and Decision-making

Guiding Question:
How does a collaborative governance group forge a solution?

Key Areas of Focus:
Agreement on framing and operating principles
Joint learning
Joint problem-solving
Consensus decision-making
Public involvement

Implementation and Adaptation

Guiding Question:
How does the group link its agreements to implementation?

Key Activities:
Structuring the agreement for implementation
Designing the future governance structure
Moving to action
Monitoring, evaluating, and adapting

SEC.2 ILLUSTRATION 1   Collaborative governance framework

Sources: Carlson, Christine. *A Practical Guide to Collaborative Governance.* Policy Consensus Initiative, 2007.

Carpenter, Susan L., and W. J. D. Kennedy. Managing Public Disputes. 1st ed., Jossey-Bass, 2001.

group finds itself stalled, or to help identify process decision points where definitional norms and core principles may be applied to help ensure the legitimacy and ultimately the sustainability of the results.

This section is organized according to the four main phases of the collaborative governance process framework. Chapter 5 focuses on how to conduct an assessment to determine whether a collaborative governance approach could be helpful in addressing a particular situation. It delves into the key indicators that point to the potential for collaborative success and offers ten strategies for conducting an effective and efficient assessment. Chapter 6 explores how to use the information from the assessment to design and organize a collaborative governance group. Chapter 7 is devoted to the joint learning, deliberation, and decision-making phase at the heart of the collaborative process. The chapter explores practices for building a shared pool of understanding within the group and how to employ that knowledge to make decisions that will achieve desired outcomes. Finally, chapter 8 describes how to link the group's decisions and agreements to implementation and action. This may involve navigating a critical hand-off to an external entity or the formation of an entirely new collaborative group devoted to implementation. The chapter also explores how to build adaptive management into the implementation of a solution that will continue to refine and improve results over time.

5

ASSESSMENT

Introduction

A collaborative governance process typically starts when an individual, a public administrator, or a small group of stakeholders wants to solve a problem or seize an opportunity that would benefit from people working together—or at least not working *against* each other—to address it. While each situation embodies a unique combination of substantive issues, political intricacies, power dynamics, and other complexities, the starting point for a collaborative governance approach is always the same—it begins with an assessment.

For example, several small coastal towns in the Pacific Northwest were overrun with elk within their city limits, which posed safety risks to drivers, pets, residents, tourists, and property. Residents of these communities were divided over a spectrum of options. Some advocated for adopting laws to allow culling, or even hunting, within city limits while others opposed these measures, instead favoring strict protections for elk. As public passions ran high about how to handle the escalating problem, public leaders considered whether a collaborative approach could be used to create a comprehensive management plan that would be supported by their diverse communities. In another instance, two rural school districts identified vocational and technical education as a gap in their students' educational opportunities. The districts and the communities teamed up to determine whether they could use a collaborative approach to develop a career technical education program to serve their whole region. In another case, the federal government required the cleanup of a large Superfund site in a river running through a major urban area. As the potentially-responsible parties entered final negotiations about how the massive cleanup costs would be apportioned, representatives of multiple community-based groups began meeting to discuss using a collaborative approach to help ensure that jobs generated by the cleanup stayed in the community.

In each of these instances, the first step was assessing whether the necessary conditions existed to support the success of a collaborative governance approach, and if so, how the process should be designed and organized to achieve the desired results. This chapter explores the value of a collaborative governance assessment, outlines the key indicators showing that a collaborative governance approach could be helpful in addressing a situation, distinguishes key indicators that are specific to an agreement-seeking process from those that apply in a collective action approach, and provides ten road-tested strategies for conducting an assessment.

The Value of the Collaborative Governance Assessment

The value of an assessment in helping to determine the viability of a consensus-based approach is well documented by scholars (Susskind & Thomas-Lamar 104; Gray & Purdy 75; Carlson 21; Carpenter & Kennedy 71) and is considered one of the most essential steps for ensuring the success of a collaborative governance process. Beyond providing valuable insight that can help determine whether conditions are ripe for employing a collaborative governance approach, the assessment sets the tone and course for the entire process moving forward. Thus, the assessment is not mere preparation. Rather, it is an integral part of the collaborative governance process itself.

A collaborative governance assessment usually involves a series of personal conversations or interviews with people who are impacted by, or have knowledge about, a public issue or who have the resources or authority needed to address the issue. These interviews provide the assessors with valuable information and allow them to inform potential participants about how a collaborative governance approach might work. With this knowledge, each potential participant can begin to prepare for collaborative engagement. A well-conducted assessment interview also provides an opportunity for interviewees to explore their needs and interests without pressure toward any preconceived outcome. Through this exploration, participants have the authentic opportunity to consider and to influence how the process might be shaped to best meet those needs and interests. Most important, this first encounter provides the assessor a chance to establish personal relationships and build trust with potential participants, laying the foundation for any future collaborative work.

Even if a collaborative governance approach is not recommended, the assessment can serve as an important intervention that may improve a situation. In many cases, the conversation itself might lead interviewees to shift their thinking. For example, tensions over a development project between the mayors of two mid-sized cities led to severed communications, which further escalated the conflict. During the assessment interview, one of the mayors recounted the history of the conflict and recognized the part he had played in its escalation. Shortly afterward, this mayor reached out to the other mayor to reestablish communication.

In another potential case, there were oil storage containers adjacent to a river running through a large city. Modeling suggested that a future earthquake could seriously damage those containers, which could pose a safety threat and create the potential for significant ecological damage. Even though the project was not ripe for a collaborative governance effort at that time, the assessment process and interview report, in part, prompted the owners of the oil storage facilities to revamp their seismic resilience committee. Overall, in this case and in others, an assessment can help bring unforeseen information to a situation, give parties a chance to be heard and better understood, and be a contributing element to improving the circumstances.

The value of an assessment is profoundly affected by who conducts the interviews. The ideal assessor is able to create a climate of trust where interviewees feel free to share—as honestly and openly as possible—their perceptions, interests, and alternatives with confidence that information will be handled sensitively and without bias. Additionally, the assessor needs to understand collaborative governance well enough to help potential participants consider whether and how it might help them meet their desired outcomes. Christine Carlson suggests that a third-party facilitator (or assessor) might be engaged to conduct the assessment "when the issues are complex or contentious, when many parties are involved, when there is a history of distrust …when this is the first effort to use consensus building, or when past efforts to resolve differences have failed" (181). Carlson further explains that by conducting the interviews, the facilitator "can begin to establish credibility with potential participants" and directly gather information that will aid in process design (181).

Key Indicators that Conditions are Ripe for Collaborative Governance

Although assessments can fulfill several purposes, the central question in an assessment is: Can a collaborative governance approach help the situation at hand? There are several key indicators that can help both the assessor and the parties determine whether that question can be answered in the affirmative. An overview of the guiding question and the key indicators is found in Figure 5.1.

The key indicators used to assess the potential success of a collaborative approach in a particular situation go well beyond whether the people involved think the process can work. For example, at the final celebration of a successful two-year collaborative governance process resulting in adoption of a

---

Assessment

Guiding Question:
Can a collaborative governance approach help the situation at hand?

Key Indicators to Explore:
Common purpose and a workable scope
Sufficient information
Identifiable interests and legitimate representation
Incentives for participation
Sufficient trust
Adequate resources and time
Opportune legal and political context
Adequate balance of power between parties
Enabling legal authorities

FIGURE 5.1   Assessment (phase one)

comprehensive conservation plan to guide the management of the federally-designated Malheur Wildlife Refuge in Eastern Oregon, participants spoke candidly about their initial skepticism at the start of the project. After years of conflict, "I never thought we would be able to agree on anything when we started," a rancher reflected, still shaking his head in disbelief. "I thought this would be a complete waste of time, but I was willing to give it a try," an environmentalist echoed. And a federal agency leader added, "While I had my doubts, I knew we had to try something different." One by one, close to forty participants representing a diverse spectrum of interests made similar remarks about their incredulity that they were able to achieve such successful outcomes, particularly given the level of conflict and distrust at the outset. These comments underscore the fact that strong doubt and cynicism are to be expected when a conflict is long-standing. Such sentiments are not in and of themselves counter-indicators to the use of a collaborative governance approach.

The assessment is a mechanism for exploring whether the situation has the necessary conditions that will support the collaborative dynamics (detailed in chapter 4) that are fundamental to the success of a collaborative governance approach. Those dynamics include the ability to "move northeast" to create mutual gain, a sense of interdependence, and the potential for trust in others. In other words, rather than seeking an actual solution to a problem, the assessment is an effort to determine whether the stakeholders have the potential to work together effectively to find or implement an appropriate and acceptable solution. This section outlines the key indicators that a collaborative governance approach might be successful. While these indicators are applicable to all types of collaborative governance approaches, the focus will differ slightly depending on whether the assessment is related to an agreement-seeking process, a process focused on collective action, or an assessment to establish a collaborative system.

Common Purpose and a Workable Scope

For a collaborative governance process to move forward, the participants must be able to agree on the overall purpose of the process. This common purpose can take a number of forms. A group might agree on the basics: that there is a problem that needs to be solved, a conflict that must get resolved, or something they want to accomplish together. More specifically, the group may want to coordinate their activities in order to accomplish a joint project, or they may want to see if they can agree on a policy recommendation to a state or federal agency. In some cases, the shared objectives may be modest, such as agreeing to undertake joint learning or fact-finding or even simply to build a relationship and promote mutual understanding through dialogue.

Clarity on a common purpose does not necessarily mean parties agree on the outcomes, over which there may be substantial disagreement at the outset. For example, the state-sponsored Genetically Modified Organism (GMO) Task Force brought together a group of stakeholders with vastly different positions on the use of GMOs in agriculture. Some representatives advocated for expanded use while others wanted to ban them completely. However, all participants agreed that there was value in producing a guide for state policymakers to help them understand the primary issues surrounding the use of GMOs, including a summary of the areas of agreement and disagreement around each of these issues.

Closely related to the existence of a common purpose is whether participants can find relative agreement about the scope of the work. For example, participants may agree that they want to seek consensus on recommendations related to natural resource management or environmental regulation. Environmental advocates may want the scope of these recommendations to apply statewide, while neighborhood groups may want the recommendations to focus more narrowly on their specific site. In another case, there may be a group of interrelated issues that could be the subject of a collaborative governance process, but participants have different views about which issues should be included in the process. Too narrow a scope might limit the effectiveness of the collaborative effort and the willingness of key parties to engage. On the other hand, too broad a scope may cause the collaboration to become unwieldy and stray into policy areas that are more properly left to political resolution. For example, a local community seeking consensus recommendations for the regulation of carbon emissions from diesel trucks might be a reasonable scope for a project, but seeking consensus recommendations on ways to stop climate change might not. To succeed, the potential must exist for participants to develop a shared purpose and a meaningful scope for their work together.

Sufficient Information

A collaborative governance process will struggle to move forward if the information upon which decisions must be based is missing, unavailable, or disputed by one or more of the parties. However, just because the necessary information is not immediately available or agreed upon does not mean that collaboration is impossible. The assessment can help clarify what information is necessary and where it might be found. Some information might be collected in advance of the collaborative effort, while some might be developed collaboratively as part of the group's efforts—such as joint fact-finding (discussed in chapter 7)—or through the initial development of an agreed-upon research plan. A collaborative approach to developing information or data may be especially helpful in situations in which there is disagreement over the legitimacy or credibility of the existing information or data.

Identifiable Interests and Legitimate Representation

It is also important to determine whether all of the potentially affected interests can be represented in a collaborative governance process. Stakeholders, as defined by Carlson, are "key individuals, groups or organizations that have an interest in the issue at hand. They may be responsible for seeing a problem resolved or a decision made, they may be affected by a problem or decision, or they may have the power to thwart a solution or decision" ("Convening" 171). Identifying representatives of each of those interests may require a nuanced and iterative approach. Some affected stakeholder interests will be obvious inasmuch as those parties may have initiated the assessment and identified other parties who have interests affected by the issue, either as allies or opponents. And other potential interests will likely be uncovered in the course of the assessment.

But, as set forth in chapters 1 and 2 it is also important to look beyond the surface to ensure that representation is robust and that the outcomes will be equitable. The assessor must seek out community members who can speak to the impacts the project may have on historically underrepresented communities and to the unique contributions these communities can bring to the ultimate solution. Oftentimes that requires the assessor disaggregate interests to determine the needs of the whole community.

Communities and interests are often more complex than they appear on the surface. For example, in constructing a particular state policy decision, the interests of cities may need to be untangled to determine whether the size or demographics of each city matters. In another example involving a project in a relatively small community, we first reached out to the local Catholic church—which held several Spanish-language masses during the week—to initiate a conversation with Latin American residents. Upon further conversation, however, we learned that while many Mexican and Mexican-American families attended the Catholic church, many Guatemalan and Guatemalan-American families attended the Baptist church, which offered services in Mam (an indigenous language of Guatemala) as well as Spanish. In the end, we did outreach in both places and in both languages. It is important to note that there may be times when it makes sense to conduct some broader community outreach and engagement as part of the assessment in order to understand the full scope of community interests.

We have also learned that the most vocal and visible spokesperson in a community may not always speak for the broader interests of the *whole* community. In such circumstances, it is often necessary to speak with several other people who might round out the assessor's understanding of the interests at play.

As the interests and stakeholders are identified, the question then emerges to what extent a more dispersed group of interests could be represented adequately and legitimately by one individual in a collaborative process. The converse question must also be considered. That is, does the identified potential participant, even someone who may have sought out the collaborative process, have the ability to represent definitively the interests of their purported constituency or community of interests?

For government entities, determining legitimate representation is relatively straightforward, as it involves selecting a representative either by virtue of an individual's positional authority within an agency or because he or she is authorized by an election. However, identifying legitimate representatives can become thornier for non-governmental interest groups, as many of the potential representatives are self-selected. The three dimensions associated with legitimate representativeness set forth in chapter 2 bear repeating here: (1) *authority* to represent a particular group; (2) the ability and willingness to exhibit *behavior consistent with the interests* of the represented group, which includes having channels of communication back to the group; and (3) *accountability* to the represented group.

These criteria can help an assessor determine who might represent an interest group or community in a collaborative governance process. Sometimes an assessor may have difficulty locating a person with the clear, legitimate authority to speak for a critical interest group. In those instances, we often turn to informal community leaders to help inform our assessments. For example, in a housing project involving a widely dispersed community, a local Zumba teacher helped connect us to the informal leadership network among Spanish speaking community members. In another instance, an employee of the county housing agency introduced us to individuals who were deeply connected in low-income and immigrant communities. One caution is in order. Because informal leadership is frequently self-appointed, the assessor may need to speak to multiple representatives of any particular community to gain a fuller picture of the interests at hand and who might represent them.

It is also important that the representative is an individual who is well-suited—or at least not ill-suited—for a collaborative process. A representative who has the tolerance for the messy pace of collaboration, the skills to negotiate, or the ability to enter the process without a history of conflict with other parties can make a difference. For example, an effective advocate for an essential interest who may fit all of the representativeness criteria but is perceived by other parties to be an inflexible bully may not be the best participant in a collaborative governance group.

One barrier to a successful collaboration arises when a party seeks to exclude someone representing an opposing interest. Sometimes that impulse to exclude a party or interest may be part of an effort to build a coalition and consolidate power as an intentional strategy to overpower opposition and advance a particular solution. If, after a thorough exploration of that party's concerns, they continue to seek to block participation of another key stakeholder, a collaborative governance process may not be an effective approach.

In some instances, however, the impulse to exclude opponents is driven by the fear that progress will not be possible. For example, one of our colleagues was involved in a project in which a county parks department sought to redesign a community green space into a sports complex. The park's manager adamantly refused to include the residents living next to the park as they had vehemently and publicly opposed the effort. Given that strong opposition from adjacent neighbors could potentially block the project and threaten the sustainability of any outcome (through litigation or other means), their exclusion would indicate that a collaborative governance approach should not go forward. However, before ruling out the possibility of collaboration, the facilitator met with a group of neighbors to more deeply explore their objections. In that meeting, the facilitator worked to understand and redefine the objections in terms of the residents' interests, such as preserving quiet times, diverting traffic away from residential areas, and ensuring adequate event parking. Upon seeing that many of the residents' interests aligned with his own, the park manager was then willing to engage the neighbors.

It is important to note that sometimes, in preparation for and during a collaborative governance process, there may be a need for like-minded groups to caucus—that is, to meet and discuss how they would like their mutual interests to be represented in a collaborative process. Such caucusing is not necessarily an attempt to exclude others or to consolidate power. Rather, it is often an effort to prepare to engage productively in a collaborative process. In a case involving negotiations on a controversial change in the ownership of a public forest, multiple environmental interests needed to be engaged. On one end of the spectrum, some advocated that no logging be permitted in the forest at all; on the other end, some groups were willing to accept limited logging as long as it met certain restoration practice standards. In that case, it was necessary for the environmental groups to meet to negotiate common ground and agree on a way to represent their diverse interests before a collaborative governance approach could be undertaken. These groups also needed to continue to meet as the negotiations continued to ensure the spectrum of groups within the coalition could live with the agreements being formed.

On a final note, the assessor should be aware that the stakeholder representation required for a collective action process to succeed is slightly different than what is required for agreement-seeking. Rather than engaging a broad set of represented interests, collective action relies on the presence of a sufficient number of public, private, and civic stakeholders, each of whom is willing to devote their time, talents, and resources to make a solution happen. Assembling that group requires intentionally looking beyond government and public resources to nonprofit and business entities that may benefit from the project and, therefore, have incentive to contribute to the solution. Resources can also be amassed by finding linkages to other projects, processes, or other public benefits or by engaging parties whose missions align with the project and may contribute to the solution. While some of the resources may still be missing, an indicator of potential success is the presence of a core group of stakeholders who are committed to contribute to the implementation of a solution over time.

Incentives for Participation

On a practical level, collaborative governance can be a slow, painstaking, and resource-intensive approach. It is not to be undertaken lightly. To make the kind of investment needed for a collaborative approach to work, parties must be motivated to do something about the situation in the first place. The problem or opportunity must be sufficiently important or a high enough priority to command and sustain their attention.

Incentives for participating in a collaborative governance process are increased when a party sees it as a likely pathway for achieving their most important interests. These interests may or may not be entirely clear even to the parties themselves. As described in chapter 4, parties typically tend to focus initially on the issue, defining what they want in terms of the desired outcome of an issue or decision. These desired outcomes are usually expressed as one-dimensional and are presented as an all-or-nothing proposition: I don't want any roads closed on those public lands, or we don't want to see these public lands torn up by recreational vehicles. In contrast, interests are the underlying reasons or motivation for a party staking out a particular position. Interests answer the question of why a particular outcome is important or what it will achieve. Interests can often be met in a multitude of ways, opening up the possibility for resolution. For example, I want to ensure access for the range of community needs from fire prevention to snowmobile trails, or we want to ensure these public lands remain healthy and accessible for wildlife movement, breeding, and migration. The assessment interviews can help parties begin to clarify what interests under-lie their positions and evaluate the extent to which these may be met through working with others.

The presence or absence of alternatives will also affect a party's willingness to participate. Of particular importance is the extent to which a collaborative gov-ernance approach offers a party more opportunity, and less risk, to get what he or she or they want. In other words, each party will undergo their own calculation to compare the potential alternatives to collaborative engagement and the risks associated with those alternatives.

This calculation is by no means simple. Often there are multiple alternatives to a collaborative governance approach, which might include pursuing legisla-tive strategies or litigation, waging a media campaign to influence an outcome, building a coalition, or doing nothing at all. In the book *Getting to Yes: Negotiating Agreement without Giving In*, the authors describe the importance of considering the "best alternative to a negotiated agreement," also known as a BATNA, as an important prerequisite to a negotiation (Fisher and Ury 100). As part of calcu-lating their BATNA, a party will also need to estimate the likely probability of getting the outcome they want out of each alternative. So, while a party might see going to court as their best alternative, the potential of winning the court case may actually be very unlikely or uncertain at best. That uncertainty and risk may create more incentive for participating in a collaborative approach. Considering the *worst* alternative to a negotiated agreement (WATNA) and its likelihood can sometimes also be important. For example, a party might gauge that the worst thing that could happen if they chose not to work with others was the high likelihood of ending up the target of a media backlash. The risk of this worst alternative may also create incentive toward a collaborative approach. Settling on the *most likely* alternative to a negotiated agreement (MLATNA) and comparing whether that stacks up to be better, more certain, and less risky than what is anticipated from a collaborative approach can also add to the calculation.

Whether a party has a better alternative to a collaborative governance approach can be difficult to discern. For strategic reasons, some parties may hold their alternative strategies close to their vests—concealing the strengths and weaknesses of possible alternatives. Or parties may have inflated confidence in alternatives. For example, a party may be deeply invested—emotionally as well as financially—in their alternative strategies for advocacy or litigation. Consequently, they may believe more fervently in the likelihood of success with that alternative than a careful analysis of strengths, weaknesses, and associated risks might otherwise suggest. The assessment interview offers an opportunity to help parties think more deeply about their long-term interests, their own best alternatives, and how much better (or not) those might be than a collaborative approach.

In some cases, external forces emerge to create compelling incentives for stakeholders to work with others. In one example, the legislature agreed to fund a rural medical center so long as the community employed a collaborative governance approach. In another, as we set forth in chapter 4, the senate housing committee chair became so frustrated by the seemingly intractable conflicts between stakeholder groups that she refused to consider advancing any potential legislation that did not have the mutual support of conflicting groups. In that case, the alternatives to collaboration were likely to be unproductive, the parties were forced into interdependence, and they were able to forge a path forward together.

If a party truly has a better alternative to a collaborative governance approach, then it may prove difficult for that party to have sufficient incentives to fully participate. The presence of the alternative frees them from being interdependent with others. They can independently pursue their own goals without the need to help other parties advance their interests in another direction. In some cases, a party's long-term and genuine interest in having a good working relationship with other parties may significantly shape their ability to participate sincerely in a particular collaborative context. But a more generalized desire to be collaborative—or to not be perceived as un-collaborative—will likely not hold up when a party is faced with the real challenges and rigor of working to meet the needs of others in a collaborative setting. When an alternative path exists to more successfully meet his or her or their most important interests, a party can, will, and—we would suggest—should choose the path that best serves their interests.

The presence of strong incentives for participation is a critical indicator that a collaborative governance approach is viable. These incentives are influenced by the extent to which parties believe that their interests can be met through working with others, that there are few or only costly or uncertain outcomes available through other alternatives, that maintaining the status quo is unlikely or unpleasant, and that a need for long-term relationships is valuable. As demonstrated by the Malheur Wildlife Refuge example discussed above, parties may be naturally skeptical, particularly when there is a long-standing history of conflict—but at the least, they need to have strong incentives to be willing to give collaboration a try.

Sufficient Trust

An assessment should also consider both the current levels of trust among the parties and the potential for trust if the conditions were to shift. As noted in chapter 4, the level of trust among parties affects their respective willingness to work together for mutual benefit. Over the course of an assessment, a party's distrust of one or more other parties often becomes apparent through either explicit articulation or is implied through their actions or unwillingness to engage. Also, as detailed in chapter 4, such distrust is often dispositional—that is, the distrust is based on prior experience with, or the impression of, the person or entity.

While it presents a substantial challenge for collaboration, a lack of trust among the parties at the outset is not necessarily a deal-breaker. When trust is low, it will be important to explore ways the process can be designed or structured to establish a sufficient level of situational or procedural trust to make engagement possible. Procedural trust evolves from confidence that the process itself will be structured in a way that will help constrain potentially adverse behavior of otherwise untrustworthy participants. The contacts that are made during the assessment phase are the first opportunities to cultivate a level of procedural trust and to gather input about procedural conditions that can be built into design of the process. For example, in the case of the Malheur Wildlife Refuge, years of conflict and litigation had led to deep distrust among the parties. Parties agreed that having a facilitator affiliated with a collaborative platform, working on behalf of the entire group, would be imperative to establishing enough procedural trust to get people to the table. Procedural trust also can be increased through the joint creation of operating principles, which can govern everything from confidentiality to decision-making processes. The more that procedural trust can be created, the more likely a collaborative governance approach can succeed, even in the face of dispositional distrust between the parties. A rigorous assessment can help determine whether that procedural trust is likely to be possible.

Adequate Resources and Time

Collaborative governance processes can be time- and resource-intensive for participating individuals and entities. An assessment should explore whether all parties have or can obtain the resources necessary to effectively participate in a collaborative process. The assessor should consider the technical and scientific complexity of the subject matter and to what extent joint technical learning or data-gathering efforts will be needed to ensure all of the participants can operate on a level playing field. For collective action projects in particular, the assessor should determine the actions and resources that will be required for a project, the sequencing of actions, and related barriers or time constraints.

Questions of inclusion and belonging will necessarily arise during the assessment. The assessor needs to consider what is required for parties to participate fully. For agency staff, participation in a collaborative governance approach is part of their job and is typically well-supported by management. For representatives of small organizations and other community members, however, participation may take away from mission-critical work and other commitments. In order for the project to go forward, the collaborative governance group may be required to provide stipends, childcare, or other resources. The group also may need to agree to hold meetings after work hours and to remove other barriers to participation. The group may need to consider accessibility issues, such as language accommodations, fully accessible meeting spaces, and equipment for the hearing impaired.

One of the most significant resources required for a collaborative governance approach to be successful is time. As noted, collaborative governance takes an investment of time on the front end to create lasting, effective solutions that will often save substantial resources and time on the back end. Thus, it is important that adequate time is available to conduct the entire collaborative process and to reach an outcome within the appropriate and necessary time frame. There is sometimes a temptation to press forward in a collaborative governance process even if there is insufficient time to do a thorough job. We will sometimes hear— or make—the argument that "something is better than nothing." But that is not always true. After a complete assessment, it is important to soberly consider whether there is adequate time (and there are adequate resources) to thoroughly consider the needs of all the parties and reach a conclusion that serves the community as a whole. If not, a rushed collaborative process runs the risk of either making things worse or wasting people's time, which may well prevent or hinder a collaborative governance approach in the future.

That said, there is an inherent tension when considering how time relates to the success of a collaborative process. Collaborative governance takes both adequate time *and* intensive engagement in order to progress efficiently. Consequently, too much time can be a problem, allowing a process to drag on unnecessarily. Participants in collaborative governance processes are almost always engaged in other governance, advocacy, or community activities beyond the process at hand. Everybody is busy, and most people have more on their to-do list than time in which to do it. When a collaborative governance process has no definite timeline, it may suffer from dwindling priority among its participants in favor of other more urgent issues on their plates—even if the subject matter is inherently important to them. This is why it is often important to consider whether there is an action-forcing deadline to drive participants to the table, increase the level of urgency, and propel the process forward. The deadline might be driven by some external factor such as a court order, an administrative or legislative deadline, or a funding opportunity. Whatever the source, the presence of some action-forcing deadline is an important factor in motivating the parties and should be considered in the assessment process.

An Opportune Legal and Political Context

At some point in the process, an assessor must take a step back and look at the external environment—the larger legal and political context in which the issues are arising. What legal or political constraints might limit meaningful alternatives or otherwise influence the outcome? For example, if pending legislation or a forthcoming legal decision would substantially affect the process, it may be appropriate to wait until the legislation is enacted (or not enacted) or until the court decision is issued. To move ahead under such circumstances could waste substantial time, effort, and resources and result in no meaningful outcome. In the Superfund case mentioned earlier, for example, the assessment revealed that the uncertainty around the liability negotiations needed to be resolved before the project could go forward, though the parties identified several steps they could take to prepare for the time when the project was ripe.

Adequate Balance of Power between Parties

As outlined in chapter 1, a group's ability to share power is at the heart of what both defines collaborative governance and makes it an effective tool for solving complex public problems. With this in mind, a key indicator of potential success relates to the power dynamics between the parties and whether they are balanced enough to support the sharing of power needed for a collaborative group to succeed. Assessing this indicator requires unpacking what is meant by power, the various sources of power, and what constitutes an adequate balance of power.

Simply defined, power is the capacity or ability to pursue one's own needs and desires and to direct or influence the behavior of others. Jill Purdy asserts that power comes from having authority, resources, or discursive power. Authority is "the socially acknowledged right to exercise judgment, make a decision, or take action" (410). For government entities, authority is tied to their legally established right to make and enforce rules. In a collaborative governance process, the governmental participants' willingness to share power with the group is so vital to the legitimacy of the collaborative group that it is its own indicator, as we will explore later in this chapter. For non-governmental organizations and other community groups, some of their authority stems "from their right to participate in governance or to pursue legal action" (Purdy 410).

Resource-based power is derived from "tangibles such as financial resources, people, technology, and supplies; and intangibles such as knowledge culture, and capabilities" (Purdy 410). Examples of resource power include a tribal community's knowledge of the history of place, a community program's ability to provide meeting rooms or staff support, a stakeholder's possession of scientific expertise, or a private company's significant financial clout.

The final source of power comes from discursive power, which "refers to the ability of an organization to represent a discourse or speak …on behalf of a societally important ideal, such as ecological preservation or racial equity" (Purdy 411). Discursive power is also derived from the ability to activate other social groups to act, such as to stage a protest. Though discursive power is often the least considered, it can play a key role in collaborative governance processes. Discursive power may be used to support the results of a collaborative process or to oppose them. It may also be used to bring others to the table or discourage them from participating.

Every entity or stakeholder possesses power derived from one or more of the sources mentioned above. Rarely, however, is the power between parties evenly distributed, nor does it need to be for collaboration to work. In fact, in a collective action project, it is the pooling of multiple sources of power that creates a successful collaboration. However, Gray emphasizes that each party must possess enough power to give them the "legitimacy, voice, and ability to influence others within the process itself" (119). This is what Iris Marion Young calls "internal inclusion" (55). This is tricky business, though, since a party must not only be aware of his or her own power (and be willing to use it), but the other parties must also understand and value that power. In collective action processes, stakeholders often underestimate the power they wield in the form of expertise, social and political capital, and lived experience. For example, in the case cited earlier in this chapter involving the transformation of a county park, the manager had to be reminded that the neighbors had the power to block an outcome before he softened to the idea of including them.

Parties may need help evaluating their own power vis-á-vis the other parties. When power is too lopsided to allow an essential party the voice and influence needed to make power-sharing work, other approaches may be more appropriate. One of the memorable examples one of our colleagues facilitated occurred right after the Vietnam War when many refugees came from Southeast Asia to settle in Portland, Oregon. Some longtime residents of the neighborhood were upset that the newcomers were coming onto their properties to glean fruit that had fallen off trees in their yards. The neighbors wanted to meet face-to-face with representatives of these immigrant communities to talk directly about their concerns. Agency staff members who were working with the refugees and who were familiar with their cultures, however, felt this kind of dialogue would be too overwhelming. In this case, power was unequally distributed between the longtime neighbors and the new immigrants because the neighbors derived power from being members of the dominant culture and being familiar with its practices and systems, placing the new immigrants at a disadvantage. So instead, the agency staff recommended hosting a lunch revolving around a panel presentation where representatives from the immigrant communities could describe their experiences after the war, what led them to immigrate, and the challenges they faced. Needless to say, few eyes remained dry after the presentation. This forum allowed both the representatives of the immigrant communities and neighbors to experience their discursive power. Afterward, the long-time residents and recent refugees formed joint committees to address a range of issues to improve how they lived together.

As set forth in chapter 1, power is not a finite resource, and parties can expand their power within a collaborative group once they understand its source. But power always intersects with systems, and Black people, Indigenous people, and other people of color have been systematically disadvantaged by some of the public, private, and civic institutions that show up in collaborative governance processes. A thorough assessment that includes a power analysis will help members of a future collaborative governance group craft procedural agreements to set the stage for a more equitable processes.

Enabling Legal Authorities

As discussed in chapter 2, collaborative governance processes are enmeshed in a variety of legal regimes. In order for a collaborative governance process to proceed, the parties—particularly the public sector parties—need to be clear about their legal obligations and restrictions. Once those boundaries are established, the participants with legal authority must be willing and able to create decision space that enables a collaborative group to share this power. According to Purdy, the legal entity's willingness to give power *to* the group rather than exert power *over* the group is what "gives teeth to a collaborative effort" (410).

To be successful, parties with the legal responsibilities for a policy or an action should see value in a process in which power is shared—power that exceeds what could be gained by a merely consultative process. Returning to the Malheur Wildlife Refuge example, the legal responsibility for development of a comprehensive conservation plan rested entirely with the United States Fish and Wildlife Service. However, the comprehensive conservation plans produced by the agency staff historically faced significant opposition and legal challenges from a whole host of stakeholders, including environmentalists, ranchers, and community groups. The Fish and Wildlife Service saw substantial value in using a collaborative governance approach in which a group of diverse stakeholders would forge consensus-based recommendations to submit for plan adoption. In this way, the agency could meet their statutory responsibility to develop the plan while ensuring it would be supported by a diverse set of stakeholders.

Relatedly, when large institutions are involved, it is also necessary to probe whether the opinions and positions of staff representatives assigned to the process accurately reflects the interests and intents of the larger organization. We describe this as the need to be aware of the "multi-headed dragon" where divisions or departments or even individuals within an organization may hold different policy orientations. In a large agency, for example, an over-enthusiastic department manager, or an under-enthusiastic one, might be articulating positions or interests that are inconsistent with those of another department or the agency's leadership. When the possibility exists that the outcomes of a collaborative process may be overturned or unsupported by those who are lateral or further up in the decision chain, this is an indicator that more work is needed to create institutional alignment before conditions will support a collaborative governance approach.

While collaborative governance is particularly helpful when there are multiple governmental entities with overlapping authorities, lack of clarity about who has what legal authority can be an indicator that more preparatory work is needed prior to engaging in collaborative governance. For example, regional leaders sought our help in assessing the use of a collaborative governance approach to address the recurring outbreak of harmful algae blooms in a lagoon on the Willamette River. The algae blooms can cause sickness and death in humans, pets, fish, and other wildlife or livestock that come into contact with the infested water. The assessment revealed that while stakeholder interest in working together was high, there was significant lack of clarity about who had legal authority to implement any coordinated actions to address the situation. We recommended that the multiple governmental entities involved take initial steps to clarify their overlapping authorities with respect to the lagoon before considering a collaborative governance approach with stakeholders.

In some situations, the decision-making authority resides with a legislative body. In those cases, it is important to consider at the outset if, or under what conditions, the political will exists or could be engaged to support potential change. The ideal condition is when one or more legislators have agreed in advance to commit to champion the policies resulting from a collaborative governance process through the legislative or other approval process.

When one or more of the key indicators are absent, it is unlikely that a collaborative governance approach will succeed. In some cases, the situation may simply not be ripe yet. In that case, an assessor or facilitator can ask what a simple next step might be. Sometimes, it requires waiting for a lawsuit to be resolved or a piece of legislation to be passed. Other times, a stakeholder or group of stakeholders may have to do some internal work to get ready. If key stakeholders are not prepared to go forward, the group could consider what goals the available parties could achieve together. Even small steps taken together can start to develop the relationships, trust, and capacity for a group to take on more extensive collaborative governance projects in the future.

Distinctions between Collaborative Governance Types

At its core, assessing a situation helps determine whether the necessary ingredients are available to complete a recipe for collaborative success. While the indicators outlined above are relevant across all situations, a few specific considerations will apply depending on whether the assessment suggests the parties should use an agreement-seeking process, a collective action process, or a collaborative system.

Agreement-seeking

When assessing whether conditions are ripe for seeking an agreement, a predominant indicator is the negotiability of issues. Some issues, by their very nature, are inherently nonnegotiable. As discussed in chapter 4, true zero-sum issues (when one party's gain is the other's direct loss) are often not well-suited to a collaborative governance approach since there is no ability to "move northeast." Issues that are rooted in fundamental values may also be nonnegotiable for one or more parties. Additional red flags include the presence of alternative forums, significant dispositional distrust, or severe power imbalances that cannot be adequately addressed in process design.

Collective Action

The success of collective action is reliant on the presence of a group of stakeholders who agree on the need for a particular action or solution. Assessing what information, resources, technical expertise, and political support is needed to implement a project will be important, and a complete assessment should include an understanding of the barriers, appropriate sequence of actions, and timelines. The assessment should identify stakeholders from the public, private, and civic sectors who can benefit, advance their mission, or link resources to the project. When conflict exists about the nature of the solution, this is an indicator that agreement-seeking might be needed before collective action is pursued.

Collaborative Systems

Collaborative systems most often arise out of two circumstances: (1) an existing agreement-seeking or collective action collaborative governance group decides it needs to continue in a long-term and more structured way; or (2) a piece of legislation or new regulation requires the formation of an ongoing collaborative governance group. In the first instance, the members of the existing group should avoid the temptation to just keep meeting without rethinking their structural and procedural needs. The most important consideration for a collaborative system is the formal structure, so an assessment focused on structural issues may be necessary even if a thorough assessment was conducted before the initial collaborative governance process began.

In the second instance—where a collaborative system is created by law— the question of whether to go forward with a collaboration has already been answered. In addition, the makeup of the group, as well as the framing of the issue may be pre-established. Any assessment conducted should be focused on open design questions, particularly those related to representativeness and inclusiveness (see chapter 1).

In either case, any assessment involving a collaborative system should identify the parties who would benefit from long-term relationships and repeated interactions over time.

Strategies for Conducting the Assessment

As mentioned above, interviews are the primary tool for conducting a thorough assessment. Though we have a strong preference for in-person interviews, they can also be conducted via videoconference or by phone depending on resources, time, distance, and other factors. While interviewing can be labor-intensive, we have not found a more effective way to ensure that the effort and resources that might be put toward a potential collaborative governance effort will ultimately yield the desired results.

Meeting jointly with members of an interest or community group can expedite the interviews and allow a fuller range of perspectives. If an assessor chooses to conduct joint interviews, it is important to ensure that the group does not have a chilling effect on other, less powerful stakeholders or on the airing of ideas that may be less developed or less popular.

Online surveys and questionnaires can be used to augment information gained from interviews and to expand the reach of input if those surveyed are sufficiently motivated or incentivized to complete the survey. In our experience, however, written responses are far less helpful than direct conversation. Written answers to questions often seem to drive respondents into more positional thinking, and the opportunity for spontaneous follow-up or deeper exploration of positions is lost.

A number of scholars and practitioners have produced comprehensive, step-by-step guides for how to conduct situational and conflict assessments for multi-party, consensus-based processes (Susskind et al. 99–136; Carpenter and Kennedy 71–91; Gray and Purdy 75). The methodologies in these resources can easily be adapted for conducting collaborative governance assessments. Rather than providing another step-by-step guide, this chapter focuses on offering ten key strategies that have guided our practice for effectively conducting assessment interviews in ways that conserve time and resources:

1. Do your homework. The interview process can be substantially aided by gathering some background information ahead of time. While too much study can begin to border on an effort to find *the* solution, having a fundamental understanding of key issues and any specialized lexicon allows valuable interview time to be spent in discussing the subtleties of the situation. In addition to reading news articles and materials related to a public issue, seeking a briefing by those familiar with the issues or people who can serve as cultural informants about the unique aspects of a situation can be essential to avoiding major pitfalls or blunders in interviews. For example, our team

led a large-scale assessment in collaboration with another center related to the complex ecosystem surrounding salmon recovery in the Columbia River Basin. The assessment team first met with several other facilitators who had worked extensively on past salmon recovery projects in the basin, as well as with a professor who had conducted an in-depth study of the decision-making framework for salmon recovery. The goal was not to become experts on salmon recovery, but rather to gain enough understanding of the history and dynamics to fine-tune the interview questions to best assess the potential opportunities for a collaborative governance approach.

2. Begin by interviewing essential stakeholders or key people who can provide a full perspective of the issues. For example, in a development-related project, interviewing the developers and local government officials would be important. If essential stakeholders indicate a lack of interest or priority for a collaborative effort, continuing with the assessment may be unnecessary. Consider organizing interviews into first and second rounds. It can be helpful to generate a list of interests and stakeholders impacted by an issue or project and create concentric circles of those most central to the issue or project. Though the line is not always that sharp, first-round interviews should include the must-have stakeholders and second-round interviews are for those stakeholders who would be beneficial but not absolutely necessary. Of course, it is likely that during the first-round interviews, new stakeholders may emerge who are high priority interviewees. Often overlooked as essential are representatives of historically underrepresented communities. Because public projects and decision-making have often disproportionately burdened Black people, Indigenous people, other people of color, and other traditionally underrepresented communities, it is particularly important to connect with those communities early in the process.

3. Interview those stakeholders who might oppose implementation or who have the power to block an agreement from moving forward. For example, in a natural resources case, consider prioritizing interviewing key leaders of an interested environmental organization that has a history of litigation.

4. Interview key elected officials, including mayors and county commissioners, legislators, and relevant staff from the federal delegation if there is a federal nexus with a project. These elected officials often have deep knowledge of their communities, and their status as elected representatives provides them with unique convening authority that might benefit a collaborative governance process should one go forward.

5. Ensure representation from all sectors. One of the primary values of a collaborative approach is the joint work of private, public, and civic entities. It is important to consider all three sectors from the beginning. For example, it might be easy to identify government and nonprofit or civil-society entities that might be impacted by the project or issue, but it may be helpful to

consider what business interests might also contribute to or be affected by a project or issue. For example, a municipal project to improve a portion of the riverfront in Eugene, Oregon, was solidly supported by the local government and environmental groups. When considering what businesses would benefit from the development, a local hotel was identified that ultimately contributed significant resources to help advance the effort. One caution is that while private sector engagement is a beneficial element of a collaborative governance approach, it is important that one company not be given an exclusive advantage over a competitor, thereby slipping into the territory of "deal making" or worse.

6. Resist the temptation to talk to everyone at the assessment stage, unless you need to. As set forth in chapter 1, the goal is to try to hear from the full range of affected interests—but it is likely impossible to hear from every individual affected. This is where relying on representatives of a wide variety of interests can be particularly helpful. On the other hand, depending on the level of conflict inherent in the situation, it may be important that many individuals feel that their voice has been heard during the assessment phase in order to build procedural trust in the process. The idea is to interview enough participants to get an understanding of the full spectrum of perspectives on a situation or to get some idea of whether a critical mass of resources or support exists for implementation of a project. One sign that enough interviews are completed is when no new information is revealed, or the same information begins to be repeated.

7. Nurture relationships between parties. Although the confidentiality of interviewees should be respected, interviews sometimes can be an opportunity to nurture relationships between parties asking about common interests or highlighting opportunities for joint action.

8. Identify potential conveners, project champions, and resources to support the process. The success of a collaborative governance approach requires a range of resources. Exploring ideas for funding, as well as identifying who might step forward to convene, lead, or champion the effort, is important in the assessment phase.

9. Think outside the box for new resources. Consider who stands to benefit from the implementation of a project or the resolution of a problem. Identifying other efforts underway or other priorities that might benefit from the effort can lead to expanded benefit from the effort under consideration.

10. Explore how affected interests can be legitimately represented. Clearly, some affected interests will be obvious from the very beginning. But it is likely that there are other potential interests or communities of interest that need to be considered in the assessment (and potentially included in any process that follows). This is especially important where these other interests are connected with historically underrepresented communities. It

may take exploring with several sources who might legitimately represent those communities' interests. The converse question must also be considered. That is, do the identified potential process participants, even those who have sought the collaborative process or supported the assessment, have the ability to represent definitively the interests of their purported constituency or community of interest? In fact, sometimes a person who is a visible spokesperson for a community or constituency represents a small but vocal subset of a larger community or constituency that includes other interests. In such circumstances, perhaps several people who represent a broader set of interests should participate in the assessment and, potentially, any future collaborative process.

Other Strategic Considerations

In some cases, resources and time may be limited. Conducting interviews with a large number of potential stakeholders simply might not be feasible. In such circumstances, it may be necessary to focus the interviews on some of the most critical stakeholders, build connections with less familiar stakeholders, or adapt the process to scale. In one such case, the director of the Oregon Department of Land Conservation and Development sought to revamp the state's highly cumbersome method of population forecasting to expedite a log jam of local and city planning that depended on these forecasts. He reached out to the director of the Oregon Association of Counties and the director of the League of Oregon Cities, both essential stakeholders, to explore whether they might all cohost a facilitated conversation with a broad spectrum of stakeholders to explore this issue. Together, these leaders convened a stakeholder meeting. During the meeting, the group confirmed their common interest in improving the state's method of forecasting city and county population, identified other interests to be engaged, and charted out some next steps. Nine months and many full-group and subcommittee meetings later, the group had agreed on a legislative concept that quickly passed unanimously in the legislature.

Sharing the Results of the Assessment

Ultimately, the assessment serves to help decision-makers determine whether to apply a collaborative governance approach to their issue. As a result, the assessor needs to communicate the findings and recommendations that come out of the assessment. What form that report will take—whether it is an oral report, PowerPoint presentation, or written document—depends on what will be of most use to key decision-makers, what suits the circumstances and timeline of the potential project, and what appropriately protects the confidentiality of those who were interviewed as part of the assessment process.

Conclusion

The assessment is the starting point for converting the possibility of using a collaborative governance approach into the launch of an actual project. If an assessment concludes that the conditions indicate a collaborative governance approach could helpful, the next step is to use the information gained from the interviews to structure a group in order to achieve the group's goals.

References

Carlson, Christine. "Convening." *Consensus Building Handbook*, edited by Lawrence Susskind et al., 1st ed., SAGE Publications, 1999, pp. 169–197.

Carlson, Christine. *A Practical Guide to Collaborative Governance*. Policy Consensus Initiative, 2007.

Carpenter, Susan L., and W. J. D. Kennedy. *Managing Public Disputes*. 1st ed., Jossey-Bass, 2001.

Colatrella, Michael T., and Anthony P. Picchioni. *Mediation: Skills and Techniques*. LexisNexis, 2008.

Gray, Barbara. *Collaborating*. 1st ed., Jossey-Bass, 1989.

Gray, Barbara, and Jill Purdy. *Collaborating for the Future*. 1st ed., Oxford UP, 2018.

Ury, William, et al *Getting to Yes: Negotiating Agreement Without Giving In*. 2nd, Houghton Mifflin Harcourt, 1992.

National Policy Consensus Center. *Oregon Solutions Project Manager Handbook*. Mark O. Hatfield School of Government, College of Urban and Public Affairs, Portland State University, 2019.

Purdy, J. "A Framework for Assessing Power in Collaborative Governance Processes." *Public Administration Review*, vol. 72, no. 3, 2012, pp. 409–417.

Susskind, Lawrence, and Jennifer Thomas-Lamar. "Conducting a Conflict Assessment." *Consensus Building Handbook*, edited by Lawrence Susskind et al., 1st ed., SAGE Publications, 1999, pp. 99–136.

Young, Iris Marion. *Inclusion and Democracy*. Oxford UP, 2000.

6

DESIGN AND ORGANIZATION

Introduction

The last chapter focused on conducting an assessment to determine if a collaborative governance approach could be helpful in a given situation. This chapter assumes that, based on that assessment, conditions are favorable for a collaborative governance process. This is where the definitional norms meet the realities of practice. This phase seeks to answer the guiding question: How is the group best organized to achieve its desired outcomes? (See Figure 6.1.)

The central task of this phase is determining how best to use the information gleaned in the assessment to design and organize a successful collaborative governance group. This challenge is complicated by the fact that participants in a collaborative governance process will come from diverse public, private, and civic organizations, bringing with them the distinct culture, norms, and ecosystem of the constituencies they represent (Emerson and Nabatchi 39).

The daunting nature of the design and organizing phase is made easier by approaching it methodically, considering one element at a time. For our purpose, there are four elements of a strong group design that "shape, support, and describe the relationships, methods, and outputs of a collaborative governance group" (Johnson et al. 5):

1. Framing the common purpose and values;
2. Identifying key roles and responsibilities;
3. Clarifying the process for decision-making and conflict resolution; and
4. Building the form to support the function.

(adapted from Morrow, "Building a Real Team")

Design and Organization

Guiding Question:
How is the group best organized to achieve its desired outcomes?

Key Elements to Design and Organize:
Framing the common purpose and values
Identifying key roles and responsibilities
Clarifying the processes for decision-making and conflict resolution
Building the form to support the function
Creating working agreements

FIGURE 6.1   Design and organization (phase two)

In designing these elements, we must be mindful of Jill Purdy's observations about the coercive power of the "deep structure" (412). By this, she means the invisible ways that interests and power can become embedded into the very fabric of the collaborative governance group's organization that over time will erode the norms on which collaborative governance rests, such as its inclusiveness and balance of power (412). For example, if a powerful voice dominates the framing of the group's purpose, that framing will then drive many subsequent decisions, such as who is invited to participate in the process, potentially undermining representativeness, inclusion, and belonging before the process even begins. Purdy's caution underscores the need for careful consideration of how each one of these elements is designed.

In this chapter, we explore each of the core elements of designing and organizing a collaborative governance group to conform with the definitional norms and foster collaborative dynamics. We cover how these elements are formed into working agreements to guide the group in its work. We also discuss some special considerations for collaborative systems.

Framing the Common Purpose and Values

How a project or policy issue is framed is perhaps the most important and foundational strategic decision underlying a new collaborative process. By framing, we mean the act of collectively defining the purpose, scope, and desired outcomes of the process. The framing defines what is on and what is off the table, what is important, and what is less so. Framing can significantly shape the perception of the issue and the process itself, implying what values are considered important.

Most everyone, of course, comes into a collaborative governance process thinking that their own framing of the group's purpose is the right one. Take for example a process involving water management in the Umatilla Basin, located in

Oregon's fertile northeast corner. From the irrigator's perspective, the essential question might be framed as follows: How can we take advantage of the opportunity for farmers in the Umatilla basin to create needed jobs and boost Oregon's rural economy, by allowing them to utilize a very small increment of additional water from the very large flows of the Columbia River? Environmental groups, not surprisingly, might frame their essential question as follows: Why should agribusiness be allowed to take even more water from the Columbia River when science clearly shows that water flows in the Columbia are already below historic levels needed for native fish?

Both questions are versions of the same policy question, but contain considerable differences. One emphasizes farmers, economic impacts, and the very large flows in the Columbia River overall. The other refers more to agribusiness, impacts on fish, and compares current Columbia River flow to historic levels. Neither framing is wrong. Both are based upon fact, but they provoke entirely different responses. However, neither would be particularly helpful in setting up a collaborative governance process that would need to be inclusive of both of these perspectives and others.

Even as the initial framing is likely to be revised later in the process when new information and challenges are better understood, it is important to start the process with a shared sense of the purpose, scope, and desired outcomes. Ultimately, the most effective frame is one that directs the effort toward shared outcomes while being inclusive of the perspectives, resources, and interests of those needed to achieve those results.

To frame an issue or project in a way that facilitates collaboration and creates a sense of shared ownership in the goals and process is a challenge and an art form. It takes a nuanced understanding of the interests and sensitivities of the various parties, and it should meet three criteria: (1) clarity about what the goal or issue is and what is at stake, (2) substantive space for agreement and alternative solutions, and (3) acknowledgment of the respective interests so that all of the parties feel included and as if they belong.

This last criterion is particularly important. Being able to see one's primary interests nested within the framing of the purpose sends a powerful signal that a party's needs and perspectives have been considered. Such a signal reinforces that the party's participation is primary, if not essential, for the group to succeed, and such a signal contributes to fostering a sense of belonging. In the Columbia River issue described above, both framing statements tend to prompt yes–no responses, providing little substantive space for agreement. Neither framing provided for acknowledgment of the other party's interests in a way that might allow them to approach the issue with open minds. Articulated in a way that could meet all three criteria, the group's purpose was ultimately framed as answering the following essential question: How can we manage Columbia River water in a way that could provide economic benefits from additional irrigation in the Umatilla Basin and improve ecological conditions for fish?

In this framing, both sides could see the potential for their interests to be furthered by a successful outcome. The challenge was clearly laid out, but in a way that provided space for creative problem solving, ultimately enabling the group to find consensus around five action items. As this example indicates, when an effort leans more toward agreement-seeking, an effective frame is one that encompasses the range of perspectives and interests without displaying a bias toward one side or the other.

A project focused on collective action can more readily be defined in terms of the project the group seeks to undertake together. Beginning in 2008, we facilitated a project in the wake of a devastating flood in the Coast Range. For the second time in eleven years, the river that flows through one town, Vernonia, overran its banks and flooded the entire downtown area. Hundreds of homes were damaged or lost, and the entire school system was damaged beyond repair. The community undertook a collaborative governance process to move the school to higher ground, which carried a price tag in the tens of millions of dollars. The collaborative governance group stated its purpose this way: "To ensure Vernonia school children have access to safe, healthy, and educationally sound school facilities, the collaborative team will work together to scout a location and leverage funding to build a new state-of-the-art school campus moving forward." That framing incorporated the group's mission, purpose, and desired outcomes.

Embedding shared values, when they exist, into the initial framing can serve an important function in continuing to build a common sense of public purpose, solidifying commonalities, and fostering a sense of belonging between group members. By including the phrase "safe, healthy, educationally sound," the Vernonia team communicated their shared values in addition to their brick-and-mortar goal of building a new school.

Collaborative governance group members, particularly in conflict situations, are often keenly aware of their differences. The articulation of common values within, or in addition to, the framing of the group's purpose starts to build a sense of shared commitment and aspiration. For example, one of our projects, Opportunity Eugene, involved working with a fifty-person task force that the mayor had asked to provide consensus recommendations for addressing the immediate and long-term needs of unhoused members of the community. The participants in the project ranged from community service managers and faith leaders to city councilors and activists in the unhoused community. Tensions were high between the various groups, as the city had recently dismantled a communal, tented living space that had developed in one of the city's public parks. In addition to the purpose and basic desired outcomes, the group also wanted to ensure commitment to shared values, both about the substance and the process. These values were stated as follows:

All people deserve to be housed, fed, safe and cared about. This Task Force presents a unique opportunity to build intentional community among segments of our community not normally together at the same table; our need to continue to treat each other with respect, listen to each other's perspective, and value each member as an equal contributor within this process is vital to the outcomes and serves as a model to the larger community.

The Task Force members recognize the importance and power of language and aim to be respectful in the terminology used to refer to those who are housed and unhoused.

Members recognize that this is a diverse group, with different established practices and that adapting language is often challenging. With this in mind, all group members agree to be open to feedback about the impact of the language they use. Conversely, when providing feedback about language, members will approach each other with the intent to educate rather than to embarrass. (Opportunity Eugene Task Force 1–3).

While these values were later operationalized in the form of ground rules, their direct articulation in the initial framing fostered trust. Despite differences, individual group members were unified by their shared commitment to fundamental values that would guide their work together. Hearing their deeply held values formally expressed helped create a sense of shared connection and belonging, particularly for the unhoused members of the group. Not all groups need to agree on such a detailed statement of common values from the outset. But when possible, these shared values can be a powerful, unifying platform on which to continue to build.

A final step in the framing process is to agree on concrete outcomes that the group hopes to accomplish. Defining the outcomes provides clarity for a group about its goals as well as how its progress will be measured. We do not expect a group to determine the substance of the outcome, of course, but rather for the participants to collectively agree on the form. The outcome might be a decision, a greater understanding, a recommendation, a plan, or a road map. In other words, members of the group should identify what success will look like to them. For example, in the affordable housing case discussed in chapter 4, the group agreed to make a shared recommendation to a legislative committee. In the Vernonia school project, the group agreed to find a new site for the school and to work together to fund its construction.

Identifying Key Roles and Responsibilities

Christine Carlson outlines four main roles required to support a successful collaborative governance effort: (1) the sponsor, (2) the facilitation team, (3) the conveners, and (4) the participants (6). This section delves into the key functions of each role and the strategic questions that need to be answered in filling them.

The Sponsor

Collaborative governance groups require resources to cover the hard costs related to the process, including meeting space, refreshments, printing, transportation, process facilitation, logistics management, and joint fact-finding efforts. In addition, Gray points out the importance of "securing enough resources to ensure that stakeholders may participate equally in the proceedings" (73), which can include costs for travel, interpretation and translation, accessibility accommodations, childcare, meals, or stipends for participation. Sponsors are those individuals or organizations that provide resources needed to support a collaborative governance process, "often by providing financial assistance" (Carlson 170).

The perception that a sponsor will exert control over the collaborative process is a real consideration in determining how to fill this role. A strategy for counteracting this danger is ensuring costs are distributed among participant interests and entities. For example, we were involved in a project intended to increase the representation of rural interests on the regional transportation authority, which determined how transportation dollars were spent in the tri-county area comprising the greater Portland, Oregon, area. Since the central issue pertained to the dominance of the largest jurisdiction, the three initiating stakeholders felt strongly that costs should be equally split between them: the most rural county in the region, the state department of transportation, and the existing regional government.

Shared sponsorship often does not mean equal sponsorship. Participants often expect contributions to be proportional to the size or capacity of the entity. For example, a larger entity may be expected to shoulder more of the financial burden than a smaller one. Often a state or federal agency may be the primary sponsor when the effort is seen as related to the advancement of their core mission. That said, all participants have something of value to contribute to support the process, whether that be office space, staffing support, refreshments, photocopying, graphic design, translation, or other expertise. More importantly, when group members contribute resources or materials to an effort, it reinforces a sense of ownership, inclusion, and belonging in the process. When resources are limited, stakeholders can be creative in figuring out ways to get space donated, engage volunteer facilitators, or solicit their own sponsors. Frequently, a project will begin with stakeholders working together to apply for grant funding to cover the costs associated with the collaborative governance process itself.

When trust is low and the effort is financed by one primary sponsor (most typically a government entity), the use of a collaborative platform to manage the process can serve to buffer the perception of undue influence from a sponsor. In one illustrative case, the Oregon Department of Education abruptly fired the director of the state's school for the deaf, significantly upsetting staff, families, and community service professionals connected to the school. In refilling the position, the department sought to hire a private facilitator for a stakeholder process to recommend criteria for hiring a new director. Given that trust of the department was low, and it was footing the entire cost, the facilitator requested that our center, in its capacity as a collaborative platform hold the contract with the department. In that way, the facilitator was employed by an entity that is designed and obligated to work on behalf of the entire group of stakeholders. This arrangement avoided the perception that the facilitator was getting their pay and perhaps their orders directly from the sponsor.

Ensuring participants have access to information about who is serving as the sponsor or sponsors is important for preserving the transparency of the collaborative governance group. While transparency does not offer complete protection from a sponsor's potential undue influence, it at least can provide the possibility of added accountability as participants are more alert to this potential abuse.

The Facilitation Team

To facilitate literally means "to make easy." The role of the facilitation team is to plan and manage the collaborative process to ease the way for participants to focus and conduct the work needed to achieve the group's purpose and identified outcomes. When students enter our collaborative governance course, they initially associate facilitation only with managing the dynamics in a meeting. However, as the course progresses, students are surprised to learn that well over half of a facilitator's work occurs outside the meeting room. Some of the tasks beyond facilitating meetings can include gathering and preparing information, identifying and engaging presenters and experts, preparing the convener and participants for engagement, preparing the agenda and developing processes for each item, managing the logistics, coordinating follow-up actions, preparing meeting summaries, holding problem-solving sessions between meetings, and managing communication with the public or other constituents. According to Carlson, "facilitators, in many ways, function as project managers in carrying out these activities" (25).

Depending on the size and complexity of a collaborative governance process, the work of facilitation can be performed by a team, with a lead facilitator or co-facilitators, process support, notetakers, and a logistics coordinator. Some of the administrative tasks also can be assigned to agency or stakeholder staff.

In order for a process to maintain its legitimacy, facilitators of a collaborative governance process work on behalf of, and are equally accountable to, all participants and to the group as a whole. As mentioned above, a sponsor may be suspected of hiring a facilitator who will help them get the outcomes they want. And, "when a facilitator treats a sponsor as their sole client—the one they work for and are responsible to—this creates a fundamental problem in terms of their accountability to the other participants in the process," writes Carlson (27).

Collaborative platforms like the one we work for at Portland State University have come to play a specialized and critical function in the facilitation of collaborative governance processes. As discussed in chapter 1, collaborative platforms can function to create a container or space that promotes shared ownership and co-creation. These platforms, often housed within university settings, carry institutional gravitas that can counter-balance the dominance of governmental or other institutional entities in order to promote greater inclusiveness. Because the mission of a collaborative platform is to serve as a resource for—and help ensure the success of—collaborative governance efforts, these platforms have developed specialized expertise in designing, facilitating, and managing cross-boundary efforts that adhere to the definitional norms.

As mentioned in the department of education example above, a facilitator working on behalf of a collaborative platform is held accountable to the mission of the collaborative platform rather than to the sponsor from whom they are receiving a direct paycheck. As a result, the presence of a collaborative platform often helps bring credibility and procedural trust to an effort. In fact, in many cases, particularly when conflict is high and trust is low, the collaborative platform will assist the group in working together to select a facilitator. The process of jointly agreeing on desired qualities and interviewing candidates can be an important starting point for helping a group work together. A facilitator selected by representatives of diverse interests establishes trust in the process by reaffirming that the facilitator is working on behalf of all interests. In addition, parties know that, should a problem with the facilitator emerge, they can appeal to the collaborative platform for assistance.

The Convener

To convene describes the act of bringing together or assembling. In a collaborative effort, stakeholders do not just magically show up in the same meeting room. Someone invites them. We like to say that the right convener is someone who can bring the right people to the table, and encourage them to act like grown-ups once they are there. While the convener role may look similar to the role of chairperson in meetings, it is quite distinct. The role of a meeting chairperson (sometimes fulfilled by the convener) is primarily functional, concerned with keeping the meeting on track, ensuring effective decision-making, and utilizing meeting skills. However, a convener's role can be considerably larger. Because the convener role is so pivotal to the success of a collaborative governance effort, yet is often overlooked or underestimated, this section delves more deeply into describing the function and design considerations for this role.

Sometimes people involved in a collaborative process will tell us they have no convener. What they most likely mean is that there is no one specifically designated to serve in that role. In those cases, the role of convening a collaborative group typically defaults to the sponsoring organizations or the key public entities. These agency leaders can be effective when they are perceived as trying to fairly consider and balance the broad range of other stakeholders' interests. The risk, Christine Carlson warns, is when a process is convened by a sponsoring organization with a strong interest in a particular outcome; stakeholders may doubt it will be fair and may be reluctant to participate or take ownership of the process (27).

One way to overcome this natural distrust is to have the agency's top executive reaffirm their commitment to the consensus-based process and the outcomes. Even better, having top-level executives involved in the process can send the signal that the work is valued and important. Openness and transparency about the purpose of the collaborative process and integration of a high level of stakeholder engagement "every step of the way...will go a long way toward establishing the credibility of the process" (Carlson 196). Carlson suggests, however, that a government entity designate an outside convener for a group "when the sponsoring organization is perceived as an advocate for a particular outcome, when multiple agencies and levels of government need to be involved, or when past history between the sponsoring organization and other parties has been difficult" (29). Information from the assessment can be helpful in considering whether someone from outside would be advisable to fill the convener role.

Experienced practitioners recommend the use of well-known public leaders who possess stature in the community and who can provide a kind of moral authority that is engendered by, but goes beyond, any official title they may hold (Carlson 29–30; Carpenter 106). What matters most, says Carlson, is the respect and trust they enjoy from a broad range of stakeholders (30). Conveners of this stature can often have a significant and pivotal influence on the success of a collaborative effort.

A respected community leader convener with moral authority establishes what we often refer to as an "elevated forum" that can attract participation, lend credibility, signal the importance of the effort, and build trust in the process. As Carlson writes, "Sometimes people will come to the table primarily because of a convener's status...[which] makes them feel they are doing something important and worthwhile" (30). Jeffrey Luke further adds that to get stakeholders to commit to a collaborative process, they must believe that it can be successfully addressed, that is, that it is "do-able" (81). That is not to suggest that moral authority is only conveyed by election or other externally conferred status. Sometimes the most-well-respected conveners draw their moral authority from their personal or professional identity or from their persistent dedication to their community.

The presence and status of the convener can convey that the effort will be worth participants' time and investment and that something positive may actually happen. In chapter 4, we established that when trust between parties is low, having trust in the process is critical. The convener's presence—particularly alongside a collaborative platform—can help engender that procedural trust, signaling that the process will be fair and will provide a forum in which all voices will be heard and no single interest at the table will be favored over others. The status and moral authority of the convener can also play a role in bringing decision-makers into the process. The higher the status and credibility of the convener, the higher the likelihood of getting decision-makers from each organization sitting at the table, and the higher the likelihood they will show up consistently. When a collaborative process is convened by a legislator, for example, we have found that there is a greater chance of getting the chief executive officer of an organization to participate.

A highly respected community convener can also be well-situated to set the context for and reinforce the public benefit of the effort. In holding and describing the intention of the collaborative effort, the convener can reinforce that the public problem is urgent, that it affects many who may not be at the table, and that the community is counting on the group to work together and produce. The convener can also emphasize why participants have been invited and what they have to offer each other, underscoring their interdependence and the likely outcome if they do not work together.

Relatedly, a convener who is a leader from a historically underrepresented community can further demonstrate that the process is inclusive and that it is intended to serve everyone. A recognizable community leader serving in the role of convener can help build trust in the process and encourage participation from communities that have been mistreated by institutions. Several years ago, we were involved in a project intended to beautify a schoolyard to benefit both the students who attended the school and the neighbors who often used the schoolyard as a playground and a park. The school is in the heart of a historically Black neighborhood in Portland. As the project progressed, a good deal of tension emerged between Black families who had lived in the neighborhood for many years and newer white neighbors. It became clear that many of the Black participants felt a great deal of grief over the gentrification of their neighborhood and the influx of new families with a lot of opinions about how it should be. The convener was a well-known Black leader who had attended that school himself and whose granddaughter was currently a student. By sharing his own experience and his own commitment to the neighborhood, he was able to both validate the grief of the participants and help them identify ways in which the project could benefit them and their community going forward.

The gravitas of conveners enables them to provide an environment for constructive and inclusive discussion throughout the process. Sometimes they can intervene when parties start to act in ways that can create distrust or an uncooperative atmosphere. Community leaders serving as conveners can also use their leverage to make space for greater inclusion, checking in with less engaged participants and creating space for less dominant voices to be heard. Throughout the process, conveners can also use their moral authority to push the group toward the best possible collaborative result, which sometimes includes letting the group know when they are falling short. A number of years ago, a group of stakeholders were assembled to develop a restoration strategy for the Willamette River. The process was convened by the well-respected president of Oregon State University. Committees were formed to draft sections of a consensus report and, after months of deliberation, a strategy was drafted. It was somewhat vague and short on specifics. Just before it was to be released to the public for comment, however, the convener addressed the group. He asked, "Is this *really* the best we can do for the people of this state, after months of work?" The group decided to delay public release, and the committees went back to work, addressing some of the thornier issues they had earlier avoided. They returned a few weeks later with many substantive improvements.

A convener may need to call on participants' better angels, as it were, and remind them that they are there to move toward solutions that have mutual benefit. A necessary aspect of this role is sometimes serving as a truth-teller, cutting through the process to get to the essential point, such as: "We have a conflict here, and we need to work it out as a group;" or "the central issue we need to resolve today is x." They can remind group members, when necessary, of the operating principles that the group has agreed upon. Relatedly, a convener with moral authority can play a crucial role in both holding participants accountable and cheering them on, serving to both push and pull groups to success.

There will be times during a collaborative process when the group's belief in their ability to make progress is tested. This is when the flipside of holding the group accountable comes into play. By their very status and reputation, a convener can provide an added sense of optimism on the part of participants and a heightened sense that success is within their grasp. In describing her role as convener for a collaborative governance process involving a recreational trail on Oregon's coast, a state senator highlighted the cheerleader aspect of her convening role. In some cases, her praise and encouragement were targeted to the group as a whole. In other situations, it involved calling out specific stakeholders for their particular contributions. In either case, public praise coming from a respected leader was a valued commodity.

A convener can often play significant roles in managing dynamics in the external environment as well. A collaborative governance process on an important public project or issue will naturally attract public and media attention. Community leaders in the convener role often serve as the spokesperson for an effort. In addition to being a public or media spokesperson for a project, leaders serving as conveners can also be very effective representatives for the process when talking to potential funders or getting other key parties involved. In the Vernonia school project mentioned earlier, the co-conveners, one of whom was

the head of a statewide business association, personally visited several foundations and private businesses to ask for contributions to build the new school.
Their status as leaders got them in the door, and their ability to frame the need
and urgency of the project helped them leave with substantial commitments.

Finally, while conveners will often chair the meetings of collaborative governance processes, they can still play an important role even when they are
unable to participate in every meeting. Such was the case for Salt Lake City
Solutions, convened by then-Mayor Ralph Becker. A broad group of stakeholders were invited to work on an important city issue by the mayor, who chal-
lenged them to come up with a solution. His staff attended the meetings on his
behalf, and then Mayor Becker returned to the group after a few months to see
the results of their work. The group benefited from knowing that the mayor was
awaiting the results of their deliberations.

So, who is the right convener for a particular effort? As mentioned above,
elected leaders, by virtue of having been voted into office, carry a democratically conferred authority that allows them to convene stakeholders from various
sectors. To serve the best interests of the group, however, the right convener
must not only bring the authority of their position, but also transcend it. For that
reason, we often look to someone without a particular stake in the outcome and
with a reputation for fairness. It is important for the convener to be genuinely
passionate about a project and to be a strong advocate, without being perceived
as trying to promote their own self-interest or to push one particular policy
response or predetermined solution (Luke 68).

The exception, which at times can be necessary, is the use of co-conveners,
whose joint message to the group is: We may have different perspectives on the
issue, but we both agree the best way to find a solution is for all of us to work
together. The effectiveness of such an approach to convening was illustrated in
the GMO task force mentioned in the last chapter. It was an extremely controversial and emotional topic, with strong value differences among the parties, and
a correspondingly low level of trust. When a collaborative group of key stakeholders was charged to frame specific decision choices, hopes were not high for
success. The choice was made to have the group jointly convened by the dean of
the College of Agricultural Sciences at the state's land grant university, and the
executive director of the Institute for Sustainable Solutions, an environmental
think-tank at the state's urban university. They were at least perceived to be from
opposite sides of the debate on genetic modification of food. Individually, they
each helped bring a certain set of stakeholders to the table. Together, they set a
tone of acknowledging differences but working things through in a constructive
manner. Participants on both sides of the issue, wary when the process began,
came to trust that it was fair, and that all ideas and positions were heard. When
the consensus report was issued at the end of the process, previous opponents
(and the two co-conveners) hugged each other in celebration.

Every collaboration, we would emphasize, has a convener, whether identified as such or not. The important aspect is to consider the most essential needs of the effort and to structure it so that the group benefits from the full range of functions that role can serve.

The Participants

Participants are those people who take part in the collaborative governance process and carry out the work of the group. As set forth in chapter 1, participation must be both inclusive and representative for a collaborative governance group to be—and to be seen as—legitimate. However, the application of these principles will differ somewhat depending on whether a group is being formed for the purpose of agreement-seeking or collective action. The composition of a collaborative system is dependent on the agreed-upon work of the group.

In agreement-seeking processes, the group should include the broad range of interests impacted, those needed to carry out the decision, and those with the power to block an agreement. As discussed earlier in this book, most of these interests are represented by an individual who is closely aligned with that interest's point of view. As Carlson points out, "a farmer who can speak knowledgeably about the perspectives of other farmers" may be invited to speak to the group "to formally represent other farmers; however, the farmer and his or her constituents will need to set up explicit linkages and clear channels of communication between them" (33). This issue of representation has been explored in more detail in previous chapters, but it is important to note that traditional notions of representativeness are rooted in elections, which create geographic representations. Collaborative governance has the opportunity to expand the notion of representativeness to include vocational affiliations, racial and ethnic identity, values-based affinities, language groups, religious affiliations, and others.

When assembling a team for collective action, the main emphasis is bringing together a group of participants who, collectively, are able to align their efforts and resources to implement a project. First and foremost, project team members should have some resources to contribute to the solution, not just a vague interest in the outcome of the project. We think of resources in the broadest sense: funding, property or other assets, staff time, local and historical knowledge, information, community leadership, political and social capital, and lived experience. It is important to strive for a broadly diverse team with a mix of participants representing all three sectors—public (governments), private (business and community members), and civic (community organizations)—who can pool their interests and resources. Finally, including interest groups already working on a goal that aligns with the project can promote linkages and synergy that benefit everyone's work.

With regard to collaborative systems, sometimes the composition of the group is dictated by legislation or regulation. To the extent that it is not, the makeup of the group depends on the type of work they set out to undertake together and the resources they need to do it. Some collaborative systems will look more like agreement-seeking. Some will look more like collective action. In addition, in setting up a collaborative system, participants need to attend to succession planning from the beginning since the system may well extend beyond the tenure of many of the participants who represent agencies and organizations at the beginning of the process.

It is important that group members come with the authority to make decisions or to commit resources on behalf of an entity. Often that requires individuals that are at the highest level in their organization. When forming the group, it is also important that the participants will be able to attend meetings. If a participant finds attendance difficult—a busy mayor or member of Congress, for example—it is important that they have a proxy in the room to avoid disruptive absences. The group may also be structured so that full group meetings (which include elected officials) are held less often while committee meetings, where work can be advanced by staff with more technical and substantive knowledge, are held more frequently.

The size of a collaborative governance group is a factor to consider for all forms of collaborative governance processes. Particularly with agreement-seeking processes, the larger the group, the more challenging it can be to reach consensus. At the same time, exclusion of parties needed to support any decision will undermine the sustainability of that outcome. For that reason, participation needs to be designed in ways that promote inclusivity while keeping the group manageable.

Because of the number of interests at play in any collaborative governance process, the group can be designed to function in concentric circles (see Figure 6.2). In the center, the core group is comprised of essential representatives responsible for crafting the agreement or deciding on the actions the group will take. The next layer consists of standing work groups or technical teams with specialized knowledge or skill that can bring that expertise to an aspect of the project, providing recommendations to the core group. An additional circle can be added when a group might need to tap into specific expertise and resources on an as-needed basis.

There likely will be a time in the process when the collaborative governance group needs to consult with the broader community or some subset of the most affected communities. That can be represented by an outer ring. Participation of the general public may be woven into the structure of the process by having an opportunity for public comment at each meeting. In other cases, the group may establish a public-facing website where meeting notes, materials, and other project updates are readily available. In yet other cases, a more elaborate public

Concentric Circles of Engagement

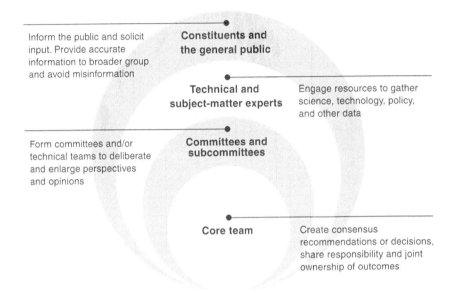

Inform the public and solicit input. Provide accurate information to broader group and avoid misinformation

Constituents and the general public

Technical and subject-matter experts
Engage resources to gather science, technology, policy, and other data

Form committees and/or technical teams to deliberate and enlarge perspectives and opinions

Committees and subcommittees

Core team
Create consensus recommendations or decisions, share responsibility and joint ownership of outcomes

FIGURE 6.2   Concentric circles of engagement

Source: Adapted from: "Core Values, Ethics, Spectrum–The 3 Pillars of Public Participation." *Iap2. org International Association for Public Participation,* www.iap2.org/general/custom.asp?page=pillars. Accessed 29 Aug. 2020

engagement process may be needed to ensure that the collaborative governance group is accountable to the broader public or to particular subsets of the community (see chapter 8).

Clarifying the Processes for Decision-making and Conflict Resolution

From the very beginning, collaborative governance groups should establish the process they will use to make decisions and resolve conflicts. As set forth in chapters 7 and 8, most decisions in collaborative governance processes are made by consensus. However, consensus is defined very differently by different groups. Some define consensus as a supermajority of the group's members, others describe consensus as an agreement that satisfies everyone and is not achieved until every member expresses that same satisfaction, while still others believe that consensus is achieved when everyone can live with the decision. Creating agreement on what consensus specifically means to them is often where collaborative governance groups will experience the most tension and debate in organizing themselves.

A group can benefit by recognizing that no matter how it defines consensus—and regardless of whether the group reaches consensus or not—*seeking* consensus as a group has value. Consensus-seeking involves a commitment to work toward understanding each other's perspectives, concerns, and interests. In a consensus-seeking context, objections to a popularly supported proposal can be taken as a sign that more work is needed to uncover new perspectives or new information that might improve the proposal.

Sometimes groups reach a point where they simply do not agree on a particular point. In order to continue seeking consensus, some groups find it helpful to delineate the specific actions they might take to resolve the conflict. For example, in some instances, representatives of differing sides meet outside the full group to mediate the disagreement. They might form a small group to work through the differing opinions and develop options to bring back to the full group, or they might opt to seek further information or input from an outside party. However, a group can be explicit that when all participants believe that further exploration or conflict resolution will not yield any more understanding or agreement, they have done their best to seek consensus.

Considering, at the outset of a process, how a group will move forward in the absence of unanimity is essential. The options may be: a group member can simply decide to stand aside, which means they do not support the decision but will not block it; the group can create a report or compile recommendations summarizing where the group agrees and noting areas where they disagree; a group can decide to advance majority recommendations and include a minority report; or they could opt to declare that they are at impasse and allow all entities the freedom to take alternative actions of their own choosing. The best option will depend on each group and situation. We advise against using voting as the fallback if the group does not reach consensus. Majority voting, even supermajority voting, can undermine a group's dedication to genuinely seeking the understanding that is a critical component of consensus-seeking. A group tends to stop listening for new information once participants know they have enough votes to pass a proposal. To foster engagement and joint ownership in the process, a group should achieve clarity about how it will handle conflict when it arises, and how to proceed when members do not arrive at unanimous consent.

Building the Form to Support the Function

Form is made up of those elements that give the group pattern and structure. The form of any collaborative governance group should be structured around the group's purpose, as well as its size and timeline. While not exhausting all the elements of form that a group might address, we highlight critical structural components that a group should consider, including committee structure, meeting time and location, a process map and timelines, and ground rules for meetings.

Committee Structure

The vast majority of collaborative governance processes rely on a committee system to accomplish their work. The committees may be composed of a subset of participants from the large group or, as mentioned earlier, may include others who have special expertise, knowledge, or connections to the broader community. Committee guidelines should define the purpose of each committee, how participants will be assigned, how leadership will be selected, and how the committee will connect its work to the full collaborative governance group. Anticipating the precise committees that may be needed at the outset of a collaborative group may be difficult. Instead, the initial organizational design might simply include a loose notion of how committees may operate until the group becomes better familiar with the issues and figures out what, if any, committees will be needed to advance the work. At the least, most collaborative groups benefit from a steering committee or leadership team that is composed of diverse interests that can work with the facilitation team to take responsibility for the progress of the project. For more complicated collaborative governance groups that are operating through multiple committees and subcommittees, it can be helpful to create an organizational chart that spells out the focus of each committee and its interrelationship with other committees and subcommittes.

Figure 6.3 is the organizational chart for the Oregon Sage-Grouse Conservation Partnership, the project described in the introduction that was convened to protect the habitat of the Western Sage-Grouse and to protect the economy of the region (Brownscombe 5). The chart details the numerous work groups and teams, their functions and expected outcomes, and the interface between these various components. This example serves to underscore how an organizational structure can be built to significantly expand the engagement of broader stakeholders through committees and work groups to draw on the expertise that extends well beyond the core decision-making group.

Meeting Times and Locations

How often, when, and where a group meets partially determines who participates fully in the process. Meetings held during typical weekday working hours may be convenient for agency staff and others participating in their professional capacity, but may be difficult for community members. Location also matters. Where a group meets sends signals about who belongs in the group. For example, holding meetings in an agency conference room may be off-putting to communities who have a history of conflict with, or oppression by, governmental

Work Groups/Teams

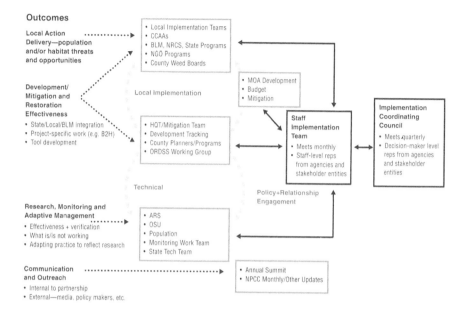

FIGURE 6.3 The Oregon Sage-Grouse Conservation Partnership organizational chart

Source: Brownscombe, Brett. "The Oregon Sage Grouse Conservation Partnership." Informational hearing presentation to the Oregon State Legislature, House Interim Committee on Agriculture and Natural Resources, Salem, Oregon, 18 Sept. 2019. PowerPoint

entities. For example, in the Opportunity Eugene project discussed earlier, full task force meetings were mainly held at a community church, rather than in a city hall conference room. That particular church had a distinct place in the community because it was centrally located, easy to access, and familiar to the unhoused members of the group. Arrangements for reimbursement for members who have to travel significant distances without the benefit of agency sponsorship, are also important to ensure inclusion and full participation.

Process Map and Timelines

A process map, often in the form of a graphic representation, provides details of the steps a group plans to take in order to accomplish its purpose. The map is designed as "a visual representation of the flow of face-to-face meetings and other activities that take place in a consensus-building process" (Straus 148). The level of complexity will depend on the work and nature of the group. Some process maps can be very simple, like the one illustrated in Figure 6.4 from the Lents Stabilization and Job Creation Collaborative Project, a collective action

2017–18 Timeline Lents Collaborative

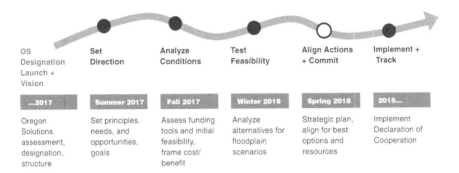

OS Designation Launch + Vision	Set Direction	Analyze Conditions	Test Feasibility	Align Actions + Commit	Implement + Track
...2017	Summer 2017	Fall 2017	Winter 2018	Spring 2018	2018...
Oregon Solutions assessment, designation, structure	Set principles, needs, and opportunities, goals	Assess funding tools and initial feasibility, frame cost/ benefit	Analyze alternatives for floodplain scenarios	Strategic plan, align for best options and resources	Implement Declaration of Cooperation

FIGURE 6.4 Process map for Lents stabilization and job creation collaborative project

Source: Meihoff, Deb. "Lents Stabilization and Job Creation Collaborative Project Overview." Presented to the Metro Regional Solutions Team, Portland, Oregon, 2017. PowerPoint

project that sought to identify and implement solutions to mitigate flooding, promote neighborhood stability, and create jobs in the Lents neighborhood in southeast Portland (Meihoff).

At a bare minimum, a process map needs to include important milestones and a timeline that will drive the pace of the work. As a group works together, the map can be adapted in response to new conditions that impact key tasks and deadlines. A process map functions as an important tool for a group to measure its progress, gives structure to what can sometimes seem like a nebulous process, and builds a shared understanding about the steps a group will go through to achieve their outcomes. The process map can also help anxious participants see when the issues important to them will be considered, allowing them to engage with more focus in all the issues before the group. In addition, seeing a path forward can provide a group with some hope at the outset—and throughout the process—that they can and will achieve what they are setting out to do and will get it done within a limited span of time.

Ground Rules

In order to create a productive and inclusive environment for decision-making, groups often need to articulate guidelines for how they will behave and treat one another. These guidelines are referred to by a number of terms, including ground rules, operating guidelines, or even group norms. The development of ground rules requires careful consideration because they relate to the culture the group wants to establish and the practices that are deeply rooted in each individual's culture. Ground rules can be an important part of what creates (or does not create) a sense of belonging in the group. Respect, for example, can mean different things to different people, and will often need to be explored in more depth before a group solidifies it into a ground rule.

Special Consideration for Collaborative Systems

For collaborative systems, designing the elements that will organize the group will often require a more robust organizational structure. This organizational structure will serve the group as an ongoing structure "to advance their strategy and achieve their goals" over multiple projects, and will include the management of finances (Johnson 5). According to Johnson, a group will likely need a higher level of structure built when the group exceeds eleven or more participants; is composed of members who may have conflict or differ significantly in their power or influence; will be accountable to government agencies, legislators, funders, or large stakeholder groups; will undertake complex work with tight deadlines; or will produce outcomes that could be a source of great public benefit or controversy requiring significant investment of time or money (12). While many of the elements in the organizational structure parallel the elements already outlined above, a key distinction is that a collaborative system will need to determine the type of entity it will become in order to fulfill its identified purpose. Entity type refers to "an organizational and sometimes legal structure that will define the group's power and formalize its obligation to others. Entity types range in formality from lightly structured (for example, a short-term committee or task force) to heavily structured (for example, a new intergovernmental agency formed by a partnership of local governments or a newly-created nonprofit corporation)" (Johnson 14).

The organizational systems also may need to create a more formal governing body than other collaborative governance groups. According to Johnson, "a governing body is a group of people who direct the affairs of the entity or organization, formulate policy, and generally make up the rules for how the group will conduct its business" (24). Considerations for the design of the governing body include its composition, how membership appointments are made, the roles and responsibilities of members, terms of office, process for removal of members, and how meetings will be conducted (25–27).

The organizational structure can be codified through a simple memorandum of understanding or a more formal intergovernmental agreement. Similar to other collective action or agreement-seeking processes, collaborative systems typically need to change aspects of their organizational structure over time. "During a start-up or entrepreneurial period, the structures needed may be simpler, more flexible, or less defined than what is needed as a group or organization further develops its purpose and structure" (Johnson 33). The initial structure should outline how these adaptations will be made by the group over time.

Creating Working Agreements

Deciding on the elements of the organizational structure is an integral part of the collaborative governance approach. While the person who conducts the initial assessment can begin to populate a draft of an organizational structure for the group to start with, convening a team representing diverse key stakeholders or interests to design the process, will "not only improve the design, but other parties will develop a sense of ownership in the structure of the process." (The Urban Land Institute 36). More important, engaging representatives in designing elements of the organizational structure "ensures that the principles guiding a consensus-based effort are consistent from the beginning" (Straus 14). An initial process design team that includes representatives of some of the diverse interests can either be brought together before convening a full group or formed as an early step in the group's process or both. Either way, the design team's work is considered a draft to be vetted, revised, and finalized by the full collaborative governance group.

The organizational elements, once agreed upon by the full group, are codified into a document that may be called working agreements, operating principles, the operational charter, guiding principles, or some other term based on the preference of the group. These working agreements will not only detail the elements described in this chapter, but can also include the group's agreements about other organizational elements such as attendance at meetings and the use of alternates, how a group will create and distribute meeting notes and communicate internally, the confidentiality of materials, how the group will handle media contacts, or other specifics particular to the group's situation. The document may either be formally or informally adopted with signatures, as long as the entire group is committed to using it to guide their functioning and relationships. As a group continues to work together and evolve, organizational elements may need to be changed. The process for how these organizational elements will be adapted can also be reflected in the working agreements. As a group may need to be frequently reminded, these agreements are written on paper not stone.

Conclusion

Each organizational element outlined in this chapter significantly influences whether the process that emerges will fulfill the promise of the collaborative governance group to promote the inclusivity, joint ownership, and the shared decision space that will produce effective, sustainable, and equitable outcomes. The definitional norms outlined in the first chapter provide guidance in navigating these design choices as applied to each unique situation. Whether building an agreement-seeking process, a collective action project team, or a collaborative system, the group's first task will be to carefully work through and reach agreement on these organizational elements that will organize how they move forward together. Working through these elements has the important benefit of helping a group practice and start to build their collective capacity for deliberation when the stakes are relatively low. How the group approaches this first group task sets the tone for their ongoing deliberation and decision-making.

References

Brownscombe, Brett. "The Oregon Sage Grouse Conservation Partnership." Informational hearing presentation to the Oregon State Legislature, House Interim Committee on Agriculture and Natural Resources, Salem, Oregon, 18 Sept. 2019. PowerPoint.

Carlson, Christine. *A Practical Guide to Collaborative Governance*. Policy Consensus Initiative, 2007.

"Core Values, Ethics, Spectrum–The 3 Pillars of Public Participation." *Iap2.org International Association for Public Participation*, www.iap2.org/general/custom.asp?page=pillars. Accessed 29 Aug. 2020.

Emerson, Kirk, and Tina Nabatchi. *Collaborative Governance Regimes*. Georgetown UP, 2015.

Johnson, Jim, et al. *Building a Collaborative Governance Framework*. National Policy Consensus Center, Portland State University, 2019.

Luke, Jeffrey. *Catalytic Leadership: Strategies for an Interconnected World*. 1st ed., Jossey-Bass, 1998.

Meihoff, Deb. "Lents Stabilization and Job Creation Collaborative Project Overview." Presented to the Metro Regional Solutions Team, Portland, Oregon, 2017. PowerPoint.

Morrow, Dennis. "Building a Real Team." Presented to the Janus Youth programs supervisors team, Portland, Oregon, 1991. PowerPoint.

Opportunity Eugene Task Force. "Opportunity Eugene Working Agreements." City of Eugene, Oregon, 2012.

Straus, David A. "Designing a Consensus Building Process Using a Graphic Road Map." *Consensus Building Handbook*, edited by Lawrence Susskind et al., 1st ed., SAGE Publications, 1999, pp. 137–168.

The Urban Land Institute in cooperation with the Program for Community Problem Solving. *Pulling Together: A Planning and Development Consensus-Building Manual*. 1st ed., ULI-the Urban Land Institute, 1994.

"Vernonia Schools – Oregon Solutions." *Orsolutions.Org*, 2020, orsolutions.org/osproject/vernonia-schools.

7

DELIBERATION AND DECISION-MAKING

Introduction

In many ways, deliberation and decision-making are the heart of any collaborative governance process, where the journey "northeast" toward collaborative solutions really begins in earnest. Indeed, as established in chapter 1, deliberation is a definitional norm of collaborative governance. This is where the real work begins. This third phase of the collaborative governance framework is where the joint problem-solving happens, guided by the question, "how does a collaborative governance group forge a solution?" (See Figure 7.1.)

While no collaborative governance process follows a cookie-cutter approach, this chapter explores how to navigate the transition from organizing to deliberation and then describes four areas of deliberation and decision-making critical to getting the best collaborative outcomes: (1) agreement on purpose and operating principles, (2) joint learning, (3) joint problem-solving, and (4) consensus decision-making. It should be noted at the outset that the process of deliberation is iterative, and steps may need to be repeated as new issues or information emerge.

We also address in this chapter a number of issues and challenges inherent in the deliberative portion of the collaborative process, including the use of technical information and experts, inclusion of public input, and the responsibilities of constituency representation. As we address these topics, it is important to recall that two of the types of collaborative governance—agreement-seeking and collective action—differ in the fundamental nature of the problems they are trying to solve. We highlight how the deliberative processes for those two types diverge to meet the needs presented by those problems. [1]

Deliberation and Decision-making

Guiding Question:

How does a collaborative governance group forge a solution?

Key Areas of Focus:

Agreement on framing and operating principles

Joint learning

Joint problem-solving

Consensus decision-making

Public involvement

FIGURE 7.1   Deliberation and decision-making (phase three)

Agreement on Framing and Operating Principles

The transition from organizing to deliberation takes place in the very early stages of the process, as the group takes ownership of some of the key tasks begun during the organizing stage.

Whether setting out to undertake agreement-seeking or collective action, a new collaborative governance group is embarking on a journey together. The first meeting of any collaborative group is filled with a certain charge of excitement, even if it is mixed with trepidation or sometimes with skepticism. Everyone is looking to see who else is there. There is often a sense of optimism in the air, or at least possibility, with participants sharing their aspirations for the process. Before the group takes its first step, the facilitator or convener has the opportunity to first acknowledge the effort it took for each participant to get there and then reinforce the moment as a promising new beginning, even if there is a history of distrust. Then the group can turn to two of the organizing tasks discussed in the previous chapter, the group's initial framing of the issue or project, and development of the operating principles. This work not only creates a sense of joint ownership in the problem and the process, it also gives the group an opportunity to practice collaboration and get a sense of early accomplishment.

Framing

We discussed in the last chapter how the framing of a project or issue can make a significant difference in how the process unfolds. In our experience, it is not uncommon for stakeholders in a collaborative process to initially bring different ideas about what the group is intended to accomplish. Group members can also be impatient to move beyond this task and get to formulating solutions. Taking the time to agree on the framing of their purpose and objectives, however, is hardly a trivial exercise. It is also a step that may need to be repeated as the deliberation proceeds and a more nuanced understanding of the issues emerges.

Operating Principles

Another initial deliberative act is ratifying the group's operating principles, discussed in the previous chapter. Collaborative governance groups often discuss operating principles at their first meeting, perhaps with a sample or two from other groups distributed and discussed. Unless there is clear consensus in that first meeting, we have found it useful to assign a smaller committee to return to the next meeting with recommended operating principles for the group to formally consider.

It is important that the members of the collaborative group own their operating principles, and take them seriously. While we sometimes expedite the process by providing examples of other groups' operating principles as a starting point, blithely adopting ground rules from another group without due consideration is rarely productive. Along with framing the goals as described above, these early ratifications can help build group solidarity. They represent early and hopefully easier wins that can help propel the group forward with a sense of accomplishment. Now they are ready to get to work.

Joint Learning

Joint learning or fact-finding is the next stage of the deliberation process, giving the parties a common informational foundation from which to engage in problem-solving. This joint learning process really involves two separate activities, learning about each other and learning about the issue or problem itself, including technical or scientific information necessary to develop solutions. These joint learning activities are equally relevant to both consensus-seeking and collective action forms of collaboration.

Learning About Each Other

Learning about the perspectives and interests of the other parties at the table is essential to "moving northeast," particularly in consensus-seeking processes. It provides a sense of what "northeast" looks like, or at least where to look for it. When parties focus the discussion on their respective interests, it begins to illuminate and open up the possibilities for potential solutions, because there may be multiple ways to satisfy those interests. It also provides a sense of which of a party's desires is higher priority for them than others—essential knowledge for later packaging of potential agreements. This process also begins to give the parties a sense of interdependence—where there are common, overlapping, or conflicting interests that will need to be worked out. "A key part of negotiating successfully," write Susskind and Cruikshank, "is understanding as much as possible about the interests and concerns of others" (187). One note of caution: in our experience, some parties come to the table without the ability to clearly articulate, or even recognize, their *own* underlying interests. Their first attempt to do so may, therefore, be imperfect, and may reasonably change over time. In addition, in agreement-seeking processes where parties start with a low level of trust or a diminished sense of belonging, some parties may initially be unwilling to divulge their underlying interests and will often lead by stating their positions.

Even in groups focused on collective action, having group members share how their interests may be served can provide a sense of the level of commitment among those assembled. However, when the collaboration is designed for collective action, the more important discovery is learning what each party brings to the table in terms of potential resources, such as expertise, dedicated staff time, social capital, data, funding, political support, regulatory authority, or community trust, to name a few. At the joint-learning stage, the parties are not seeking binding commitments. Those come later. Rather, joint learning provides the parties a sense of what is possible by combining their resources and knowledge and increasing their confidence that they can solve the problem. It also creates an important group norm and expectation that each will contribute to the solution in some way. Finally, it can help identify the resource gaps the group needs to fill. It is helpful to keep in mind, however, that in this early stage some parties may hold back from mentioning all potential resources, especially financial resources, until they see what others offer.

Finally, for collaborative processes focused on collective action, the joint-learning process is a chance to learn about and explore the participants' interdependence. Are there places where government can amplify and support projects that have already taken root in the community? Are there existing or planned activities that some parties need help with? Are there specific resources or help needed by some of the parties that others could provide? Are there people who should be at the table who are not? What are the relationships between the parties who could provide resources?

For example, for many years, we facilitated a collaborative system focused on sediment management at the mouth of the Columbia River (the Lower Columbia Solutions Group). Near the beginning of that process, there was concern among representatives from the crab fishing industry that sediment deposits near the shore would disrupt crab habitat. In order to determine whether that concern was valid, the group needed to monitor the impact of sediment on the crab population. One federal agency was able to provide underwater cameras but needed someone to provide locational buoys. The crab fishing association, it turned out, had extra buoys available, and the monitoring was able to move forward. By becoming more aware of their interdependence, a monitoring program was made possible.

Learning About the Problem or Issue

Through background documents, guest speakers, panels, commissioned research, and other sources, collaborative governance group members need to jointly learn about the substantive and technical information necessary to complete their task. It is important to develop a common base of understanding about the history, context, legal and statutory framework, and technical or scientific aspects of the issue. Taking the time to develop shared understanding, although it is not always easy, will result in "agreements that are more credible and more durable than they would be otherwise" (Ehrmann and Stinson 377).

As discussed in chapter 1, joint learning is a place where a collaborative governance group can foster a sense of inclusion and belonging. By using plain language and avoiding agency jargon, the group can begin to create a culture of shared discovery. It is also an opportunity to value and respect multiple ways of knowing and various kinds of expertise. For example, in the Vernonia school example discussed earlier, there were several meetings in the wake of the flood intended to help the team and the community get a handle on what happened and what some of the alternatives might be. At one meeting, agency representatives repeatedly referred to the flood as a 500-year flood. Several older members of the community disputed that characterization, sharing that damaging floods had always been an issue and that, many years ago, flooding had been partially controlled by a community-built, makeshift dam up river from the town.

In addition to readings and guest speakers, one of the more effective techniques we have found for joint learning is field trips. Getting people in a van and traveling to a site that is relevant and important to the project not only provides everyone with a common—usually pleasant—experience, but it makes the ensuing discussion less theoretical. After a field trip, participants have a common and more tangible image of what the issues are and what the actual impacts are likely to be. This is also a place where direct observation and careful attention is more important than technical expertise. The relational benefit of riding in a vehicle together and sharing information about themselves is an added bonus.

Particularly when it comes to technical or scientific information, the importance of joint learning cannot be overemphasized. Rather than one party, or even a third-party facilitator, deciding who the expert is, collaborative governance groups will be better served if all key interests at the table are involved in framing the research questions, jointly identifying the best scientific or technical sources of information, and once the information is received, analyzing it together. We saw this play out in one agreement-seeking project we were involved in, a process that was time-constrained due to legislative deadlines. In the interests of time, we relied on one party's recommendation as to the best, most universally-accepted expert and invited that person to make a presentation to the group. It did not take long to realize our mistake. Others at the table had very different ideas about that expert's credibility, and our attempted short-cut ended up taking more time, not less. In fact, the subsequent outcry nearly derailed the entire process. In complex cases requiring expertise from various disciplines, we will sometimes work with the group to develop a list of potential experts that they will then choose from together as the process unfolds.

Other considerations for joint fact-finding that we have learned from experience include the following:

- There will be various levels of comfort with technical or scientific language represented at the collaborative table. As set forth above, it is important for the material to be presented in ways that are accessible to all participants, such as in plain language, graphics, video, or translations;
- It's important to dedicate adequate time for this joint fact-finding, even when (or particularly when) stakeholders are anxious to jump to solutions;
- It is often important to disaggregate data in order to set equitable goals and to determine whether burdens fall disproportionately on historically under-represented communities;
- The acceptance and credibility of facts and data used to make decisions is critically important. Therefore, the selection of informational resources and experts should be deemed fair and reasonable by all the parties;
- If financial resources are needed to bring in an outside expert, the source of those financial resources must not taint the information provided;
- Perhaps most important, the effort should be focused on helping the group answer necessary questions.

With regard to the last point, we have seen agreement-seeking processes in which the participants have spent years looking at data, without a clear sense of what question the group is trying to answer. When collaborative groups keep looking for more and more data, beyond some reasonable point, we suspect one of two things is happening—either some members of the group are using data collection as a way to delay potential changes that may negatively impact them, or group members are hoping that the science will save them from doing the difficult work of actual deliberation and decision-making.

Adler and his co-authors advocate for what they call "disciplined inquiry," for which they recommend a third-party facilitator. A disciplined inquiry is characterized in six ways:

- Multiple stakeholders are involved, representing the sometimes very different perspectives;
- The multiple stakeholders work together to identify and review the necessary data;

- The effort is focused on the data needed;
- It is a robust exploration of the information;
- It is not an attempt to reinforce a political position;
- It is multi-disciplinary.

(Adler et al. 2)

Joint learning and fact-finding bring both credibility and a sense of shared ownership to the information the group collectively gathers. The challenge, particularly with highly contentious issues, is that each side often has already chosen a slate of experts whose opinions support that side's policy position. The question then arises whether experts or sources of information can be found that are seen by all parties as legitimate. And, if such universally-acknowledged experts cannot be found, how will the available experts and information sources be balanced?

On many issues today, the "dueling scientists" approach is the norm, making disciplined inquiry both more challenging and, at the same time, more impactful. For contentious issues, where science plays a critical role, we have developed what we call a science-policy workshop. This intensive workshop format is structured to identify and utilize relevant science in public policy deliberations. Interestingly, in order to better integrate science and policy, we find it is best to separate them. We first bring together scientists to consider the scientific evidence, followed by a meeting of decision-makers. We take the following approach:

- Take the time to carefully identify and frame the key scientific questions, the answers to which are most likely to impact policy decisions;
- Ask scientists questions about science, and leave policymaking to the policymakers;
- Bring together the broadest range of principal scientists doing work on a particular subject, including those whose research findings seem to conflict. Doing so reveals what the latest science says, where scientists agree, where they disagree, and where they feel further study is needed;
- Provide policymakers with information about the places where scientists agree, as well as where they still disagree;
- Facilitate a deliberative conversation among policymakers, using the science as the basis for the conversation.

Joint Problem-solving

The process of exploring options, developing strategy, identifying barriers, and ultimately solving problems jointly is the most exciting, and often the most challenging aspect of the collaborative governance process. This is the stage that everyone has been preparing for, the reason for the proper framing, working principles, relationship building, and joint discovery that have come before it. Because the problems and challenges that agreement-seeking is trying to address are quite different from those in collective action, the joint problem-solving steps for each type of process will be discussed separately below.

Joint Problem-solving for Agreement-seeking Processes

As set forth in chapter 3, policy agreement-seeking processes are focused on reconciling diverse interests to reach agreement on the question of what is to be done. Agreement-seeking is used most often, though not exclusively, when there is a conflict. The major challenges it must overcome include positional bargaining, disparities in power, and trust issues.

Challenges

When trying to resolve conflicts, parties often resort to positional bargaining, staking out their opposing positions before engaging in a struggle to see who can compromise the least. A developer wants to build 120 housing units, for example, while the neighborhood organization's position is a maximum of 65. Each may have a less extreme position they would be willing to accept, but they begin the negotiation with their optimum number, giving themselves room to eventually compromise. The problem with this positional bargaining approach in a collaborative governance setting is that it frames the problem as win-lose, making mutual benefit—and agreement—more difficult. Consensus may eventually be reached, but opportunities for greater mutual gain go unrealized. Focusing instead on underlying interests, that is, why the positions were taken, expands the range of potential solutions and opportunities for agreement.

In our example of the proposed residential development, residents' interests in retaining the neighborhood's more rural character may conflict with the developer's interests. However, the neighborhood residents may have other interests as well, such as maintaining a neighborly atmosphere, preserving easy access to commercial services such as groceries and pharmacies, protecting pedestrian spaces, easing traffic circulation, and so forth. Packaging solutions that address multiple interests is one way of finding agreement when a group finds itself stuck on a particular issue.

Another challenge for agreement-seeking processes is disparity in power among participants. These disparities are often created by asymmetries in the interdependence between the parties (Coleman et al. 288). Some parties are simply more dependent on the actions or resources of others. Put another way, if the negotiations do not work out, some parties may have better options than others. When this happens, two conditions often follow that create barriers to agreement. The first is that those who perceive themselves as having relatively good alternatives to a collaborative agreement are likely to be less committed to the process. They will be less willing to work hard to find mutually-beneficial outcomes; in other words, they will be less cooperative. Then, as we discussed in chapter 4, this less cooperative behavior will elicit distrust and, therefore, less cooperative behavior in return. Addressing this challenging cycle is important to success.

Some would say the biggest challenge to agreement-seeking, particularly in situations requiring resolution of historic conflicts, is distrust. We previously discussed in chapter 4 the role that trust plays as social capital, enabling exchanges to happen between parties. When there is an atmosphere of distrust, however, the exchanges necessary for agreement-seeking become far more difficult. Therefore, the joint problem-solving approach needs to take into account the levels of trust between parties, and incorporate procedural elements that can either repair trust or create situational trust through contingencies, joint monitoring, and other measures. We discuss some of these procedural elements below, and delve into them further in chapter 9.

To solve the problem of reconciling diverse interests, and addressing the challenges presented above, we focus on three problem-solving steps for agreement-seeking projects: developing criteria together, exploring potential options, and jointly evaluating those options against the criteria.

Developing Criteria Together

The problem-solving process can often be aided by first developing objective criteria for evaluating solutions. These criteria should derive from the parties' interests and incorporate legal and other constraints for potential solutions. They will be most helpful if they are as objective, straightforward, and measurable as possible. Subjective criteria, such as "best looking design," may elicit entirely different responses, depending on the stakeholder making the judgment. More helpful and measurable criteria might be a ranking based upon cost or greenhouse gas emissions.

The establishment of objective criteria, as Carpenter and Kennedy point out, contrasts with the often common approach of every party evaluating each option based upon how closely it resembles their own proposal (53). These objective criteria, however, should be used to help the group reach consensus, rather than to rigidly constrain it, or prohibit creative solutions. The criteria should be intended to clarify trade-offs and develop the best solution, or package of solutions, rather than dictate what the solutions should be.

The joint development of criteria is also an opportunity to shift the focus to underlying interests by incorporating the various interests in the criteria. In the Columbia River project discussed earlier, for example, the agreed-upon criteria for the placement of dredged material included economic development impacts and ecological impacts, as well as other technical criteria. Particularly in high conflict situations, when each party sees their interests reflected in the criteria adopted by the group, the belief that "we're in this together" is reinforced. Similarly, when there are disparities in power among the participants, having all interests reflected in the criteria can help foster a sense of belonging and can help ensure more equitable outcomes.

Exploring Potential Options

Before a group begins the process of moving toward a decision, it is often helpful to engage in creative thinking, opening up the range of possibilities by brainstorming ideas. Susskind and Cruikshank call this process "inventing." It is important to refrain from jumping to evaluation during this brainstorming step to discourage group members from immediately responding with—that will never work! Get as many ideas out on the table as possible, expanding the range of possible solutions, before beginning the process of winnowing them down. As Susskind and Cruikshank say, "the more good ideas, the better" (90).

In the Tillamook flooding project described in chapter 1, the group consisted of federal and state agencies, community groups, landowners, environmental groups, and local governments. All participants, it seemed, had different ideas about the best solution. They developed an early list of eighteen actions, from wetland restoration and channel widening to dredging the bay. That list of actions served a unifying function, representing everyone's ideas. While they subsequently identified clear priorities for action, and some of the ideas have yet to be implemented, none of the original ideas were taken off the list.

As the joint problem-solving process moves toward the evaluation of options and developing agreements, a second phase of brainstorming may be needed, this time to brainstorm possible packages of solutions.

Evaluating Options

As noted previously, the evaluation of options is intended to aid the decision-making process rather than constrain it, to focus the discussion so that decisions can be made. In the Eastern Oregon water policy process discussed in chapter 6, where the group was attempting to improve conditions for migrating fish as well as increase irrigation water for farmers, the brainstorming phase created a full range of options, based upon the group's fact-finding and technical analysis. After the group went through the first round of evaluations, however, there was a clear separation between the top nine options and the others that followed, and the group chose to focus their deliberation on the nine that had the best chance of being approved by the whole group.

Evaluating the potential options using the adopted criteria, as described above, is one of several techniques that can be used for winnowing options. Another method for moving toward agreement is to agree first on a general plan or principles, and then to dive into a deeper round of negotiation on the details. A third approach is to develop a single negotiating text, which becomes the starting point for parties to make revisions and additions until they find agreement. As we stated at the beginning of this chapter, there is no unified approach that fits all collaborative processes.

As we have previously emphasized, the people at the collaborative governance table are representatives of organizations or constituencies. As such, they need to take the critical step of keeping their constituencies informed and up-to-date. When moving toward agreement, it is critical that the representatives have checked in with their constituencies along the way to ensure that those constituencies understand the new information gathered in the fact-finding stage, their interdependence with others at the table and in the community, and the alternatives to a collaborative outcome. The representatives at the table should also bring interests, information, and concerns back from their constituencies to the collaborative group so that those interests and concerns can be considered as the group moves toward agreement. A reminder of this responsibility by the group's convener or facilitator can ensure that a broad range of interests is considered and that the agreement will not be unraveled because the essential constituencies were not fully consulted and represented.

Joint Problem-solving for Collective Action

The basic problem that a collective action process is trying to solve is fundamentally different than an agreement-seeking process. The goal of collective action is to create a public good. The problem is that no one party has the authority, expertise, or resources to do so on its own. Because the basic problem to be solved is quite different than that for agreement-seeking, it is not surprising that the principal challenges are different as well.

Challenges

The classic and most well-documented challenge of collective action is the problem of free riders. Because a public good can, by definition, be enjoyed by everyone, every party has an incentive to take a free ride, that is, enjoy the benefits while leaving others to step up and contribute to those benefits. The paradox is that if everyone acts on that incentive, no one contributes, and no public good is produced. Think about a public transit system that depends upon the honor system for riders to pay their fare before riding. Each rider may ultimately think they will get to ride whether they pay or not, and, therefore, choose to ride for free. But if all riders do that, the transit system itself will not survive, and nobody will get to ride. This problem of free riders becomes more pronounced the larger the group and the smaller each party's relative contribution.

Another key challenge to collective action stems from the horizontal nature of collaborative relationships. Even when parties understand they need the help and cooperation of others, they are often wary of entering into an enterprise where their success is dependent upon the actions of those they can't control. This can result in either a lack of commitment to the collaborative process and reduction in their own contribution or an attempt to control the process and others who are participating in it. Both become challenges to the success of the enterprise.

One of the more difficult challenges that can face a group trying to initiate collective action is the lack of what we call a principal implementing party. Nearly all projects or programs require someone to step up to take on a kind of principal administrative or coordinating role, convening the other partners when needed to address an unanticipated problem, for example. Without someone playing this role, there is no foundation for others to add to. We discuss this particular challenge in more detail in the next chapter.

Given this different set of challenges, the joint problem-solving phase for collective action, therefore, involves a slightly different series of steps and questions designed to solve the specific problem and challenges surrounding the creation of a public good.

Developing a Preliminary Strategy

The first step is usually development of a preliminary strategy for solving the problem. Once a group agrees on the initial strategic approach, it can then make an initial assessment of what potential resources are represented at the table. We normally help groups make this assessment by simply asking each party at the table in turn why they support the project and what they might be able to contribute. For example, in a project to improve the structural integrity of the Columbia River levee system in Portland, Oregon, participants first agreed upon a general strategy of conducting engineering studies and sharing the costs of levee improvements among a number of public jurisdictions.

The initial strategy and commitments provide the group with a starting point, and a road map for the work ahead. Depending upon the resources available, the problem-solving strategy may need to be revised over time. Most often, the details of the strategy need to be filled into more specifically identify the resource needs (discussed further in the section below). More important, the group needs to identify remaining barriers, challenges, and what resources are missing or might be added to complete or improve the project. Adding details to the problem-solving strategy, identifying gaps and opportunities, and finding missing resources then become the collaborative problem-solving work for the group.

Adding Detail to the Problem-solving Strategy

While there is often broad agreement about the general strategy, moving to implementation usually requires greater detail to better clarify the actions and resources actually needed to make implementation successful. Groups will often charge committees with tackling the detail of various parts of the initial strategy, bringing recommendations or options back to the larger group. The collaborative group working on the Portland levee project may have found agreement on the general strategy relatively easy, but the devil was in the details. A committee of key stakeholders subsequently spent months detailing, negotiating, and vetting the cost-sharing formula before finally bringing it back to the larger group for approval.

Identifying Gaps and Opportunities

Depending upon the type of collective action (fixed goal, incremental improvement, or coordinated interdependent actions) required, the group must identify what resources or actions are needed. What are the political or resource challenges? Potential resources at the table may have been identified earlier, but they now need to be quantified and reaffirmed. As the group approaches success and gets more resources committed, the effort to fill the gap gets more and more targeted. In the Vernonia school project, the known price tag was $38 million to replace three schools in the community that had been destroyed by flooding. At every meeting, the group would report new commitments, and the gap would get smaller. In the rural transportation project discussed in chapter 4, every meeting would include reports of additional resource commitments, but the need for a principal implementing party was still reported as a gap, until ultimately that gap was filled. In addition to filling gaps, a collective-action group should also identify opportunities. There may be ways to magnify the impact of a project by adding additional resources or actions.

Assembling the Needed Resources

Finding and aligning the needed resources and other commitments to create a public good is the essential problem of collective action. A good starting point is to identify who might particularly benefit from the public good, as these are the stakeholders who have a vested interest in making sure the effort succeeds. Economists would argue that the degree to which a party benefits should be relatively proportional to the degree to which the party is willing to contribute to ensure that benefit.

In one project that we facilitated, the City of Eugene, Oregon, approached our center to convene a collaborative process to transform unsightly riverside gravel pits into an urban natural area with pedestrian trails and viewing plat-forms surrounding scenic ponds that fill during the high-water months. When the project—which became known as the Delta Ponds project—began, one of the first steps was to identify and contact the owners of property abutting the ponds. If the project was successful, the city reasoned, those property owners would not only enjoy the improved amenities, but also have the value of their own properties substantially increased. Each of those property owners had an incentive to help make that project successful, and many of them ended up con-tributing to the project's success.

Successful groups also look for how they can combine their individual assets to create greater public value. If one party has already committed actions or invested resources to address a problem, for example, others at the table may be able to add additional resources to boost that effort. By piggy-backing on the existing commitments, group members can produce something bigger, better, faster, or cheaper.

The challenge, as we described above, is the free-rider problem, and each party's fear that others will be free riders. If one party steps forward, they risk having others take less responsibility for the solution. This risk is real, and often prevents parties from stepping forward to fill the necessary gaps. One way to deal with this problem is to arrange for joint or simultaneous commitments. The transparency of the collaborative governance process, with its face-to-face interactions that encourage accountability to the group, can foster these joint commitments. It is, in fact, one key advantage of transparency. When multiple parties make a commitment in the same meeting, it starts to become a group norm, and other commitments are likely to follow. The research is clear that creating a group norm of contributing is an effective way to solve the free-rider problem (Ostrom 9). It is one of the reasons we recommend against having a significant number of interested stakeholders with no incentive or ability to contribute participate in collective action projects. The more non-contributors are involved, the more difficult it becomes to create a group expectation that everyone contributes, paving the way for free riders.

Another strategy for reducing the incidence of free riders is for participants to make contingent offers. For example, I will commit my organization's staff time, *if* other organizations can commit financial resources to pay for the materials. We have seen parties successfully leverage their resources by making them contin-gent on a commitment by others. In the Lakeview project discussed in chapter 4, one company offered to construct a new mill that would process small-diameter logs, creating needed jobs in the community. That offer, however, was contin-gent upon federal agencies guaranteeing a supply of small-diameter logs. Both commitments were ultimately kept.

One of the most effective antidotes to the free-rider problem is creating a sense of momentum. One way to engender belief in potential success is to recognize and celebrate resource commitments as they are made rather than waiting until the end of the process. This approach not only provides greater belief in the enterprise, it reinforces the group norm that everyone contributes. We have observed that when a certain critical mass of resources and support starts to accumulate, increasing the chances of success, other parties become more willing to contribute. For example, in the project in which the neighborhood was working with the city to build a community bike park, the neighbors were raising money to build the park with mostly small donations obtained through a crowdfunding platform. As they got closer to their goal, they held a press conference, and the media reported their success. Then, seemingly out of the blue, a major corporation—with no previous connection to the project—made a $25,000 contribution. Everyone, it seems, wants to be associated with a winner.

These unexpected synergies are why it is important to mark success along the way and to publicly recognize the contributions or efforts of various parties. We've seen project teams utilize news articles, widely-distributed newsletters, joint appearances, or almost any opportunity to celebrate and recognize their collaborative success. The project to repair the Portland Columbia River levee, described earlier, began with a relatively narrow geographic scope. After nearby jurisdictions learned of the successful initial stage of the project, however, they soon petitioned to join the group. They did not want to be left out of a good thing.

What should be done if the needed actions and resources are not found around the table? If needed resources can be identified outside the group, the parties that control those resources should be invited to join the group. Indeed, one of the questions the group should ask itself in the early stages of the collective action process is: Who else can help? Celebrating the resources that have already been harnessed can help in that regard. The project to rebuild the Vernonia schools began with a number of substantial commitments, not least of which was the passage of a local bond measure that raised $13 million. Still, the group faced a major gap, and began to approach private foundations and businesses that had not previously been at the collaborative table. Eventually, this effort to enlarge the circle of contributors filled the gap.

Whether for agreement-seeking or collective action, joint problem-solving is truly the heart of the collaborative process, one which hopefully leads to a group decision. It is to that decision-making process that we next turn our attention.

Consensus Decision-making

In chapter 6 we said that most collaborative groups utilize consensus-based decision making. While the exact definition of consensus may engender its own debate, the primary distinction between consensus decision-making and majority rule is that consensus decision-making attempts to ensure that minority views are considered and addressed well enough that all participants consent to the ultimate decision. This raises the questions: Why do collaborative governance groups, even those involved in collective action, tend to make most of their important decisions by consensus? What's wrong with majority rule? Hasn't it worked as a decision-making process for most governing bodies in the United States since the country's founding?

The use of consensus decision-making in collaborative governance stems from two of the inherent characteristics of collaboration we identified in chapter 4, the voluntary nature of collaboration and the interdependence of the parties. The parties are all, in one sense, autonomous actors. That is, they are not under the control of any other party at the table. No one is forced to go along with a group decision made by a majority with whom they disagree. The only way one can get reasonable assurance that all parties will go along with the decision and support its implementation is if that decision is made by consensus.

Further, the parties are engaged in a collaborative process precisely because of their interdependence. While they lack direct control or authority over one another, they also need each other to support the group decisions and direction in order to get the desired outcome. Therein lays the value of decision-making by consensus. When you need everyone on board in order to move forward with confidence, consensus works better than majority rule. A majority vote can, particularly with contentious issues, leave a minority of the group unhappy with the decision. They may then work to prevent implementation.

Not all decisions, however, require consensus. Sometimes decisions need to be made quickly, such as when there is an emergency. Other times there are minor decisions, where the value of the decision is not worth the time required to get consensus (for example: Where should we meet next time? or what color should the invitations be?). Consensus is required when the implementation of a decision requires that all key parties are on board, or at least that none of them oppose the decision.

We do not suggest that consensus decision-making is easy or expeditious. It can take longer for a group to reach consensus. Indeed, some participants cringe when they hear the word. To them, it conjures up images of endless debate and delayed decisions. The investment of time and effort spent reaching consensus, however, can often yield large dividends in the long run. We describe below a method for using consensus decision-making that respects everyone's time.

Defining Consensus

There is an ongoing debate in the field of collaborative governance about what consensus really means, usually couched in terms of numbers. Does consensus require unanimity? Is it unanimity minus one? Does it require striving for unanimity, but allowing for a majority vote if unanimity is unreachable? We believe that this debate over numbers is slightly misplaced. Instead, we argue that the defining characteristics of constructive consensus decision-making are: (1) each party feels like their opinion truly matters to the others, (2) each party is given a genuine opportunity to weigh in, and (3) conflict is seen as a call for creative problem-solving, rather than something to be avoided. A focus on these three characteristics can result in better decisions and greater support for the decisions, without causing undue delays. When these characteristics are present, we find that parties acting in good faith are more willing to consent to a decision, even when it is not their preferred position.

In one instance, we were approached to facilitate a planning process for a local city council. The council was trying to reach consensus on their annual priorities. A disagreement emerged over a particular initiative—one councilor felt it should be a high priority, while the other six rated it as a lower priority. Those in the majority worked hard to understand the underlying reasons for the other council member's position and how they might address his overall interests. They asked: "Is there a way to combine this activity with one of the other high priority activities? Can we study the issue in the upcoming year?" For his part, the lone dissenter tried to find a way that he might amend his own approach to garner their support. This went on for some time, without apparent success. It appeared they simply could not reconcile the two positions. After a while, however, the objector acknowledged his fellow council members' sincere attempts to address his concerns and was willing to move on and support the decision favored by the others.

It may also be helpful here to contrast the above scenario with some distorted versions of consensus decision-making. One might look something like this: the chair or convener calls the question on a proposal and asks if anyone disagrees. There is a pause of perhaps two to four seconds after which the chair or convener promptly announces that consensus has been reached. A slightly different version of this scenario involves two or three influential group members dominating the discussion, voicing support for a proposal, and based on that discussion, the chair announcing that a consensus decision has been made. A third version involves one lonely soul who dares to speak up when the chair asks if there are any objections. Others around the table roll their eyes as if to say, here we go again. The objection might then be simply ignored, or the person who raised it might be marginalized by the rest of the group.

While all three of these scenarios are actually quite common, none of them are true consensus decision-making. When this kind of process takes place under the guise of "consensus," those around the table who have not spoken up can receive a very clear message that their opinion does not matter. This is the opposite of the central reason for consensus decision-making—that everyone's consent matters. Participants in a false consensus process end up having neither a voice nor a vote. The deliberation and decisions instead get dominated by a vocal minority, and dissent or objections may be seen as unwanted obstruction. Sometimes things can even appear to be going smoothly, but previously suppressed questions or conflicts arise when it comes time for implementation, and the false consensus falls apart.

Consensus Process Guidelines

True consensus decision-making, in contrast to false consensus, is a distinctly collaborative process with all parties working together for mutual benefit. It is a process where conflict is seen as a natural occurrence rather than a flaw, where it is safe to express true opinions, and where the focus is on reconciling competing interests as a way of "moving northeast." In a true consensus process, each party has two essential responsibilities: to speak up about his or her or their interests and concerns, particularly if they disagree, and to actively work to satisfy the needs of the other parties at the table.

During a collaborative governance group's discussions, it is important to provide every party at the table with an opportunity to ask questions or express their opinion. Often we find it helpful to poll participants along the way to get a sense of which aspects of a proposal have consent and which require further work. When polling, we give every participant, in turn, three options to choose from:

- *I agree*: They support the proposal;
- *I have concerns, but they are not serious enough to cause me to block the decision*: It may not be their preferred option, but they won't block a group decision in support of the proposal;
- *I would block the decision*: They oppose the proposal and do not give their consent.

If a more nuanced approach is necessary, we sometimes use five fingers to demonstrate the level of support for a proposal, with one being lowest and five being highest.

If a party opposes and blocks the proposal, they cannot simply fold their arms and stonewall until they get their way. Instead, the group should agree in advance that anyone blocking a proposal must do both of the following: 1) provide their reasons for blocking in a way that gives others something to work with and 2) work actively to create a proposal that would be acceptable to them *and* to the other parties at the table.

These decision-making guidelines are designed to encourage joint problem-solving behavior, encouraging parties in conflict to work together on the shared problem of reaching consensus. We once observed an experiment where two groups were given the same difficult policy problem and given one hour to reach consensus. Only one of the groups was given the process guidelines offered above. That group immediately set to work addressing the two or three individuals who were blocking a proposal. The other participants approached them with questions, such as what are your specific objections to the proposal? And what changes would it take for you to support it? The dissenters, in turn, responded by offering their own counter-proposals designed to elicit the support of the others. This group came to consensus within about twenty-five minutes. The other group, without the more detailed guidelines, floundered. After one hour they were still nowhere close to agreement. The lesson of this experiment was powerful: if certain principles and rules are followed, consensus decision-making can be far more efficient than many think.

Challenges and Problems in Consensus Decision-making

Group Size

Consensus decision-making becomes more challenging as group size gets larger. Finding a way to give everyone an opportunity to voice their opinion or articulate their concerns becomes much more difficult and time-consuming with groups larger than fifteen or twenty people. In these circumstances, we resort to facilitation techniques such as hand signals (thumbs-up for agree, thumbs-down for disagree, flat palm for "do not agree but will not block"), holding up cards (green, red, yellow), and compiling written post-it notes to combine ideas and concerns. Initially breaking into smaller groups also helps enable meaningful dialogue and deliberation, and key points can then be reported back to the larger group.

Differing Interpersonal Styles

Consensus guidelines have implications for different types of people. Every collaborative governance group is made up of a mix of personalities, some of whom process information more by talking and some of whom process information more by thinking. Good decisions depend on both.

In order for the group to gain the benefit of both types of people, it is important to give each type an opportunity to process information before they are asked to commit to a position through a poll or other means. For example, we often give all participants a few moments to think and write a few notes in response to a question or poll. This provides everyone who needs it a chance to collect their thoughts. In order to meet the needs of those who are oral processors, it is important to ensure that the topic has been thoroughly discussed before polling commences, without allowing them to dominate the conversation. If the group is too large to support a thorough discussion, small groups or even pairs can be helpful.

Bad Faith

Sometimes parties show up, but they are not there to collaborate. Rather, it seems, their aim is getting to "no," or sometimes it is to delay or prevent action, without any openness to a consensus outcome. They may be grandstanding, believe they have a better alternative, or be an adherent to old-school positional bargaining. Or they may be using the process to take advantage of others' cooperation. It can be extremely frustrating for the other parties at the table, who are working hard to find mutually beneficial outcomes, when one party simply refuses to engage in principled negotiation. It is why we recommend that the consensus decision-making guidelines described above be incorporated into a group's working principles ahead of time. If one party refuses to abide by those principles, the group may wish to adopt consensus decisions without them or, if the situation is severe enough, remove them from the group.

Public Involvement

Because collaborative governance concerns itself with public policy and the public good, its impact extends beyond the group represented at the collaborative governance table. As discussed in chapter 6, participants in that core group should consider how best to seek input from the broader public.

This is where the delicate balance between the norms of representativeness and inclusion come into play. Whether it is for agreement-seeking or collective action, decisions made in a collaborative governance process will affect the general public. Consequently, the public should be informed and offered the opportunity to give input in some way.

We have seen several ways in which the general public can be engaged in a collaborative governance process. First, most collaborative governance groups have a list of interested persons who are not participating at the table but who are able to observe the meetings, receive meeting notes, and so forth. Some project teams provide public comment or questions at each of their meetings. Many attend or schedule special public gatherings to hear additional public input.

We've also seen collaborative governance groups design and execute a full-blown public engagement process to inform their work, proactively reaching out to educate and hear from broad segments of the public, including historically underrepresented communities and multiple language groups. There is a growing recognition in the United States of the need to dismantle barriers that have prevented Black people, Indigenous people, and other people of color from fully participating in community decision-making. In one recent collaborative project with a high potential for controversy, representatives from the collaborative governance team spent two years attending neighborhood meetings, hosting information booths at street fairs and community celebrations, sending out a periodic newsletter, and scheduling a series of special meetings to inform the community and answer questions. In another project involving school boundaries, our staff spent six months engaged in a community involvement process conducted in six languages and using many culturally specific forms of outreach. We conducted small deliberations in a sewing circle for Somali mothers and held community conversations during the Spanish-language coffee hour at an elementary school. Each of these conversations eventually informed the framing of the issues, as well of the makeup of the collaborative governance group. Only after that process was complete and a full report was issued summarizing the results did the collaborative governance group begin deliberating in earnest.

Public involvement is its own democratic art form, and we will leave a detailed discussion of its theory and techniques for another day. We wish here only to emphasize its importance as an adjunct to the collaborative governance process.

Conclusion

As always, how a collaborative group goes about its deliberative work makes a difference. Paying attention to the steps in the deliberative process can result in better decisions and help a group overcome the inherent challenges, whether in agreement-seeking or collective action. If done well, tending to such details should also make groups' decisions or agreements easier to implement.

Note

1 Though we often distinguish how practices play out in collaborative systems as well as the other two types of collaborative governance, in this instance there are no such distinctions.

References

Adler, Peter S., et al. *Humble Inquiry: The Practice of Joint Fact Finding as a Strategy for Bringing Science, Policy and the Public Together.* Mediate.com, 25 Feb. 2011.

Carlson, Christine. *A Practical Guide to Collaborative Governance.* Policy Consensus Initiative, 2007.

Carpenter, Susan L., and W. J. D. Kennedy. *Managing Public Disputes.* Jossey-Bass Publishers, 1988.

Coleman, Peter T., et al. *The View from Above and Below: The Effects of Power Symmetries and Interdependence on Conflict Dynamics & Outcomes.* IACM 21st Annual Conference Paper, 9 Nov. 2008.

Ehrmann, John R., and Barbara L. Stinson. "Joint Fact-Finding and the Use of Technical Experts." *The Consensus Building Handbook: A Comprehensive Guide to Reaching Agreement,* The Consensus Building Institute, 1999, p. 375–399.

Ostrom, Elinor. "A Behavioral Approach to the Rational Choice Theory of Collective Action: Presidential Address, American Political Science 1997." *American Political Review,* vol. 92, no. 1, Mar. 1998.

Susskind, Lawrence E., and Jeffrey L. Cruikshank. *Breaking Robert's Rules.* Oxford UP, 2006.

8

IMPLEMENTATION AND ADAPTATION

Introduction

In the previous two chapters, we described the elements of collaborative govern-ance preparation and process that can produce extraordinary results. Nonetheless, all of that rigorous process—the assessment, the convening, and the hard work of deliberation—means little if the agreements reached are not actually *implemented*. Participants in collaborative governance processes sometimes believe that once the agreement is reached, their work is done. They frequently find out, however, the real work is just beginning.

In this chapter, we cover how to move from the decision-making stage to implementation so that the potential public benefits of a collaborative govern-ance process are realized. The guiding question for this phase of a collaborative process is: How does the group link its agreements to implementation? (See Figure 8.1.) In answering that question, we will focus on the following topics:

- Structuring the agreement for implementation;
- Designing the future governance structure;
- Moving to action;
- Monitoring, evaluating, and adapting.

A project in the Columbia Gorge National Recreation Area near Portland, Oregon, illustrates how important effective implementation is, even after an agreement is reached. The area had become so popular for hikers from all over the region that parked cars along the scenic highway were creating a major safety hazard. A group of federal, state, and local agencies met with local residents and

Implementation and Adaptation	

Guiding Question:
How does the group link its agreements to implementation?

Key Activities:
Structuring the agreement for implementation
Designing the future governance structure
Moving to action
Monitoring, evaluating, and adapting

FIGURE 8.1 Implementation and adaptation (phase four)

community groups in a collaborative governance process to try to solve the problem. After months of deliberation, they decided to institute a low-cost bus service to transport visitors from the Portland area to the gorge scenic area, though at the time they were not sure anyone would actually use it. However, when the bus service was finally launched, some weeks after the group's collaborative governance process was done, the system was overwhelmed with demand. Complaints about long lines and waiting times threatened the feasibility of the solution and required the agencies to regroup and adapt. The group reconvened and found the resources to expand the shuttle service to meet the demand. The collaborative agreement, they learned, is not the actual solution. It is implementation that ultimately matters. In the end, the implementation roles the group had collaboratively agreed upon enabled them to quickly respond and address the problem.

One of the greatest challenges for collaborative governance, we find, is ensuring implementation of agreements over the long term. Over time, as politics and circumstances change, the alternatives available to the parties may evolve, budget priorities may shift, and the people who once forged the original agreement and made commitments on behalf of their constituency may move on and be replaced by representatives who may not fully understand the history behind the agreement. Indeed, they may even be unaware of the agreement.

This long-term vulnerability of collaborative agreements is due in part to the horizontal nature of collaborative relationships. No party is directly accountable to another unless they create legal accountability. Maintenance of the agreement over time is, therefore, often uneven unless the agreement is officially adopted by an individual organization or is memorialized through some official means such as a contract, intergovernmental agreement, ordinance, or some other legally binding act.

Structuring the Agreement for Implementation

Whether for agreement-seeking or collective action, the product of most collaborative governance processes is an agreement of some kind. While not every collaborative agreement is in writing and signed by the parties, we believe most of them should be, particularly in complex cases or projects. This is true whether the group is convened as a stand-alone process or is the off-shoot of an ongoing collaborative system. Agreement-seeking first requires coming to a mutually-agreed-on decision on a policy or direction going forward. Then a second round of agreements is needed to determine implementation roles, monitoring, and adaptation. For collective action, there should be an agreement on the overall strategy for creating the public asset and the commitments of the parties. In either case, the culmination of the deliberation should be written agreements that all parties feel comfortable signing.

Without a *written* agreement, there is a greater chance each stakeholder group will hear what they want to hear or misinterpret what parties are committing to. There is also a risk that important elements of the agreement will be lost or forgotten over time. A written agreement helps illuminate questions, gaps, or omissions that need to be addressed. Perhaps most importantly, we find that stakeholder groups take the agreement and negotiations far more seriously when they know they will be signing their names to something in writing. In memorializing the agreement and getting all the parties to sign, however, there are a number of challenges and opportunities that deserve mention.

Structuring the Agreement

Because of the less formal nature of collaborative relationships, the collaborative agreements we are referring to are generally not legally-binding documents, rather they are statements of intent and good faith. Nevertheless, how written agreements are structured can make a significant difference in how successfully they are implemented. Furthermore, while these written agreements tend to use less formal language, they may shape future legal agreements.

A common question from those involved in a collaborative governance project is: When do we know we are done? Put another way: How much detail needs to be in the agreement, and how much can be deferred to individual parties in the implementation stage? Those questions are important because, by the time participants get to the agreement stage, they are often worn out. As groups approach the finish line, they may develop "a willingness to rush past an unresolved issue and simply act as if it's resolved" (Susskind and Cruikshank 133). Not all details need to be included in the collaborative governance agreement. There are some details that can and should be left to the implementing parties. In the Tillamook flood control project, for example, the group decided that floodgates should be replaced, and the group decided where they should be located. The actual design of the floodgates, however, was left to the implementing agency.

Our answer to the question, "how much is enough?" is a functional one. The agreement should have enough detail to make it clear how the important issues or implementation questions have been resolved. The level of detail should provide all the stakeholder groups with an acceptable level of assurance that the spirit of the agreement will, in fact, be implemented and the implementation will be sustained over time. It should, therefore, clearly define roles and responsibilities, that is, who is to do what and by when. The level of detail needed will be different for each situation, depending on the project and the stakeholders involved.

What are some of the key components of a written agreement? For agreement-seeking groups, we recommend that the components for implementation include the following:

- A description of the policy approach or resolution agreed upon;
- A commitment to abide by the agreement;
- Any action items central to the agreement, that is, who is to do what and by when;
- A plan for monitoring adherence to the agreement with stipulated consequences for noncompliance; and
- A procedure for reconvening if, and when, circumstances change that require amendment or adaptation of the agreement.

Collective action agreements will need to include a slightly different set of elements. The National Policy Consensus Center incorporates these elements into what we call a *Declaration of Cooperation* signed by all the participants:

- A description of the project;
- A description of the general strategy the group has adopted to create a public asset and, in particular, how collaboration will help;
- The combination of resources and information needed to solve the problem;
- The contributions individual parties commit to solving the problem;
- The governance structure for future implementation (Who will be responsible for what aspects of the program or project? Who will be the principal implementing party?);
- A description of the formal or legal actions will need to be taken and by whom; and
- A designation of who will reconvene the group, and when.

Specificity of Commitments

Implementation requires action, information or expertise, and commitment of resources (both financial and in-kind). A common challenge, particularly with collective action agreements, is a tendency for some stakeholder groups to be vague about their commitments. Phrases, such as, "We will continue to support x" or "we will actively participate," make it difficult for the collaborative group to ascertain whether they have marshaled the necessary resources to complete the task. Without specific actions and timeframes and plans for monitoring results, it is difficult to know how the agreement will actually be implemented.

Written agreements that include tangible commitments of information, staff time, financial resources, or actions not only give collaborative groups a better understanding of their ability to implement the project or program but also pro vide a measure of accountability. Indeed, it may be concerns about accountability that motivate some parties to make their commitments vague. It is difficult to determine if a stakeholder has or has not followed through on a commitment like this one made in a recent project: "Where practical and appropriate, [we will] provide public and political support."

By contrast, the Declaration of Cooperation for the Jade Greening Project in Portland, Oregon, provides an example of tangible commitments explicitly tied to actions on the ground. This project was intended to address the health and wellness disparities experienced by residents of the Jade District, which is home to a significant percentage of Portland's Asian community and is one of the most racially diverse districts in the city. The project team adopted a strategy of increasing urban green spaces and roadside trees and improving pedestrian access to services throughout the district. The Declaration of Cooperation included the county health department's commitment to provide "current data on health and air quality, in accessible formats" ("Jade Greening" 9). A local nonprofit committed to develop a series of three to six "green-space improvement pro-jects" in the neighborhood over a year (12). An Asian-Pacific Islander advocacy organization committed to "form a neighborhood 'green team' to...encourage tree plantings" (14). And the city transportation agency committed investments totaling $100,000, including an offer of roadside trees to commercial and indus-trial property owners (10). The specificity of these and other commitments ena-bled the group to move forward with a shared sense that their strategy would be implemented.

Phasing a Collaborative Project

When an issue or a project is highly complex or difficult, a collaborative govern-ance process can take years. In those cases, when energy and motivation start to lag, phasing a project can be helpful. If the finish line is too far in the distance, the group can create multiple finish lines. Doing so sets achievable milestones and helps the group keep track of what they have already achieved. It also pro-vides a structured opportunity for a reset to evaluate what is working and what is not before going forward. Sometimes the group needs to shift its focus or add a new objective from their original work plan. There may be a need to reconsider adding stakeholders who were not part of the previous phase. Of course, cel-ebrating the end of a phase with a signed agreement can raise broader awareness of the effort, potentially attracting additional members or resources.

In the levee repair project described in the previous chapter, the first phase involved the completion of an engineering study of the two areas most in need of repair. The first phase provided a springboard for the more difficult work to follow: prioritizing and paying for the needed repairs, incorporating neighborhood and ecosystem improvements, and so forth. The Declaration of Cooperation signed by the parties at the end of phase one memorialized the commitments that led to the study completion, and it set the objectives and changes in the collaborative structure needed for the next phase of work.

Designing the Future Governance Structure

Beyond policy agreements and commitments of actions or resources, the written agreement may also need to include a governance structure, that is, how the group will actually work together to implement the agreement. At times, this involves the establishment of a collaborative system. In that case, without structure, the group may tend to meet indefinitely, without a clear sense of purpose or accountability. In fact, any collaborative governance process that lacks an agreed-upon governance structure creates the possibility that some stakeholders will be diverted, that necessary actions will fall through the cracks, or that turf battles will ensue. Given the informal nature of collaborative relationships, an agreed-upon governance structure is needed to clarify roles, responsibilities, and process. We discuss four common governance issues below: (1) identifying the principal implementing party, (2) outlining the responsibilities of other stakeholders, (3) continuing the collaborative process, and (4) establishing a new governance entity.

Identifying the Principal Implementing Party

In the case of the rural transportation project that we discussed in earlier chapters, several jurisdictions came together with the intention of creating a joint transit system. Many of those jurisdictions and other organizations had contributions to offer, but nobody initially volunteered to actually run the transit system. The group met for months without much progress. It was only after one of the parties stepped up to serve as the principal implementing party that the other stakeholders felt confident enough to follow through with their own contributions to the solution.

Collective action projects, such as that rural transit system, nearly always require a principal implementing party, someone responsible for ensuring that all the necessary information, resources, and authorities come together as envisioned in the agreement. The principal implementing party may take on legal ownership or responsibility for implementation of the project. And they may be given the authority to reconvene the collaborative parties as needed. One important benefit of identifying this principal implementing party in the group's written agreement is that it legitimizes the role. In essence, all of the parties are agreeing that, within this informal set of collaborative relationships, one organization has authority to convene them, ask for progress updates, and so forth. The principal implementing party is thus able to confidently take ownership of key tasks.

In the case of the collaborative governance group that developed the Malheur Wildlife Refuge plan, which we have discussed several times, the United States Fish and Wildlife Service was the clear principal implementing party. All of the other parties understood and acknowledged the agency's role as the manager of the wildlife refuge, while many of the key parties had their own distinct responsibilities in the implementation of the agreed-upon plan.

Sometimes a separate entity needs to be created to play this role. Over a number of years, we were involved in a project in which the parties worked to continue operation of the Willamette Falls Locks. The locks had been owned and operated by the United States Army Corps of Engineers for more than 100 years before they fell into a state of disrepair and the Army Corps decided to decommission them and not allow boat traffic to pass. There was an uproar from the local community, however, because recreational boaters and others used the locks as a way to go up and down the river. Parties from around the area came together in a collaborative process to save the locks. As they began to garner resources, the Army Corps of Engineers started out as the principal implementing party, but later declined that role. At that point, any potential resource commitments were rendered ineffectual without someone to actually own and operate the locks. Several years went by as efforts to find an existing party to play that role proved unsuccessful. The collaborative governance group has recently made a proposal to the state legislature to establish a new legal entity to own and operate the locks, with the hope of creating a principal implementing party around which the stakeholders can coalesce.

Outlining the Responsibilities of Other Stakeholders

The written agreement should specify who is responsible for the various actions related to implementing the agreement. Who has legal authority or responsibilities? Who will be monitoring performance? If legislation or a city ordinance will be needed, who will draft it? Who will be responsible for public outreach and engagement? If these and other governance questions are addressed in the agreement, there is greater certainty that the agreement will be implemented in a satisfactory manner even after the collaborative group stops meeting.

We find it helpful to think of governance roles as divided into three categories:

- *Ownership/leadership tasks.* These tasks include legal ownership and responsibilities, convening of other partners or stakeholders as needed, and the other tasks of a principal implementing party;

- *Management/operational tasks.* These tasks include oversight of specific operations, including work projects, monitoring, and evaluation;
- *Support tasks.* These include responsibilities, such as communications, public engagement, and financial management.

The Sage-Grouse Conservation Partnership (SageCon) demonstrated the value of having these responsibilities spelled out. The project, as we have described previously, was part of a larger multistate effort to respond to the significant decline of the Western Sage-Grouse. Federal agencies were identified as principal implementing parties in this project, and the comprehensive plan detailed the responsibilities, actions, and commitments of other stakeholders in the agreement. One agency agreed to adopt administrative rules, another committed one million dollars in financial support, another committed financial assistance to private landowners implementing conservation agreements. The group's agreement clearly addressed who, what, and by when, and it provided needed accountability.

Continuing the Collaborative Process

Establishing the governance structure requires determining whether and how the collaboration between parties will continue during implementation. Do participants simply go back to their respective silos now that the agreement has been signed, or will subcommittees or task groups continue to meet? How will members of the collaborative group work out unforeseen implementation issues that may arise? Will there be specific legal or financial agreements needed? Are there any constraining deadlines? Stakeholders signing the agreement should do so with a common understanding of the answers to these and other implementation questions.

As the collaboration moves from agreement to implementation, reality sets in. Unforeseen circumstances pop up in the implementation of nearly every collaborative agreement. Designating, in the agreement itself, a timeline for reconvening the group not only saves time and effort later but also provides a built-in mechanism for accountability. When the parties know they will be gathering again in several months to see how they have performed, they are more aware of their accountability to each other and have an incentive for following through with their commitments.

Establishing a New Governance Entity

One of the reasons for collaborative governance, particularly for collective action, is to address public problems when no single entity has the authority or resources to address the problem on their own. At times, these conditions require the establishment of a new entity to take ownership or carry out leadership tasks.

Sometimes this is the very purpose of a collaborative system. This new entity may be formed through an intergovernmental agreement, as was the case in a long-term project to construct a recreational trail, the Salmonberry Trail, along an abandoned rail corridor in Oregon. Sometimes the creation of a new government entity such as a special district is required, as was the case in the Columbia River levee project, which spanned multiple municipalities and special districts.

When a new entity is required, formation of this new governance structure becomes a significant topic of the deliberation itself. Deliberating over the future governance structure was a central focus of the Salmonberry Trail project. This project, spanning eighty-six miles, three counties, numerous special districts, a state forest, and multiple private properties, required a governance structure that took into account dozens of interests. A large group of public and private stakeholders deliberated for months before agreeing to form a new intergovernmental agency authorized under state law to oversee work on the trail. The charge for this new agency was agreed to in writing by all parties. It included a detailed set of authorities and responsibilities, including that the new agency "maintains effective open and transparent communications, including a trail-related website and regularly scheduled meetings of the coalition to discuss status and priorities and to coordinate policies that affect design and implementation of the trail" and that it "provides a neutral forum to work directly with local partners in facilitating their interests with the final design and implementation of the trail" (Oregon Solutions, "Salmonberry" 2).

Moving to Action

How a group moves from the written agreement to action, and how quickly, are critical factors in the ultimate success of a collaborative governance process. What happens in these first steps of implementation sets the tone and later expectations for the enterprise.

Moving from Informal to Formal Agreements

A standard part of the implementation process is moving from informal collaborative agreements to more formal legal agreements and contracts. Collaborative governance, we have noted previously, does not substitute for the legal authorities and responsibilities that lie with governmental bodies. It does not, for example, replace a city council's or county commission's budget authority. Rather, the process helps parties work out the necessary interlocking steps for a decision to be implemented. So, while every organization at the table remains legally autonomous, the collaborative governance process provides a clear path forward for the key stakeholders. Those stakeholders, then, must take the next steps to create the necessary legal structure to ensure that the agreement is implemented.

An example of an informal agreement that required formal action on the part of the stakeholders arose in the Columbia River levee project we have discussed several times. In that project, the parties worked out a cost-sharing formula for the levee improvement project, but that formula required several stakeholders to take formal action. After the parties worked out a preliminary collaborative agreement regarding who would contribute to an engineering study and how much each party owed, each jurisdiction went through their own process to officially approve their share of the costs.

In the Delta Ponds project discussed in the previous chapter, one of the stakeholders was the Oregon Parks and Recreation Department, which provides grants to local governments for projects precisely like Delta Ponds. While the parks department was supportive of the Delta Ponds project and participated in the collaborative group, they had their own legally-mandated process for deciding on the distribution of those grants. Their participation in the collaborative governance group did not replace or undermine the legitimacy of the parks department's process, and the city had to formally compete for a grant that later substantially aided the project.

Planning to Action

Despite having succeeded in reaching a collaborative agreement, participants may retain some skepticism at the end of a project. In an agreement-seeking process, a party may not completely trust that others will fulfill their part of the bargain or that the result will conform to the agreement. In a collective action project, parties may be concerned that their agreement will be another in a long line of reports or recommendations that end up on a shelf and that nothing will really happen. Past experiences with unstructured collaboration may feed these fears.

The best way to counteract this skepticism is to get moving, to start to implement a part of the agreement, no matter how small, as quickly as possible. In the Tillamook flood control project, there was significant disbelief that anything would come of the group's efforts. After all, the same stakeholders had attempted to address the problem years before, without results. This time, however, the group immediately set about implementing one of the action items in their agreed-upon plan, the removal of the Dean dirt pile, a build-up of sediment that worsened flooding in high-water events. Although it was not a high-priority step in the plan, it was an attractive first step because the necessary resources and participants could be quickly mobilized to implement it. The speed and success of that first action sent an important message to the group: this time the solution was going to be real. This early momentum inspired the group to follow up on other parts of the agreement, subsequently implementing projects of increasing scope and complexity.

These initial actions need not be large to provide a significant boost to the implementation process. We recall the state of Washington's early efforts to implement an unprecedented program of water development in the eastern portion of the state. The first projects were quite small, in the range of two to three thousand acre-feet of water, negligible in the big scheme of things. But these projects demonstrated that this major policy initiative was real, and they established a successful track record. Soon projects were being implemented involving hundreds of thousands of acre-feet.

As we discuss in a subsequent chapter, one of the participating organizations in a collaborative process will sometimes be poised to initiate some small action on their own. Using their action as a springboard, other members of a collaborative group can add their own expertise, authority, or resources, multiplying the impact or effectiveness of the initiative. Such was the case when public and private stakeholders in a collaborative process began planning a new riverfront park in Milwaukie, Oregon. Two dilapidated commercial buildings on the site were being demolished, significantly changing the landscape. After demolition, the Oregon Department of Transportation improved pedestrian access along the adjacent state highway. These complementary activities provided an enormous sense of momentum and affirmation that the group's work wasn't going to be just another plan on a shelf. The park was soon completed and became a source of civic pride and subsequently sparked new economic activity in the adjacent downtown area.

Moving quickly to action, even on lower-priority portions of an agreement, creates momentum in a number of ways. The shorter the time interval between a signed agreement and actual implementation, the less likely parties will move on to other priorities. Swift action also demonstrates that the group is serious about making something happen. It provides an opportunity for parties to show they can be trusted to follow through, and provides a shared experience of success that increases group trust and solidarity. Finally, quick implementation of one part of an agreement fosters important learning about working relationships and technical challenges that can be applied to subsequent planning or actions.

Keeping Communication Flowing

In the early stages of implementation, the lines of communication established during the collaborative process are still open, making implementation easier. As implementation advances, it is helpful to make sure that the entire group is still kept up-to-date. Without this communication, organizations go back to their respective corners and may not even be aware of the positive results of their work. Communication is also critical to maintaining accountability to the group, especially when new challenges arise or some parties fail to follow through with their end of the agreement. This communication can happen in a number of ways: periodic email or text updates, social media, press releases or media events, and good old-fashioned live conversations.

Keeping the other parties informed of progress is usually one of the roles assigned to the principal implementing party. Even if the group is no longer meeting, it is important that someone feel responsible for communicating with the group. Letting stakeholders know that certain parties are implementing a part of the agreement is a way of giving credit to the parties who have taken action and reinforcing the expectation for others that they, too, will follow through with their commitments.

We should note here that ongoing collaborative systems, such as forest collaboratives or education collaboratives, provide an existing forum for communication about the implementation of individual projects or policy agreements. It is, in fact, one of their primary advantages. Because they may initiate multiple collaborative processes over time, they will be involved in a cycle of agreement and implementation. As a result, they are likely to already have a website or other communication media, regularly scheduled meetings, and even monitoring systems in place to oversee and aid the implementation of each respective collaborative agreement.

Monitoring, Evaluating, and Managing Adaptively

Evaluation of collaborative governance is fraught with challenges. One such challenge is the often blurry distinction between process performance and outcome performance (Emerson and Nabatchi 184). We separate monitoring and evaluation of collaborative governance into three separate activities: (1) monitoring of each party's individual performance with regard to their commitments and agreements; (2) evaluation of group performance in addressing the public problem or issue; and (3) monitoring and evaluation of the collaborative process itself, including relationship impacts.

Monitoring Individual Performance

Accountability in a collaborative governance process, as noted in chapter 4, is inherently horizontal; the parties are accountable to each other for following through on their agreements and commitments. For this to work, Susskind and Cruikshank point out, performance monitoring mechanisms need to be in place (150). Did each of the parties follow through with their commitments and the spirit, if not the letter, of the collaborative agreement?

Even when individual performance falls short of commitments, accountability mechanisms in these horizontal relationships are more indirect and informal. It is the threats of social embarrassment and reciprocity (others not cooperating in turn) that are the primary consequences of noncompliance. In an environment of horizontal relationships, says Ostrom, reciprocity is the glue that holds these collaborative agreements together. If one fails to honor commitments to others, they may do the same in the future (10). Martin Nowak argues that reputation (what he calls "indirect reciprocity") can have a similar effect. If you have a reputation as someone who cooperates for the good of the whole, Nowak writes, it brings you a certain power to negotiate future agreements, even with people you have not dealt with before. Word gets around, Nowak writes, and it is your reputation that counts, whether good or bad. If people see you as someone who does *not* follow through with your cooperative commitments, people will be less willing to engage in cooperative arrangements with you. Your social credit rating, in effect, will suffer (60).

The importance of reputation that Nowak describes is one reason we now regularly include a date for reconvening in the written agreements for many of the collaborative processes we facilitate. We commonly observe a striking increase in stakeholder activity in the weeks and months leading up to the reconvening date, suggesting that stakeholders are paying attention to that date and wanting to uphold their reputations for following through.

Evaluating Group Performance

We stated in chapter 1 that the intention of collaborative governance is ultimately to advance some public purpose. Therefore, some evaluation mechanism is needed to determine if the collaboration succeeded and, if it did not, what course corrections may be in order.

Collaborative groups should be thinking about accountability and evaluation from the very early stages of their work together. Evaluation of group performance is aided by a clear framing of the goal and purpose of the collaboration itself (see chapter 6). Emerson and Nabatchi emphasize this point by recommending that collaborative groups have explicit discussions up front about what will constitute success (222).

At the end of the process, the agreement should reflect who will monitor and evaluate progress, whether it is a participant in the original collaborative governance group or an agreed-upon third party. We recommend that, at least at a general level, the method of performance evaluation be included in the group's initial agreement, describing what will be monitored, who will monitor, and how it will be reported to the group (and, potentially, the public). A number of collaborative groups we have worked with have created websites that provide transparency on current activities, monitoring, and progress.

Reconvening the group, we find, is also a way to help the group evaluate progress. The value of this evaluation, however, is directly linked to its use in adaptive management. Circumstances frequently change, beyond the control of those signing a collaborative agreement. A local government may have a change in political leadership and priorities, or new grant funding may become available. The agreed-upon strategy to address the public problem may simply not work, or it may work better than expected. Such changes are to be expected, say Carpenter and Kennedy, and parties should not be alarmed when adjustments are needed. "Something *will* go wrong" (149). Monitoring progress toward the public policy goal can help the group evaluate and adapt its approach.

Emerson and Nabatchi recommend that collaborative groups evaluate their work from a variety of perspectives, including those of the participants, the groups represented by the participants, and the intended beneficiaries of the public policy or program (84). One of the most effective monitoring and adaptive management programs we have seen, one that incorporates the multiple perspectives recommended by Emerson and Nabatchi, is that used by the Lower Columbia Solutions Group project, the collaborative system that we discussed in chapter 7. This group established an elaborate monitoring program as part of its initial agreement, with roles assigned to specific parties. Part of that program was a commitment to hold periodic adaptive management meetings. The group now conducts an annual workshop open to all stakeholders to review the year's activities, evaluate the results, and plan for needed changes or adaptations for the next year. Their annual workshop keeps everyone accountable and focused on their goals. It is one of the reasons, we believe, for the group's successful performance.

Monitoring of the Process

In addition to performance monitoring, Emerson and Nabatchi emphasize the need for evaluating the *process* as well (185). One of the challenges of evaluating collaborative processes is that their context is not uniform. When no two collaborative groups are alike, how does one determine which has been more effective? How does one compare a group process involving fifty stakeholders, for example, with a group of nine stakeholders? How does one compare a process addressing water supply issues in the western United States with one addressing child health in Malaysia?

Some of the challenges related to evaluating and comparing the effectiveness of collaborative processes derive from the frequent attempt to measure collective action and agreement-seeking in the same manner, when, in fact, they are different types of processes, solving fundamentally different types of problems. Those differences should be kept in mind as a group evaluates the effectiveness of its collaboration.

Our work over the last two decades with several hundred collaborative groups tells us that a rigorous approach to the definitional norms, fundamental dynamics, and process design leads to better outcomes in collaborative governance. For that reason, our process monitoring and evaluation has focused on those elements. Common questions, therefore, include the following:

- Was the process seen as fair and inclusive?
- Did the parties work toward mutual gain?
- Was there a strong sense of interdependence among the parties?
- How high was the trust level in the collaborative relationships?
- How high was the trust level in the process?
- Was the framing of the group goals clear and agreed upon?
- Was there shared ownership of the problem and process?
- Did the convener promote a fair environment for discussion?
- Did the parties feel like their voices were heard and appropriately considered by others?
- Was there broad participation in the discussion among those at the table?
- Was there a willingness to deal with conflicts as they emerge?
- Were communities of color and other historically underrepresented communities meaningfully involved in the process?
- Was the process equitable and inclusive?
- Was there attention to results and accountability?

We have used several methods for evaluating our collaborative processes, some more elaborate than others. For agreement-seeking processes, we used to administer a pages-long, comprehensive survey of all participants, but the lengthy survey was off-putting for some participants. We have found we get a better response with a more concise format that is administered soon after the collaborative process is concluded. We have also conducted process evaluations, both formally and informally, *during* a process in order to determine what midcourse corrections may be needed. For example, we ask: Is the process transparent? Is it fair and equitable? Is the decision-making seen as effective? Is the convener or facilitator performing to expectations? We then adapt the process in response to the feedback.

In other instances, we have enlisted research teams to perform more detailed process evaluations on a few projects, including the Oregon Sage-Grouse Conservation Partnership. These types of evaluations have generally been conducted as academic research, usually months or years after the agreement is reached, and include detailed interviews of participants.

Conclusion

The unifying message of these last four chapters might be: process matters. An assessment will provide indicators as to whether a collaborative governance approach can be helpful, and if so, provide input about how best to organize and design the collaborative governance group. How a group comes together, how the process is designed and convened, and how decisions are made can all make a difference in the performance of the collaborative governance group. But even after all of that, it is the attention to implementation, the last step in the process, that ultimately determines if the intended purpose is actually met. Without implementation, there can be no public benefit.

References

Carlson, Christine. *A Practical Guide to Collaborative Governance*. Policy Consensus Initiative, 2007.

Carpenter, Susan L., and W. J. D. Kennedy. *Managing Public Disputes*. Jossey-Bass Publishers, 1988.

Emerson, Kirk, and Tina Nabatchi. *Collaborative Governance Regimes*. Georgetown UP, 2015.

Nowak, Martin, and Roger Highfield. *Super Cooperators: Altruism, Evolution, and Why We Need Each Other to Succeed*. Free Press, 2012.

Oregon Solutions. "Jade Greening Declaration of Cooperation." Portland, Oregon, 2017.

Oregon Solutions. "Salmonberry Trail Declaration of Cooperation." Tillamook, Oregon, 2015.

Ostrom, Elinor. "A Behavioral Approach to the Rational Choice Theory of Collective Action: Presidential Address, American Political Science 1997." *American Political Review*, vol. 92, no. 1, March 1998, pp. 1–22.

Susskind, Lawrence E., and Jeffrey L. Cruikshank. *Breaking Robert's Rules*. Oxford UP, 2006.

SECTION 3

Skills to Improve Collaborative Governance

Although the theoretical grounding provided in section 1 and the nuts-and-bolts view of process set forth in section 2 are essential to understanding and practicing collaborative governance, the questions we get most often are related to what might be called the "people challenges" inherent in collaboration: How do you collaborate with someone who is not collaborating in return? How do you prevent one or two people from dominating the conversation? What do you do when the parties just don't trust each other? In this section, we take a pragmatic look at these and similar challenges that frequently arise in collaborative governance.

Rosemary O'Leary and Lisa Bingham have written that "[c]onflict resolution is effectively group problem solving" (6). Indeed, we would argue that group problem solving is actually the common element linking agreement-seeking, collective action, and collaborative systems. In all three cases, various parties are attempting to solve a public problem by working together. Why are some groups better at it than others? What does effective group problem-solving look like? In chapter 9, we explore these questions and set forth some of the practices and interventions that can maximize the effectiveness of collaborative governance groups.

In chapter 10, we describe what individual participants can do to provide leadership and improve collaborative outcomes.

While the practices we explore in this section are based on theory and research, our intent is to provide pragmatic advice and suggestions that will help make collaborative processes more effective and more rewarding for participants and will provide guidance for those charged with facilitating or convening these processes.

Reference

O'Leary, Rosemary, and Lisa Blomgren Bingham. *A Manager's Guide to Resolving Conflicts in Collaborative Networks*. IBM Center for the Business of Government, 2007.

9

STRENGTHENING COLLABORATIVE GOVERNANCE GROUPS

Introduction

Over the course of the previous chapters, we explored the preconditions that can either promote or constrain collaboration. We also described some of the elements of process design and structure that are important to success. However, even the right preconditions and the right process cannot guarantee positive results. How the elements of process are put into practice can make a substantive difference. In this chapter, we address group traits that can make the difference between extraordinary public solutions (what Huxham and Vangen call "collaborative advantage") or long, drawn-out frustration ("collaborative inertia") (59). These group characteristics speak directly to the quality of the deliberative process that is central to collaborative governance.

First, we define what we mean by success in collaborative governance, and then we highlight five characteristics found in the most successful collaborative groups:

- Joint ownership of the problem and the process;
- Broad and balanced participation;
- A willingness to deal with conflict and difficult issues;
- Ability to rebuild trust;
- Attention to results and accountability.

Defining Success

What does success look like in a collaborative governance process? As Emerson and Nabatchi have noted, evaluation of collaborative governance has measured both substantive accomplishments and the relationships that arise out of the processes (185). This approach conforms with Robert Bales' conclusion that successful groups exhibit behaviors that attend to both the task and to relationships (or process). Keeping both task and relationship in mind, our four criteria for success include: (1) real public benefits, (2) equity and fairness; (3) process-focus and efficiency; and (4) improved relationships.

We should emphasize that success in a collaborative governance context is not binary. There are degrees of success (or failure). However, while a collaborative process that accomplished only one of the four criteria might not be considered a failure, neither would it be much of a success. Achieving all four criteria should be the goal of any collaborative governance process.

Real Public Benefits

As set forth in chapter 1, a governance group must be seeking to achieve a public purpose in order for their work to be collaborative governance. In the case of agreement-seeking, this means the collaborative governance group reaches an agreement on the key policy issues. In the case of collective action, it means co-creating an outcome, project, or program that is bigger, better, faster, or cheaper, and one that would not have come about without the collaboration. The results should be real and tangible, the more specific the better.

In the case of collective action, what constitutes real public benefits can be deceptive. Too often, groups exhibit interaction patterns that are akin to the behavior in young children known as "parallel play." When very young children start to play with others, often they are able to play in the same sandbox, but one is building castles, while the other is playing with a truck. They share the space and get along, which is good, but they are not collaborating. The next stage is more like "integrated play," where one child might build a tunnel or a bridge in the sandbox for the other child to use for the truck, thereby enhancing the experience of both.

Parallel activity in collaborative governance is when parties come together and share what each is doing on a certain problem or issue, but their relative contributions are disconnected, the impact is cumulative rather than integrated. The resulting public benefit may be measurable, but it is not particularly *collaborative*. Nobody is really doing anything different than they would have done otherwise, and in many cases, the outcomes might well have occurred without the collaborative process. This is not to say that sharing information about what everyone is doing is inherently unproductive. It certainly can serve to spur later integrated actions and can help build relationships, but it is only a starting point if the goal is to gain the full value of collaboration.

In a collective action process, the work of the collaborative group becomes more integrated when the parties seek to identify what we refer to as "complementary assets." These are resources that when combined, produce a result that is better than the sum of the parts. It is only through this integrated work that the real synergistic potential of collaborative governance can be realized, a potential we will explore further in chapter 10.

In addition, the public benefits of collaboration are real only as long as they are sustained. A collaborative governance process will be successful to the extent that agreements hold over time. Indeed, it is this staying power that many argue is one of the key advantages of collaborative governance. Agreements made collaboratively are far less likely to be reversed in the next election cycle, and the transparency of commitments that are made by people sitting across from one another in a public setting adds to this staying power. Taking steps to retain what might be called the collaborative memory of the group, for example, by posting agreements on a website or reconvening the group periodically after the project is completed, is important for ensuring the continuity of those public benefits.

We have observed collaborative processes where no agreement on the key issues was reached or no substantive public benefit was gained, but participants still pointed to improved relationships as a successful outcome. We believe this stretches the definition of success, and that tangible public benefits should be the primary goal of any collaborative governance process.

Equity and Fairness

The second substantive criterion for success is a fair and equitable outcome. While the definitional norms we presented in chapter 1 emphasized the fairness and equity of the *process*, here we look to the *outcome* to define success. We have previously described collaboration as an exchange between parties (of resources, information, benefits, and so forth). For a collaboration to be successful, particularly in the long term, the distribution of costs and benefits among stakeholders needs to be fair and equitable and perceived as such. If it is not, then a collaborative agreement is unlikely in the first place, or at least will not build social capital for future exchanges.

Considerable research has identified fairness as one of the principal motivations that influence interactions with interdependent others (Eek and Biel 197). This concern for fairness helps explain why some parties act in ways that are different than would be expected if they were only looking at their own short-term self-interest. That is, they will often accept an outcome that is less beneficial to them in order to achieve a more equitable outcome for the group. Conversely, parties will sometimes walk away from a deal that would benefit both sides if they perceive the distribution of benefits is unfair or inequitable (Rand et. al. 2581).

For groups involved in agreement-seeking, this sensitivity to fairness manifests itself as an often unwritten (and unspoken) goal that there should be relative symmetry in the degree to which the parties "move northeast." In a collective action process, for example, Eek and Biel suggest that a fair distribution of contributions to the public good takes into consideration both the ability to pay and the level of interest (198).

In our classes, we utilize a variation of a game described by Nowak and Highfield (209). In our variation, a group collectively invests in a fund to combat climate change, while still trying to conserve funds for other societal needs. The object of the exercise is for players to conserve as many of their own resources as possible, while still adequately addressing climate change. If the group's combined investment in the climate fund does not reach a certain threshold amount after ten years (with years represented by rounds of the game), every player loses all funds (presumably because climate change brings catastrophic costs that wipe out everyone's treasury).

As one group of students played the game, they needed a substantial investment in the last round in order to avoid catastrophe. One participant, though he had given liberally in earlier rounds of the game, chose to give zero dollars in the last round. As a result, the group failed to reach the minimum threshold in the fund and he (and everyone else) lost everything. We were a bit puzzled and asked his reasoning. He replied, somewhat indignantly: "I already gave my fair share earlier."

It should be noted that perceptions of what constitutes a fair outcome will quite often vary among parties (Raiffa 268), and the definition of fair is often not synonymous with equal. In the levee repair project we have referred to before, several jurisdictions decided to share costs for a major engineering study that affected them all. However, some jurisdictions were much larger than others, so splitting the costs of the study equally did not seem particularly fair. After a brief deliberation, the group members agreed to each contribute between $100,000 and $500,000, depending on their relative size and perceived degree of benefit. As mentioned before, the discussion of what constituted a fair distribution got more serious once the stakes got higher. Before the project could move to the next phase, the group spent months negotiating a more precise and complicated cost-distribution formula. They were ultimately able to move forward, but only after each party felt the distribution was fair.

Although there are many factors that drive fairness and perceptions of fairness, we note that collaborative governance processes often intersect with systems that are historically discriminatory and inequitable. In the United States, for example, Black people, Indigenous people, and other people of color may be asked to collaborate with institutions that play a part in systemic racism. A collaborative group may well need to consider that history in attending to the fairness of its outcomes, as well as to the process itself.

Toward this end, the concept of "targeted universalism" may be useful in setting goals and measuring outcomes: "Within a targeted universalism framework, universal goals are established for all groups concerned. The strategies developed to achieve those goals are targeted, based on how different groups are situated within structures, culture, and across geographies to obtain the universal goal" (powell et al. 4). In the case of collaborative governance, it means that the group must not only be attentive to the shared goals, but also to how those goals will play out for each subpopulation in the group. The targeted universalism framework allows decision-makers—including collaborative governance groups—to disaggregate the needs of communities and demographic groups and make decisions accordingly. That kind of disaggregation allows collaborative governance groups to respond to the needs of historically underrepresented groups, and it applies in a variety of other contexts, as well. As we mentioned in chapter 5, a group of small towns and residential areas on the Oregon Coast have been working together to address a recent surge in the local elk population that has created safety concerns. All of the towns share the goal of better management of the local elk population, but each town is not affected equally by the problem, nor should the solutions or the financial resources allocated to the problem be applied equally. The solution needs to take each local area's situation and needs into consideration for the outcome to be fair.

Process-focus and Efficiency

Collaborative governance can often be challenging and time-consuming. Not letting the process drag on unnecessarily is a way of improving its value to stakeholders. Process-focus and efficiency is, therefore, a third criterion for success.

By bringing stakeholders together, collaborative governance actually reduces what economists refer to as transaction costs for parties who would otherwise still need to interact. The collaborative group interactions replace otherwise sequential interactions, reducing time to complete certain tasks (Jones et al. 921). Further, the trust and reciprocity produced by repeated face-to-face interactions, as was discussed in chapter 4, also help bring about collaborative agreements more quickly and easily. That trust and reciprocity help prevent the group from having to renegotiate the agreement every time the balance of power shifts.

Nevertheless, collaborative governance usually demands a substantial investment of time for the participants, sometimes involving months or even years of work, not to mention actual investments of money or other resources. The transaction costs can be particularly burdensome for low-income communities and organizations with limited resources. For the collaboration to be seen as worth the effort, the benefits need to outweigh the costs. And, while participants rarely, in our experience, perform an actual calculation of those costs and benefits, they are constantly weighing the fundamental question in their minds: Is the time spent in these meetings worth the effort?

The point here is that the whole team needs to take a rigorous approach to the process in order to reduce unnecessary transaction costs. By utilizing best practices, groups can avoid endless meetings or discussions that seemingly lead nowhere. A prime example of the difference that process-focus and efficiency can make is the Lower Columbia Solutions Group, mentioned in earlier chapters. Before they entered into a formal collaborative governance process, some of the members of that group had been trying for years to resolve their differences, but like a lot of groups, were more focused on defending their positions than finding shared solutions. Consequently, little progress had been made on the issue of where and how to deposit dredged sediment. They finally decided to invest in one intensive multi-day session, professionally facilitated and co-convened by the Oregon and Washington Governors' Offices. Using the principles and best practices of collaborative governance, they were surprised at the results. "We made more progress in three days," said one political leader, "than we've made in the previous ten years."

Efficiency and efficacy also help lead to a more equitable process. Black people, Indigenous people, other people of color, and other historically underrepresented communities are often asked to donate their time to represent their communities or to stretch the resources of small organizations in order to participate in processes that are adjacent to the organizations' core missions. For many such organizations, time and capacity are at a premium. A focused and efficient process might make it easier for grassroots and culturally specific organizations to participate. On some occasions, collaborative governance groups have also offered stipends for participation for smaller organizations or individuals or have created other ways for those organizations to stay connected to the process, even if they are not able or do not want to participate as group members.

Efficiency aside, there will be occasions when a collaborative governance group simply needs to invest the time to get everyone up to speed on critical information, ensure broad participation, build trust, or explore creative solutions in order to move the process forward. In difficult circumstances, finding "northeast" can take time, and that investment of time at the front end is necessary to reaping efficiency dividends later on when agreements are implemented. We are not suggesting that these important investments of time be eliminated.

However, the group dynamics discussed below are specifically designed to reduce unnecessary transaction costs (that is, time spent in meetings) without sacrificing either substantive or relational outcomes. When best practices are not used, groups can become mired in endless meetings and unproductive, drawn-out processes. Indeed, if a process drags on and on without much progress, the commitment of the parties wanes, the relationships suffer, some stakeholders are no longer able to participate, and substantive agreements can actually become more difficult to achieve. Apprehension over these transaction costs is, in fact, often a barrier to parties deciding to pursue a collaborative approach.

Improved Relationships

We are all familiar with public policies forged through court decisions or legislative actions that have come at the expense of the relationships between the affected parties. In a collaborative governance process, the substantive public benefits can and should be gained while actually improving relationships and increasing social capital, ultimately improving stakeholders' capacity to work together on future-related issues and perhaps even their willingness to work across divides in other unrelated public settings.

What does it mean to improve relationships and increase social capital? In its aspirational form, it means that each party feels heard, understood, and respected by the other parties, even when there are divergent interests or opinions. It means that the parties understand the underlying interests and values of others and where those converge with and diverge from their own. It means that the parties are comfortable expressing and working through differences of opinion with each other. And it means there is an atmosphere of trust and reciprocity, with a sense that the process was fair.

As set forth in previous chapters, the beginning of the collaborative governance process involving the Malheur National Wildlife Refuge was rife with distrust. The participants began tentatively, suspicious of each other because of a history of acrimony and legal action. Then, discovering they shared a common concern about invasive fish species in Malheur Lake, they built upon that issue to slowly and steadily increase levels of trust. That improved relationship had a spillover effect on subsequent issues, as ranchers, federal agencies, and environmental groups all continued working together to solve other problems and issues, including undertaking a collective response to a major range fire a few years later. This social capital and collaborative capacity came into even sharper focus during the community's response to a group of outside protesters who took over and occupied the Malheur Wildlife Refuge (ostensibly in support of local ranchers). The community's rejection of the protesters' approach is well documented by Peter Walker in his book, *Sagebrush Collaboration: How Harney County Defeated the Takeover of the Malheur Wildlife Refuge.*

As it did in Harney County, collaborative governance should not just solve the problem at hand, but should also enhance the community's collaborative capacity, in other words, its ability to solve the next problem, by improving working relationships between stakeholders.

Real public benefits, fairness, process efficiency, and improved relationships—those four criteria are the standards of success we look for in collaborative governance. Let's now turn our attention to the attributes that enable groups to meet those standards.

Group Attribute 1: Joint Ownership of the Problem and the Process

One can usually tell whether there is joint ownership by observing a group in action. In an agreement-seeking process, when there is a lack of joint ownership, parties often restate and defend their positions rather than engage in the search for overlapping interests. Without joint ownership of the problem and process, there is less commitment to finding solutions. This lack of commitment often manifests as participants showing up late or leaving early, attending inconsistently, and not completing assigned work between meetings. When there is little or no joint ownership of the problem and process, everyone can feel the lack of energy in the room.

By contrast, when group members do have joint ownership of the problem and process, they also assume responsibility for the impact of their own behavior on the group's task. They look for ways to contribute to the group's success. Everyone is leaning in.

In the Lower Columbia Solutions Group project, during an impasse over scientific uncertainty about the biological impacts of the proposed sediment disposal strategy, one representative of a federal fisheries agency suggested the group could learn the answers by conducting joint scientific monitoring. He was, in essence, suggesting they collectively take ownership of resolving the scientific uncertainty. Up to that point, many of the stakeholders had viewed the problem as owned by the United States Army Corps of Engineers and were there to either support or criticize the Corps' actions. Once the suggestion was made for joint monitoring, however, a few of the parties stepped up to contribute in-kind resources, and then all helped design (and revise) the monitoring program. The group took joint ownership of the monitoring, which led to them taking ownership of the results, greatly accelerating progress in resolving the issues. The entire project became *their* project.

In the Tillamook flooding project described in the first chapter, most of the parties at the table were residents or business owners in the community and experienced the flooding at a personal level. Though they had differing interests, they all had a stake in the success of the collaborative process. Attendance and engagement were correspondingly high. There was a sense of joint ownership and pride in their collaboration, and, when it paid off with tangible results, they celebrated together.

How do groups engaged in collaborative governance attain a sense of joint ownership? As discussed in chapters 1 and 6, it is important that the conveners, the facilitators, and the other staff of the collaborative platform work on behalf of, and are equally accountable to, all participants and to the group as a whole. That broad accountability enables all of the parties at the table to take ownership because the message conveyed is, "this is *our* problem, and we need to work together to solve it." If participants do not believe the problem at issue affects them or that the process is accountable to their communities, they are less likely to do the hard work necessary to reach agreement. If they do not believe the forum recognizes or respects their interests as equal to others, they are unlikely to trust it. Joint ownership is forged through a shared forum that considers and serves the interests of all the parties.

Group Attribute 2: Broad and Balanced Participation

Early research by Lewin, Bales, and others demonstrated that groups perform better than individuals on many kinds of tasks. One of the major advantages of groups is their diversity, or more pointedly, their diversity in pursuit of a common challenge.

The only way to access this diversity advantage is to meaningfully engage all the voices at the table (and have a diverse set of voices at the table in the first place). When the participation in a group process is less broad, that is, some members are silent and others are more dominant, the group loses this diversity advantage. In that sense, the definitional norms of inclusion and belonging are not just about creating fair processes, but are also about creating better outcomes. Inclusion does not just require that affected communities are invited to the table, it requires that the process maximize the participation of all affected groups. It requires that everyone's interests are seriously taken into consideration. When a collaborative governance group creates the conditions where all participants can contribute at their highest level, the group is most likely to generate both a fair and a creative outcome.

Broad and balanced participation also improves the group process by strengthening relationships. When there is a real commitment to hearing everyone at the table, group members feel like their opinions and contributions matter, creating greater group cohesion, joint ownership of decisions, and a stronger commitment to the group's success (Bresson 238). The opposite is also true: when a group is dominated by one or two individuals or one public agency, other members of the group do not see themselves as particularly valued or needed, and the group fails to cohere.

How does a collaborative group ensure broad and balanced participation?

Pay Attention

In the heat of trying to accomplish a group task, people often become unaware of imbalances in the distribution of participation in the group process. People get focused on the task and neglect the process. Observers of groups sometimes utilize a simple analytical tool called a "sociogram" to diagram who is talking to whom and how often in a group process (see Figure 9.1).

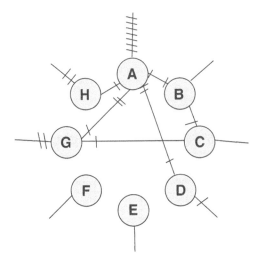

FIGURE 9.1   Sociogram of group interaction

We aren't recommending that anyone physically use a sociogram at their next meeting, unless they are strictly observing the process. Even when used by as an outside observer, the tool begins to lose its value when applied to groups of twenty or more. It is nevertheless useful as a mental construct for keeping track of the group process. Paying close attention to who is participating and who is not, or who is talking to whom, can reveal potential process issues. For example, if one or two people begin to dominate the discussion, or one or more group members are withdrawing, there may be a process problem.

Use Polling

As described in chapter 7, polling the group during agreement seeking is a technique to ensure that each person gets a chance to weigh in on an important decision. Polling is not quite the same as voting. It is a way for each person, in turn, to quickly voice or show their level of support for an idea. As each person weighs in on their current thinking, it helps quickly surface any disagreements and focus the group's discussion. It also prevents the discussion from being monopolized or dominated by a few powerful or talkative individuals. It is particularly helpful when dealing with variances in power among group participants. Polling group members on an issue sends the message that every person's opinion is important.

Caveat

When we advocate for broad participation, we distinguish it from open-ended, "come one, come all" processes, which really are more about public involvement than collaborative governance. Collaborative governance, as we defined and described it in chapter 1, involves *representation* and *deliberation*, both of which require consistency in group membership to be successful. If a group changes membership from meeting to meeting, it is virtually impossible for the group to build collaborative relationships and to actually deliberate toward agreements on public policy or collective action.

That said, reaching out and involving the broader public frequently becomes an important task for the collaborative group. Citizens need to be kept informed and given an opportunity to weigh in on important matters that affect their lives. Collaborative governance teams we have worked with have found various ways to keep the public informed and involved, using everything from deep, culturally specific outreach to crowdfunding, which enables citizens to contribute to the projects that are important to them.

Group Attribute 3: A Willingness to Deal With Conflict and Difficult Issues

Every once in a while, we will hear someone bragging about a group they participate in and how collaborative it is. "Nearly every one of our votes is unanimous," they say. This is when we know they are in trouble.

One of the key characteristics of successful collaborative governance groups is their ability to acknowledge and deal with conflict. The very purpose of many collaborative governance processes, of course, is precisely to help group members resolve differences of opinion. This requires that differing opinions are heard and respected.

In too many groups, unfortunately, the group norm is just the opposite. The very notion of consensus often suggests to participants that raising concerns will be seen as unwelcome obstructionism. Particularly when conflict is strong, or there are wide disparities of power, there is often a tendency to go through the motions, to act "collaboratively" while skirting the real issues. These meetings then become, as McCarthy says, little more than theater, where everyone has their mask on and a role to play (58). The resulting atmosphere in the room is often one of guardedness or resignation, leading ultimately to cynicism about the process. Everyone involved is aware that there are issues or opinions that are not being expressed. Everyone can feel the tension. When the chairperson or convener asks if there are any objections, and no one speaks, the other group members can see the two people at the end of the table, jaws clenched and arms folded over their chests.

It sometimes takes courage to express authentic concerns or feelings in these settings. To be real is to be vulnerable. To be vulnerable requires trust in the group and the process. When group members express their own disagreements, questions, and concerns, they demonstrate trust in the group's ability to accept and handle it. As game theory instructs us, that kind of trusting behavior often begets trusting behavior in return. However, unfortunately, that is not always the case. In our work with collaborative groups, we have found that the initial response to someone expressing concerns, emotions, or conflict can make all the difference. If those comments are ignored, put down, or responded to with embarrassment, it discourages others from expressing their own concerns.

It is healthy for groups to allow and sometimes even encourage the expression of emotions, including anger. When anger is suppressed, pent-up grievances can sometimes build up until there is an outburst. In fact, the longer a conflict is not openly dealt with, the more power it takes on, and the greater the emotions behind it grow.

When anger takes the form of a personal attack, it can be difficult for the group to respond. There are, fortunately, responses that a group member or facilitator can offer in this circumstance to acknowledge the grievance and help the group work through it. We recall one collaborative process where an industry representative, in the process of voicing his disagreement to a proposed solution, angrily accused the federal agency involved of disregarding the law and causing the death of one of his colleagues. With this accusation, the room fell silent. The facilitator tried re-framing the message for the group: "Based on his history with (the federal agency), George (not real name) just does not trust them to follow through. And he feels pretty darned strongly about it. What could be done that might raise his level of trust, and reduce what he sees as his level of risk?" At this re-framing, everyone seemed to exhale a bit, and suggestions soon were forthcoming. By the day's end, the industry representative who had raised the concerns agreed to the proposal.

When a group member shares an experience of harm or historic discrimination or oppression, the role of the collaborative group is first to listen and then later to determine how best to address those harms in the context of the project. There will not be a perfect response, but listening closely and working to repair harm in the group's own context are some important first steps.

Group Attribute 4: Ability to Rebuild Trust

In chapters 4 and 5, we discussed the crucial role that trust plays in collaboration. Here we explore distrust and how to rebuild trust once it has been lost. Distrust can manifest in an instant, with just one betrayal, but can take considerably longer to be rebuilt. When there is a history of distrust, rebuilding it can take even longer.

Distrust leads to behaviors that reinforce that distrust (Gambetta 234). Halting or reversing that vicious spiral is one of collaboration's biggest conundrums. To rebuild trust requires one party to act cooperatively first, and no one wants to be first because that requires accepting vulnerability in the face of little evidence that the vulnerability will be reciprocated. Both sides are wary, rationally so.

So, how does one attempt to rebuild trust? Is it possible to ever work together once that trust has been breached? Can trust somehow be restored to the relationship? In each instance, the answer is yes, but it requires commitment and patience. The actions discussed below can help the parties get there.

Use Contingencies

As discussed in chapter 7, by utilizing contingencies, parties can turn dispositional distrust into situational trust. That is, even if one party may not trust another party to act cooperatively under normal circumstances, they can create consequences for noncompliance or untrustworthy behavior. An example of a contingency is the deposit that hotels commonly ask for when someone makes an advance reservation. If the prospective guest does not show up for their reservation, they lose the deposit. The deposit—a contingency—creates a much higher level of situational trust that the guest will actually honor their reservation.

When there has been a history of distrust, some are inclined to make such contingencies air-tight, to reduce their risk to zero. If one is attempting to re-establish trust in the relationship, however, reducing the risk to zero is a mistake. For example, in the Lower Columbia Solutions Group process, the crab fishing industry representatives originally did not trust the United States Army Corps of Engineers to deposit sediment near the shore without impacting the crab population. The industry forced the Corps to deposit the dredged sediment in deep water, far from shore. This eliminated any direct impact on crabs, but it also did not do anything to improve trust. It was only when both parties agreed to a small test run using an enhanced near-shore disposal method, that the Corps was able to demonstrate its good faith and the effectiveness of the method. There needs to be some potential for uncooperative behavior or risk of poor performance, in order for someone to demonstrate that they can be trusted.

Start Small to Minimize Risk

Reaching collaborative governance agreements when there is a history of distrust can take a lot of time and hard work. In order to justify that investment of time, some participants wish to raise the stakes to ensure that the reward is worth the effort. While the desire is understandable, it is not entirely rational. When there is a history of repeated noncooperative behavior, it is entirely rational to believe that the other party will seek to take advantage of any cooperation. It, therefore, makes much more sense to reduce the stakes, in these circumstances, rather than raise them.

The best advice to rebuild trust might be: make the stakes small and the joint-monitoring large. Starting small and increasing the stakes incrementally over time reduces risk while providing a potential pathway to creating a new, more cooperative history. In this way, trust can expand incrementally, with the parties accepting ever-greater levels of risk, as each party demonstrates trustworthiness. As Ansell and Gash put it:

> A number of the case studies suggest that collaboration is more likely to ensue when…"small wins" from collaboration are possible…we represent them here as critical process outcomes that are essential for building the momentum…These small wins can feed back into the collaborative process, encouraging a virtuous cycle of trust building and commitment. (561)

Once again, we return to the Lower Columbia Solutions Group as an example. As discussed above, the question before the group was whether or not the United States Army Corps of Engineers should dispose of 300,000 cubic yards of clean dredged material near the mouth of the Columbia River. The crab fishers, however, trusted neither the Corps nor the thin-layer disposal method it proposed. They were concerned that depositing the material on prime crab-rearing grounds would decimate the catch. The group met for more than two years and could not get past this stalemate. Finally, one of the corps managers suggested a "trial run" of 30,000 cubic yards, a minimal amount that—even if everything went awry—would not do appreciable harm to the nearshore crab population.

After months spent in regulatory review, the pilot study was finally conducted, and no discernable impacts on crab or other marine life were found. In subsequent years, the program expanded to 100,000 cubic yards, with continued monitoring. There were still no significant impacts to crab or other marine life, so the amount was later raised to the originally proposed level of 300,000 cubic yards. After a few years at this level, however, it was the crab fishing industry representative who proposed that the amount be increased to 500,000 cubic yards. By starting small, they were able to not only break the stalemate, but also ultimately raise the stakes over time.

In a related way, starting small is effective for addressing trust issues that arise in collective action processes. In those cases, stakeholders often have a low level of confidence that anything will actually come of their efforts. Just as trust begets trust, we have found that action begets action. By incrementally implementing even a small part of the larger project, it sends a message that the group means business, and that their collaboration will produce real on-the-ground results. The Tillamook Flooding project's early removal of the Dean dirt pile, as set out in chapter 8, demonstrated this concept. This small early action got people's attention, creating momentum for further actions.

Group Attribute 5: Attention to Results and Accountability

It may sound overly simplistic, but paying attention to results and accountability can produce, well, better results. Unfortunately, it is all too common for public advisory committees, stakeholder meetings, coordinating committees, and yes, collaborative governance processes, to produce little of consequence. Based upon their past experiences, it is no wonder that so many participants enter these processes with low expectations.

The problem has several sources. Let's start with the voluntary nature of collaboration outlined in chapter 4. Government agencies, businesses, and other organizations at the table are more familiar with vertical relationships of accountability. Collaborative relationships are horizontal: no one participant has any direct authority over another participant. Consequently, people are not quite sure how to create and enforce accountability in the group.

In agreement-seeking processes, this problem can be compounded when parties start with a history of bruised relationships. In collective action processes, participants may know they cannot accomplish the task or project by themselves, but they are also not sure they can count on the other members of the group to really keep their commitments. They are uncomfortable being dependent on others to accomplish the goal. Conversely, they may also worry that other parties will steal the credit for any success the group does have, and their own institution or agency may not get the recognition it deserves.

Below we discuss a number of ways to attend to results and accountability in a collaborative process.

Frame the Goal

Framing the goal from the outset in a way that is clear and measurable provides a kind of compass that the group can continually use to keep itself on track. A number of years ago, we helped a collaborative group that was trying to establish a coastal marine education center on the southern Oregon coast. The hope was to draw tourists to a town that supports one of Oregon's largest commercial and recreational fishing fleets. The group's focus, as they looked for funding, shifted to a solution that would involve cohousing a number of marine-related state and federal agencies. Over the next year, changes in budgets and staffing led to a number of false starts, and the group felt adrift. By returning their focus to their original framing, however, the group eventually worked with the Oregon Institute of Marine Biology to acquire the needed financial resources. Soon after, the new marine education center, with an aquarium and museum, was built and opened to wide acclaim.

Create a Norm and Expectation of Being Part of the Solution

People come to the table with different expectations. For collective action processes in particular, parties frequently come to the table with an expectation that they will be offering recommendations about what other organizations or government bodies should do. Results are far better when participants embrace the expectation of collective *action*. As participants, they are part of the collective, and, therefore, expected to contribute in some way to the solution (through actions, information, or resources). Susskind and Cruikshank advise that, to achieve collaborative success, "the people at the table need to get into a problem-solving mindset as soon as possible" (84).

Group norms can create conditions that support cooperative behavior, in particular norms of fairness and reciprocity (Irwin and Simpson 1058). During the SageCon project first discussed in the introduction, a major sticking point in the negotiation between ranchers, counties, federal agencies, and environmental advocates involved how the habitat mitigation rules would apply to private lands. At an impasse over the question of how stringent and enforceable the rules would be, the counties made the first overture by agreeing to new land-use regulations that would include habitat mitigation requirements. In response to this, environmental advocates agreed that they would not seek to bar development altogether. This began to establish a norm for reciprocity within the group, with the federal agencies subsequently assuring landowners they would not be liable if they followed the new rules. This group norm motivated ranchers and other landowners to show they too were contributing to the solution, committing to taking action on invasive species that were affecting sage-grouse habitat.

Maintain Momentum

In many collaborative processes, there is high attendance and excitement at the first meeting, but as the process continues and participants get down to the hard work of actual collaboration, the energy and participation begin to wane. One way to break that pattern is to maintain a sense of movement, particularly in longer processes. Success, we find, breeds more success. A feeling of momentum, the sense that the group is actually getting somewhere, provides positive reinforcement and the encouragement to keep going.

Marking a collaborative group's progress, noting the accomplishment of every step toward the goal identified in the framing, is an easy way to help create this sense of momentum. It is also helpful to highlight the role that working together played in taking that step, and to use it as an opportunity to celebrate the contribution of individual parties and give them credit. This can be done in group meetings, in written communications or social media, and sometimes in press releases. Almost no step, we have found, is too small to celebrate. Some groups illustrate their path to the goal graphically, charting their progress along the way, even starting each meeting with a reminder of where they are. Among other things, this helps reinforce the sense of a shared mission, and helps keep the discussion focused on the task at hand.

Use Written Agreements and Commitments

As set forth in chapter 8, written agreements and commitments are important tools in collaborative governance processes. Susskind and Cruikshank put it like this: "It is…appropriate to ask each individual involved to sign the agreement… to sign a statement that indicates their personal support for the package and their personal promise to work to implement the agreement (and to follow through on any commitment they have made)" (186). Especially for collective action, it changes participants' mindset when they know, from the beginning, that they will be asked to develop and sign such an agreement. It helps provide a sense of gravitas to the proceedings, a sense that it is more than a group that meets to share reports of individual progress.

Address the Problem of Free Riders

Collaboration for collective action involves the creation of a public good. By definition, all parties can enjoy a public good (for example, a program, public service, or facility) once it is established, and there is a built-in temptation to enjoy it while limiting one's own contribution. As discussed in chapter 7, the classic challenge to the problem of creating public goods is that if everyone acts on the incentive to limit their contribution—operating as "free riders"—there is no public good and nobody gets to enjoy it.

Some economists would say that each party should be willing to contribute up to the level of value they put on that public good. While not every party that benefits from the public good has to contribute, it takes enough parties who place high enough value on the public good to contribute enough resources to create the solution. The collaborative governance process becomes the forum for identifying and bringing these parties together.

The challenge, as we have stressed previously, is that there remains an incentive for each party to let others step up, while limiting their own contribution. How do groups successfully address this challenge?

- Identifying the level of commitment to the project in the assessment process, before ever beginning the collaboration, is critical. Having even a few parties identify the kinds of contributions they would be willing to make provides a model of collaborative behavior for others to follow;
- The collaborative governance process itself helps create a sense of collective accountability. The transparency offered by face-to-face meetings, and publicly making one's commitment, provides a sense of accountability to the group (Ostrom 6);

- Early in the collaborative governance process, it is helpful to have each party at the table publicly identify how they might be able to contribute to the solution. Besides creating a group norm of contributing, this also provides a boost to the group's confidence that they can actually succeed.

Adapt Collaboration to the Realities of the Project

As with most collective endeavors, no matter how much a collaborative group plans ahead, things do not always work out the way they are originally envisioned. The following are real-world challenges to implementation that sometimes need to be addressed:

- Staff changes take place, things get lost in the shuffle, and some organizations do not follow through with their commitments;
- Priorities change;
- Elections change the balance of power;
- Opportunities open up that were not there before;
- New resources become available, while others dry up; and/or
- New problems or challenges arise in the implementation phase.

As Emerson and Nabatchi point out, a collaborative group "must adapt to both ongoing changes in the external system context and to internal changes within itself and between its participants and parent organizations" (85).

In response to these challenges, as we described in chapter 8, we sometimes do mid-project evaluations in order to adapt to the needs of a collaborative governance group. In addition, a few years ago, we began to add into some of our collaborative agreements a plan for the group to reconvene at a time certain (for example six months or eighteen months after the project) to review progress in the implementation.

Conclusion

Successful collaborative governance processes result in both substantive and procedural accomplishments, including real public benefits, equitable and fair outcomes, an efficient process, and improved relationships. Those outcomes need not be left to chance. If the collaborative governance group attends to the five characteristics laid out above—joint ownership of the problem and the process, broad and balanced participation, a willingness to deal with conflict, rebuilt trust, and attention to results and accountability—it will greatly improve the likelihood that the group will accomplish both their substantive and procedural goals.

References

Ansell, Chris, and Alison Gash. "Collaborative Governance in Theory and Practice." *Journal of Public Administration Research and Theory*, vol. 18, no. 4, October 2008, pp. 543–571.

Bales, Robert F. "A Set of Categories for the Analysis of Small Group Interaction." *American Sociological Review*, April 1950.

Bradford, Leland P. *Group Development*. University Associates, 1978.

Bresson, Tree. "Consensus Decision-Making: What, Why, How?" in *Practicing Law in the Sharing Economy: Helping People Build Cooperatives, Social Enterprise, and Local Sustainable Economies*, edited by Janelle Orsi and Jenny Kassan, ABA Books, 2012.

Eek, Daniel, and Anders Biel. "The Interplay between Greed, Efficiency, and Fairness in Public-Goods Dilemmas." *Social Justice Research*, vol. 16, no. 3, 2003, pp. 195–215.

Emerson, Kirk, and Tina Nabatchi. *Collaborative Governance Regimes*. Georgetown UP, 2015.

Gambetta, Diego. "Can We Trust Trust?" *Trust: Making and Breaking Cooperative Relations*, edited by Diego Gambetta, U of Oxford, 2000, pp. 213–237.

Huxham, Chris, and Siv Vangen. "Doing Things Collaboratively: Realizing the Advantage or Succumbing to Inertia." *Organizational Dynamics*, vol. 33, no. 2, 2004, pp. 190–201.

Irwin, Kyle, and Brent Simpson. "Do Descriptive Norms Solve Social Dilemmas? Conformity and Contributions in Collective Action Groups." *Social Forces*, vol. 91, March 2013, pp. 1057–1084.

Jones, Candace, et al. "A General Theory of Network Governance: Exchange Conditions and Social Mechanisms." *Academy of Management Review*, vol. 22, no. 4, October 1997, pp. 911–945.

Kelly, H. H., and John W. Thibaut. *Interpersonal Relations: A Theory of Interdependence*. John Wiley and Sons, 1978.

Lewin, Kurt. "Frontiers in Group Dynamics." *Human Relations*, vol. 1, no. 1 June 1947, pp. 5–41.

McCarthy, Robert E. *Navigating With Trust: Transform Your Organization With Energy, Direction and Joint Effort*. Rock Bench Publishing, 2012.

Nowak, Martin, and Roger Highfield. *Super Cooperators: Altruism, Evolution, and Why We Need Each Other to Succeed*, Free Press, 2012.

powell, john a., et al. "Targeted Universalism: Policy & Practice." *Othering & Belonging Institute*, 8 May 2019. https://belonging.berkeley.edu/targeteduniversalism

Raiffa, Howard, et al. *Negotiation Analysis: The Science and Art of Collaborative Decision Making*. Belknap Press, 2003.

Rand, David, et al. "Evolution of Fairness in the One-Shot Anonymous Ultimatum Game." *Proceedings of the National Academy of Sciences of the United States of America*, 2013.

Susskind, Lawrence E., and Jeffrey L. Cruikshank. *Breaking Robert's Rules*, Oxford UP, 2006.

10

INDIVIDUAL LEADERSHIP TOOLS

Introduction

As should be clear by now, we believe that collaborative governance requires a rigorous approach to (1) the definitional norms of collaborative governance; (2) the fundamental dynamics of collaboration; (3) the assessment, design, and structure of the process; and (4) the particularities of group interactions. In this chapter, we focus on what individual members of a collaborative group can do to provide leadership and make collaborative governance more productive and rewarding.

There are many definitions of leadership. In a collaborative governance setting, we define leadership as taking actions that help enable the group to succeed in its task, regardless of one's own interests. Helping a group to take a more productive course requires paying attention to both the task and the process, to think about what the group needs at any given moment to move it forward. Under this definition, leadership is not relegated to those at the head of the table or associated with any particular role, title, or position of power. Nor is leadership confined to one particular person. Every participant in a collaborative governance process has the potential, and indeed the responsibility, to provide leadership at certain times, in other words, to look for opportunities and act in ways that help the group succeed in its task.

We provide below ten practical leadership tools any member of a collaborative governance process can use to make their group more successful. Used strategically, these tools can help build trust and collaborative relationships, ensure more authentic and productive conversations, and lead to agreements or outcomes that serve the interests of all the participants.

Leadership Tool 1: Collaborative Listening

Effective collaborative governance requires a certain quality of listening. We use the term *collaborative listening* to mean listening with the intent to understand the other parties. More specifically, it is listening for information that enables the listener to analyze the collaborative landscape and connect the dots. This includes being alert to mutual affiliations, for example, which may help build more trusting and productive relationships. It means picking up on subtle cues from other parties that might indicate how much they value the program or project in question and listening to understand what they want or need from the process.

Collaborative listening is often the only way to discern the information necessary for successful collaboration. In agreement-seeking projects, for example, it enables the listener to discern underlying interests from stated positions, identifying what is valued most, and where interests may overlap. It can illuminate where there is high potential for agreement and the avenues for getting there. As Roger Fisher and Scott Brown nicely summarize, "You can't solve differences without understanding them" (65).

However, it is not just about having the skill, but also the intent to understand that is important. Too often we may listen to someone while simultaneously constructing a rebuttal in our heads or impatiently awaiting our turn to express our thoughts. But to truly capture the value of listening in a collaborative situation, one needs to suspend judgment, at least momentarily, and engage in what others have called "active listening" or "empathetic listening" (Covey 239), trying to see things for a moment from others' point of view. We call this "collaborative listening" when it involves being alert for the type of information critical to collaborative success.

Collaborative listening involves giving the speaker complete attention, that is, not checking a cell phone for messages or interrupting to give one's own point of view. It is not, however, just about being undistracted and silent while others talk. It involves asking clarifying questions (as opposed to those designed to challenge) to make sure the listener fully understands. And it involves listeners communicating their understanding back to speakers occasionally, not only to ensure that messages were properly understood, but also to let speakers know they've been heard. It may also involve following up later to either ask further clarifying questions or to assure speakers that their concerns were heard and considered.

Collaborative listening requires listening across differences, be they political, racial, economic, gender-related, or some other difference, while at the same time listening for commonalities. The critical information gained can surely aid the collaboration, but almost as important as what listeners learn is what they communicate by truly listening. Roger Fisher and Daniel Shapiro identify the need to be appreciated and valued as one of the core needs in human relationships. Biological research shows that when someone feels appreciated and valued there is a measurable physical response, a reduction in the secretion of stress hormones and shifts in the neuro-endocrine system (McCraty and Childre 247).

When a person truly listens to another, with the intent to understand them better, they are effectively saying that the other person's perspective is important, directly feeding that basic human need identified by Fisher and Shapiro. This is true regardless of whether or not the listener agrees with the speaker. This kind of deep listening also communicates a willingness to be vulnerable. To really listen implies that the listener is open to new information. This act of vulnerability is correctly interpreted by others as a sign of self-confidence and trust. And it engenders trust in return. People are far more likely to listen to someone if they first feel that they have been truly heard.

Real listening is powerful in part because it is all too rare, even in collaborative governance processes. Remarkably, this can be especially true for agreement-seeking groups trying to work through disagreements. These conversations can easily devolve into a debate where all parties are simply lobbing arguments at each other. Collaborative listening can have a powerful effect because it has the potential to change the entire tenor of a conversation.

A former member of the governor's staff in Oregon tells the story of once receiving a phone call from a woman who was upset at her local city council. The caller had a number of complaints about the direction of the city and the council's unwillingness to take her concerns seriously. She went on, quite heatedly, for about twenty-five minutes, at which point the governor's staff person summed up the essence of her grievance, "You really don't trust these people to look out for the city's interests." There was silence on the other end, a long pause. Then, in a much calmer tone the caller said, "Why, yes, that's exactly right. You understand!" The conversation lasted only another minute or two, at which point she thanked him for listening and hung up. That the governor's staff person did not necessarily agree with the caller was beside the point. The caller was just grateful to be heard.

Collaborative listening cannot be faked. If a person tries to employ a listening technique on someone without really trying to understand, the insincerity will become apparent to the speaker in seconds, actually creating greater distrust. This is in part because our emotional and relationship messages are primarily communicated nonverbally through visual and auditory cues such as facial expressions, body language, and tone of voice (Mehrabian and Ferris 251). People know whether someone is really listening to them or not.

In our teaching, we sometimes utilize an exercise where the group breaks into pairs and each person shares with their partner their own experience of a particular concept. The pairs are given a limited amount of time to do this and then asked to individually rate the quality of the conversation on a scale from one to ten. They then hear a presentation on the value of listening, including what one can learn and what one communicates by listening. After the presentation, we have the same pairs discuss a different question or concept, followed by their rating of that conversation. The second conversation almost universally receives a higher average rating than the first, often by a significant amount. Simply by listening better and more intentionally, the participants come to realize, they have the power to improve the quality of their collaborative conversations.

Leadership Tool 2: A Focus on Underlying Interests

As we have discussed before, focusing on underlying interests rather than positions is a way to shift from positional win-lose bargaining to mutual gain. Focusing on the underlying interests, as we have said previously, expands the palette of potential solutions. Parties, therefore, need to be clear not only about their positions when beginning collaborative agreement-seeking, but also must think through what their underlying interests are. Almost as importantly, they need to seek out and consider the underlying interests of the other parties. Many people enter into a collaborative governance process without giving much thought to either their own underlying interests or those of others. For this reason, a party's first response to questions about their underlying interests may not be entirely accurate, and should not always be taken as the final word on the subject. They may become more aware of their underlying interests as the process proceeds.

Finally, referring to others' interests, while deliberating, can be very helpful in building trust and developing collaborative relationships. We are not suggesting that anyone presumptuously speak for other parties. However, when making a proposal or framing an issue, we have seen some participants very effectively refer to another party's interests or ask one of the parties whether an action might help meet their interests. This demonstrates that the other party has been heard. It also shows that their needs have been taken seriously and that their interests (if not their positions) have been recognized as legitimate.

In a collaborative governance process, it is not just the convener or facilitator who can shift the conversation from positional bargaining to a focus underlying interests. Anyone at the table can provide leadership by first articulating their own interests and inviting others to do the same. This can be done through a series of questions, such as:

- Why is that important to you?
- What would that solution accomplish?
- What changes would that solution make in your life?
- How would you experience that?

If the group has been stuck on positional bargaining, shifting focus to underlying interests begins to open up other possibilities for a mutually agreeable solution. It also has a relationship benefit, as it legitimizes the interests of all parties, and shifts the discussion from who is right and who is wrong to answering the question, how do we together find a way to meet our interests? This is the first step toward true collaboration.

Notwithstanding the benefits listed above, it is common for agreement-seeking groups to occasionally gravitate back to positional bargaining. In the heat of the negotiations, helping a group refocus on interests provides valuable leadership, expanding potential avenues for agreement and collective action.

Leadership Tool 3: Communication

It may seem obvious that communication is an important leadership tool for building collaborative relationships. Collaborative governance, by its very nature, is about bringing people and institutions together for productive interactions, parties that might not otherwise talk to one another.

Collaborative relationships and outcomes depend on high-quality and frequent communication. Building trust among the parties, for example, requires open communication. Those who hold their cards close to their vest are sending a message that they do not trust the other participants at the table. And as McCarthy suggests, when one is not trusted, the natural instinct is to become guarded and withhold information (21).

The frequent, iterative face-to-face communication afforded through collaborative governance, Ostrom points out, is itself a significant factor in building trust among parties, and in encouraging them to act cooperatively (7).

Face-to-face Communication

It should be emphasized that an important characteristic of the communication cited by Ostrom is its synchronous face-to-face nature (6). Numerous studies underscore the advantage of face-to-face communication over communication through email or text in building trust and dealing with emotional content (such as working through conflicts). This statement comes with a caveat. As we write this book, in the throes of the COVID-19 pandemic, we (along with the rest of the world) are learning rapidly about the potential and limitations of the widely expanded use of video conferencing. Zoom, a suddenly ubiquitous teleconferencing application, became a household word overnight. This technology seemingly incorporates some of the advantages of both face-to-face and electronic communication by allowing participants to call in from anywhere while providing a wider range of visual and auditory cues than teleconferencing. More research will be needed to compare its relationship-building capabilities to actual face-to-face communication.

Even prior to the pandemic, email, instant messaging, texting, and social media were making up an increasingly large share of social and professional communications. Our ability to communicate nuance and emotion electronically is evolving (Thrimm 348). However, as noted above, it is primarily nonverbal cues that communicate relational and emotional information. And it is precisely these nonverbal cues that are lacking in electronic communication such as email and texting. In one comparison study between face-to-face and electronic communication, participants who interacted face-to-face felt "greater oneness with their partner" (Okdie et al. 156). Much of the research in this area, we should note, does not consider the experience of participants who are visually impaired or hearing impaired or the experience of those who are navigating a process outside their first language or original culture.

Text and email communications, when used for politically-sensitive or emotion-laden topics, carry significant risks, as short, quickly written electronic messages may be open to multiple interpretations. Humor that might work in face-to-face communications, for example, can be entirely lost and misinterpreted when included in a text or email message. These limitations become a problem, research shows, because everyone tends to think they are more competent in communicating ambiguous messages via electronic media than they actually are (Kruger et al. 933). The less direct nature of text and email may sometimes tempt people to use it to express anger or conflict. While it may feel less confrontational, communicating anger or conflict electronically almost never facilitates resolution of the conflict, and in fact, often escalates it.

Another risk of electronic communication, particularly email, is the potentially public nature of what feels like a private communication. We may communicate confidential or sensitive information in these seemingly private communications, which can then be easily or even inadvertently passed along to others. In addition, public agencies are also subject to public records requests, meaning that emails are almost always public documents.

In summary, while using email and text communication in a collaborative setting can be tempting and is an efficient way to disseminate factual information, it is far from ideal in establishing collaborative relationships or when dealing with emotional content. For this reason, initiating face-to-face discussions or phone calls (which at least incorporate auditory cues), is a form of leadership. When the interaction is likely to have a meaningful impact on the relationship, non-electronic communication is almost always better.

The Two-minute Phone Call

Communication may be most important when there is bad news to communicate. If one party promises to get back to the group with certain information but is late in following up or if somebody is about to take action that could be interpreted by some at the table as a sign of bad faith, the best approach is to pick up the telephone and let people know in advance. One axiom that collaborative groups sometimes put into their operating principles is "no surprises." No one likes to be the bearer of bad news, but making that two-minute phone call to give someone advance warning is a wise investment that can pay dividends for the future of that collaborative relationship.

In fact, sharing bad news can actually *strengthen* a relationship. In a recent collaborative project, one of our colleagues reluctantly shared some bad news about the delayed schedule with participating stakeholders. She worried that it would exacerbate existing skepticism about the process. To her surprise, several participants responded with messages of gratitude that she had let them know.

Even when there is not bad news, but simply a lull in the process, silence is seldom beneficial. When parties are starting with low trust, silence is likely to be interpreted in the worst possible way: What are they up to now? Perhaps more importantly, making that phone call or setting up that brief office visit is a sign of respect for the other party and a sign that the relationship matters.

Paying attention to the quality and frequency of their communication with others around the table is, therefore, a leadership tool that any party can utilize. It is precisely because it is often more difficult in the moment than electronic communication, or not communicating at all, that it exemplifies leadership.

Leadership Tool 4: Reciprocity

Some would say that reciprocity is the very basis of civil society, the under-pinning of the Golden Rule. We take in our neighbor's mail when they are away because they do the same for us. We pick up our litter at the campground because others did so before us. We stop at the red light, even if it appears safe to go, because we need to trust that others will do the same. In the context of the COVID-19 pandemic, conversations about the ethics of mask-wearing have become heated debates about the line between individual freedom and com-munal reciprocity.

We have spoken at some length in this book about social dilemmas. Each party's outcome is based in part on what others do, and, consequently, each party's behavior is largely based on what they predict others will do. For the repeated interactions over time that characterize most collaborative governance processes, successful strategies for any party will be based on reciprocity (Axelrod 7). Simply put, if cooperation by one party is not reciprocated by another party, cooperation is unlikely to continue. Once someone's cooperation has been taken advantage of, the party is likely to suspect (and reasonably so) similar behavior in the future.

When two or more parties have very different interests and are trying to resolve a conflict, negotiations can get difficult. Sometimes, to break the logjam, one party will offer an olive branch, a small token of compromise. Those who view themselves as being tough negotiators or in a power position might inter-pret this olive branch as a sign of weakness or surrender. In fact, offering an olive branch is often a test. It is a test to see whether or not the other party will recip- rocate, that is, whether they will offer some small compromise in return. The advantage of an olive branch is that it minimizes risks even if all goes bad. If, on the other hand, all goes well, and the other party reciprocates, it creates a safer environment to explore bigger compromises in the future, with bigger stakes. However, those who attempt to take advantage of a goodwill gesture without reciprocating will have failed the test, and they should not expect another olive branch any time soon.

In an agreement-seeking process, reciprocity is an act of leadership because it is an act of engagement, one that recognizes and rewards the trust shown by the party offering the olive branch. As noted previously, when two or more parties have a history of distrust and competitive behavior, no one wants to be the first to compromise. The initial offer of an olive branch is, therefore, an act of great trust and courage, even when the risks are small. It can be a watershed moment in a process, the point where things begin to come together, but only if there is a reciprocal response. Reciprocity creates a sense of movement, the beginning of momentum toward consensus. This is why we consider it a true act of leadership.

For collective action, reciprocity plays a similar role. In one project we were involved with, the state department of transportation offered $300,000 to keep a project going, but only if others also contributed. Had no one responded, not only would the $300,000 have been forfeited, but the entire project likely would have stagnated. One of the first to respond, however, was a small non- profit, immediately committing $1000 toward the match. This reciprocal act immediately inspired others at the table to contribute, and the project was off and running.

Leadership Tool 5: Finding Opportunities for Integration and Synergy

One reason collaborative governance processes can sometimes feel unproduc- tive is the "parallel play" phenomenon discussed in chapter 9. In the absence of actually working together to integrate their interests or resources, some col- laborative groups spend a lot of time simply sharing opinions or information about their individual activities, producing little of additional value. Agreement- seeking groups can trade arguments back and forth, like ships passing in the night, or gravitate to a lowest common denominator of consensus where noth- ing is required to change. For many participants, unfortunately, when they hear the term collaborative governance, this "parallel play" approach is what they envision.

In the case of collective action, the process of integration provides an oppor- tunity to leverage the resources of each party, aligning those resources to have a much bigger impact. Years ago, we were contacted by a group of businesses and organizations in the Eugene-Springfield area of Oregon. These organizations wanted to shift to cleaner fuel for environmental reasons. However, they balked at the significantly higher premium they would have to pay to the existing distributor because of high shipping costs. By aggregating their clean fuel purchases through a collaborative governance process, the parties were able to create sufficient demand for clean diesel to support a distribution facility in their own community. As a result, the cost was significantly reduced. Moreover, once the price for clean diesel became more affordable, the additional demand from others in the community (including those who had not been at the collaborative table) eventually led to the distributor making a further investment, building a facility to manufacture clean bio-diesel fuel.

This kind of synergy occurs when parties put together what have been referred to as "complementary assets," those which, when combined, produce an effect that is more than cumulative. In one of our projects, for example, there was a civic organization with a large number of potential volunteers, and a private business with heavy equipment to donate. When the two organizations combined these complementary resources, the result was a nearly one-mile recreational trail that could not have been built with either resource alone. That action subsequently leveraged a multi-million-dollar federal grant to create a pedestrian bridge over a highway, connecting a nearby neighborhood to the new trail.

This is the ultimate prize, where the value-added by working together can be transformative. To get there requires an understanding of the other parties' interests and constraints, deep listening, creative problem-solving, and sometimes working through tough conflicts or trust issues. But that is the real work of collaboration.

Former Nebraska state senator David Landis likes to illustrate this point with a story about a phone call he received from the Flatwater Shakespeare Festival. The festival director was angry about a radio advertisement for the Nebraska State Fair. The advertisement said something like: "Tired of TV reruns or a boring old Shakespeare play? How about exciting live horse racing instead?" The Shakespeare Festival was about to open a performance of *Macbeth*, and the director did not appreciate the tone of the ad. He wanted it taken off the air, and called the senator, a supporter of the festival, for help.

Senator Landis called the state fair leadership and, perhaps because his position had some influence over their budget, the state fair director was contrite, apologized for the inadvertent slight to the festival, and offered to take the advertisement off the air. "Why don't we all talk about it first?" replied the senator, who is a trained mediator. Senator Landis convened a meeting with the Shakespeare festival director and the state fair director to see what might be worked out.

The agreement they struck at that meeting played out over the next several days. First, the Flatwater Shakespeare Festival wrote a letter to the editor issuing a challenge: Shakespeare was as exciting as horse racing, it said, and to prove it, the Shakespeare festival offered to present a scene from their upcoming performance of *Macbeth* at the state fair. If the crowd cheered, they proposed, the original advertisement would come down. A few days later, the state fair wrote the editor back, accepting the bet. Before long, local radio and television stations began playing up this unusual wager, and it was only a matter of time before the story was picked up by National Public Radio. All of this was free publicity, of course. The broadsword fight and Macbeth's decapitation on the fairgrounds were filmed for television news and prominently covered in a statewide newspaper. Who won? They both did, of course, with thousands of dollars of free publicity for both the fair and the *Macbeth* production. By working together, the two organizations both benefited from addressing their conflict.

Like the Nebraska State Fair and the Flatwater Shakespeare Festival, each organization or interest group generally has a range of interests, and while some of those interests are disparate or in conflict with those of other parties, not all of the interests conflict. Just as the ranchers and environmental groups around the Malheur refuge found a common interest in reducing the invasive fish species in the lake, smart collaborators are always looking for those overlapping and harmonious interests.

The good news is that every party at the collaborative table has the ability to provide leadership by engaging with others and connecting the dots to go as far "northeast" as possible. If Angela is running a program that provides meals to low-income seniors, and Malik is a local farmer trying to figure out what to do with surplus produce, maybe they could work together. Anyone can set an example for "integrated action" by actively exploring ways to expand the pie, find complementary assets, identify common or complementary interests, and pursue opportunities for synergy. Through these actions, they can help lead the way to a more productive collaboration.

Leadership Tool 6: Asking for Ideas, Opinions, Proposals

Why do collaborative groups sometimes get bogged down? And when it happens, what can be done to get back on track?

To answer these questions, we look to one of the early pioneers in the field of group process, Robert Bales, who first developed a scale of possible behaviors or interventions that group members could use to impact either their task or their relationships (see Figure 10.1). Those behavior categories included things like, "show solidarity," "give opinion," and more. Other categories involve asking questions such as "ask for opinion" or "ask for orientation." This Bales scale has been used, in many variations over the years, to observe and take data on groups, and analyze group process (258).

Our own use of the Bales scale suggests that when groups get bogged down, it is often because the group members are talking past each other. There is a surplus,

Socio-emotional positive	1	**Shows solidarity** — Initially: greets, welcomes, praises. Congratulates, defends, thanks, encourages, gives credit, elevates opinion, expresses desire for cooperation, harmony, reassures. In response to tension: assists, offers help, mediates, sympathizes.
	2	**Shows tension release/dramatizes** — Jokes or stories with a double meaning, e.g., "that sure was fun!" while displaying a face that says it wasn't. Expresses relief after tension, satisfaction, gratification, enjoyment, thrill.
	3	**Agrees** — Shows passive acceptance, understands, concurs, complies, "I see" "mmhmm." In response to disagreement: admits error, withdraws politely, cedes point.
Task answers	4	**Gives suggestion** — Gives instructions, makes proposals, facilitates guidance, delegates authority, gives direction, all imply automony for other.
	5	**Gives opinion** — (opinion, evaluation) Analyzes, expresses feeling sentiment or desire, wish, assessment.
	6	**Gives orientation** — (facts/observation) Gives information, references back to something, repeats, clarifies, recounts, reflects content back, summarizes information.
Task questions	7	**Asks for orientation** — (re: facts/observation) Asks for info, asks for repetition or confirmation. Examples: "What?" "Who did we appoint?" "What did we decide?" "It isn't clear to me."
	8	**Asks for opinion** — (opinion/evaluation) Seeks others' feelings, intentions or inclinations. Example: "What do you think?" "Is this the most effective way?"
	9	**Asks for suggestion** — Asks for direction or possible ways of action, e.g., Where do we start?" "What do we do now?" "What shall we talk about?"
Socio-emotional negative	10	**Disagrees** — Negative toward content not person, not so strong as to be unfriendly. Rejects anothers statement of information, opinion, or suggestion.
	11	**Shows tension** — Any verbal or motor expression of fear, apprehension, worry, dread, agitation. Appears disconcerted, confused, flustered. Nervous laughter that is not accepted by the group as a release of tension, appearance of being mortified, chastised.
	12	**Shows antagonism** — (seems unfriendly) Overridding: Interrupts, interferes with others' speaking. Deflating others' status: belittles, disparages, reduces others' remarks to absurdity, finds fault. Anti-authority: rebellious, disorderly, badgering, flippant. Reprimands, scolds, indignant, apalled, blocks, obstructs, withholds resources. Inattentive, bored, withdrawn.

FIGURE 10.1 System of categories for group observation

Source: Bales, Robert F. "A Set of Categories for the Analysis of Small Group Interaction." *American Sociological Review*, April 1950

you might say, of giving opinions, offering proposals, and so on. Fisher and Brown describe the problem as too many people "telling" something to others (88). Unfortunately, there is much less receiving, in part because there is little, if any, asking for opinions or ideas. Rather than real engagement and working together, the group feels more like a debating society, each party arguing why they are right and others are wrong. When a group operates this way, they are highly likely to experience problems reaching collaborative agreements. One can almost predict a group's success, we have found, by the number of questions they ask each other. It is the asking and answering of questions that creates true engagement.

When a group gets bogged down, what if instead of restating his or her or their position, one party was to turn to another, or to the group as a whole, and ask: How would *you* suggest we reconcile the differing views here? It is an intervention that facilitators often use to good effect, but its use need not be restricted to third-parties. Asking the right question is a powerful leadership tool for creating a collaborative atmosphere and getting things moving again.

In a collaborative project, we worked on several years ago, a state agency and local government were at odds over how to solve a groundwater problem, going back and forth with opinions and arguments about why each of them was right. After hours of this, we started the afternoon session by summarizing that both of the principal parties had made reasonable points, but their positions were not compatible. The facilitator then asked: "How can two reconcile your positions?" There was a brief silence, as they considered the question. Finally, one of them offered a proposal that clearly incorporated the interests of the other party. Somewhat startled by the offer, their counterpart replied, "I am pretty sure we could go along with that." They had been bogged down for hours (months, actually), but the right question led to a proposed solution literally within minutes.

It is not always that easy, but asking for an idea or a proposal can often break an impasse and move a group to a solution. The question can be directed to a specific individual or the entire group, as circumstances dictate. Preceding it, as happened in the example above, with a framing of the issue often helps remind the group that they are there to work on the problem *together*.

Asking for ideas, opinions, and proposals can also provide an additional boost to collaborative relationships. A group member may be silent during a discussion due to their unfamiliarity with the process. Perhaps the silence stems from group power dynamics. Or, maybe they just don't want to compete for airtime. Whatever the reason, asking for someone's opinion on an issue can sometimes help draw them back into the group, ensuring that their unique perspective gets incorporated into the deliberation.

When one party asks another party for an opinion or proposal, particularly when the other person's perspective may be different, is not unlike the relationship benefits of listening that were described earlier in this chapter. The underlying message is that the other party's ideas matter. It also underscores the collaborative nature of the relationship, metaphorically moving them to the same side of the table to address the problem together. It is a very different message than the one too often implied in collaborative agreement-seeking groups: "This is why I am right."

Asking for a proposal can also help shift the dynamic of participants critiquing every suggestion made by someone else without offering their own. A gentle, "what would you suggest?" can help shift the conversation in a more productive direction.

To be effective, asking for someone's opinion or ideas should be done in a way that does not feel aggressive or extractive. It should be done with the implicit permission for the other person to decline the offer. Depending upon the situation, rather than asking: What is your opinion?, it may be better to ask, Do you have an opinion on this issue? Or: Do you have anything you would like to share? Other times, it may be best to ask a question during a break or in a less public setting. Applied with sensitivity and judgment, however, asking for opinions, ideas, and proposals is a leadership tool that can help a group improve both their task accomplishment and relationships.

Leadership Tool 7: Reframing Issues for Discussion

Chapters 5 and 6 explore how framing is an important step in designing a collaborative governance process. Here we address the framing or reframing of various issues or disagreements that may arise *within* the process.

Framing, as we have previously emphasized, is an essential leadership skill. How an issue is framed has a major impact on how it is shaped in the mind, how one thinks about possible solutions, and how one views the parties involved. Reframing an issue or problem is frequently needed during a process when new information or new issues arise. This reframing, if it is to create conditions for collaborative success, needs to incorporate clarity and focus, respect for all the interests involved, and creative space for a range of options or solutions.

An example of new issues being reframed in mid-process occurred a few years ago in a collaborative governance process intended to address flood control issues along the Columbia River in the Portland metropolitan area. A steering committee, made up of the project sponsors, was set up to develop the agendas for each meeting. Two neighborhood associations objected, based on years of mistrust and bad relationships, asserting that the steering committee members were the "same old power players calling all the shots." They essentially framed the issue in historical terms as "us against them." However, the question, when presented to the collaborative group, was reframed as: What should the criteria be for serving on the steering committee? As the discussion ensued, the issue was reframed again as: How do we ensure transparency in our subcommittee work? Each of these questions met the criteria listed above, resulting in a lively and productive discussion. The two neighborhood associations were consequently added to the steering committee, among other changes, and both ultimately became vocal supporters in the community of the collaborative governance process.

Reframing as a leadership skill can be applied in other circumstances. In the course of a group discussion, it is not uncommon for the group to sometimes lose track of the issue at hand or its relevance to the larger issue or project. Reframing an issue, in this circumstance, fulfills the function that Bales calls "providing orientation," that is, clarifying: What are we trying to decide? Or what's at stake here? Or what are the choices on the table? Providing this kind of framing to help a group get back on track and to provide a context for the discussion is an important leadership tool.

It is also not uncommon, when disagreements arise within a group, for the emotional temperature in the room, along with discomfort and frustrations, to rise. It is easy, in these situations, for the participants to forget that conflicts are to be expected in collaborative governance and that the existence of a disagreement does not imply there is something wrong with the group. In these situations, reframing the disagreement and question can help the group deal with these bumps in the road more quickly and easily. And although this responsibility often falls on a convener or a facilitator, any member of the group can do it.

It is also important to note that successful framing of issues is not about smoothing over difficult issues. As Bernard Mayer writes, "Frequently, the hardest conflicts to resolve are those that people present in vague, indecisive, and confusing ways in order to avoid confronting serious disagreements. If reframing attempts to minimize the seriousness of a dispute, it will not in the end be constructive" (132). Sometimes reframing can and should be used to actually sharpen a disagreement so that the parties can clearly see and attend to the interests at stake.

A few years ago, at a meeting of a nonprofit board, one of the board members made a proposal to establish a political action committee, to which another member immediately and curtly replied, "I strongly oppose this. That is *not* the kind of organization we are." There had been a long-standing rift on this issue, though never directly addressed, and now it had finally boiled over in plain sight. Everyone could feel tensions rise around the table and the palpable fear of what would happen next. Many probably wished they could be somewhere else. Then the board chair addressed the group by framing the issue:

> This is an important question, and not easy. There are reasonable arguments to be made for both sides, but we really do need to make a policy decision as a board about this. Let's take a ten-minute break, and when we come back, we'll give [John and Hazel (not their real names)] each an opportunity to make those arguments. We'll all then discuss it and make a decision.

That simple reframing, while not diminishing the seriousness or difficulty of the issue, helped lower the tension level in the room immediately. It acknowledged the disagreement and the importance of the issue without making it personal (who is right and who is wrong). It took the focus from the two initial "combatants" and put it on the group. And it provided creative space in which to work. The board members returned after the break, had an informative and thoughtful discussion, which was not nearly as contentious as they had feared, and made a consensus decision not to form a political action committee at that time, but to be ready to do so should the need arise. The board left the meeting with relationships intact and a renewed confidence in their collective ability to face difficult issues.

Framing an issue or disagreement in this way, when tension levels and tempers are rising, actually fulfills a number of necessary functions, including the following:

- Clarifying the issue so the group discussion can be focused;
- Letting people on all sides of the issue know that they have been heard;
- Depersonalizing the issue, helping the group focus on the issue, not the people;
- Defusing the issue, turning down the heat without minimizing the strong feelings or the difficulty of resolving the issue;
- Helping the group move, metaphorically speaking, from opposite sides of the table to the same side, so they can work together to resolve the issue.

It is also worth noting that some issues should not be reframed, even if the original framing causes discomfort or even stalemate. Many Black people, Indigenous people, and other people of color have had the experience of having white authority figures and even white allies reframe their experiences and grievances to make their statements more palatable to white listeners. In a collaborative governance process, it is often the role of white participants to listen and learn before making any move to reframe an issue based in racial or other oppression.

Leadership Tool 8: Disagreeing

We understand that it may seem counter-intuitive that one of the most effective ways to help a group reach a better collaborative outcome is to allow them to disagree. It is nevertheless true. We should clarify here that we are not trying to turn collaborative governance meetings into shouting matches—quite the contrary. Disagreement can and should be expressed in a way that respects all participants in the process. Collaborative governance, however, especially agreement-seeking processes, can sometimes create conditions where people are too nice; for example, they passively agree to principles, plans, or policies they do not actually agree with. When the chair asks if there are any objections, people may not speak up, even if they *do* have objections.

The reason a participant may avoid speaking up is, as we discussed in chapter 9, that people in a group may simply not trust the group process enough to disagree. In our experience, this is a common phenomenon, particularly when there are significant power differences among the members. Consequently, when participants do not feel they can express disagreement, any so-called consensus is likely a false one, spelling trouble down the road.

We spoke at length in chapter 9 about how successful groups are willing to deal with conflict and difficult issues, and that it is better to express anger than keep it pent up (and have it eventually explode). One of the barriers to dealing with conflict may be the language associated with collaborative governance: phrases like "civil discourse," "conflict resolution," and "collaborative agreements." Disagreement in this setting can, therefore, sometimes be seen by some as inappropriate or unwelcome behavior. The goal is to prevent or resolve conflicts, some might say, not create them. This line of thinking stems, in part, from some people's natural discomfort with conflict and their inexperience in dealing with it in productive ways. It also comes from a misunderstanding of the purpose of collaboration, which is to work through conflicts, not avoid them. It is through confronting conflicts and working through them together that the group achieves a better outcome.

Unfortunately, many collaborative groups establish an unwritten group norm through their behavior. They place a higher value on completing the task on time and maintaining the peace, and consequently discourage disagreement, objections, concerns, or sometimes even questions. The underlying message— heard loud and clear—is that it is not going to be a real collaboration or discussion. It is intended to get the task done in form only, with a minimum of fuss or discomfort, particularly for those in power. It is also worth noting that norms of civility and politeness have often been used against people of color, particularly women of color, as a way to label them as angry or difficult.

When someone does speak up about a real concern or disagreement in a way that invites others at the table to help resolve it, the result can be transformative. First of all, the person who raises the disagreement often finds out that others in the group share the same or a similar concern. Perhaps more importantly, disagreement is an act of trust. It implies trust that the group can handle disagreement and will act constructively in relation to the concerns expressed. It tells everyone that maybe this is an environment where real conversation can take place after all. In that way, it helps the group raise its sights a little bit. Perhaps more importantly, it makes it easier for others to raise their own concerns.

All of these benefits are predicated on disagreement being expressed in a way that invites the others at the table to help resolve it. Simply saying, "I disagree!" isn't particularly constructive or informative. We recommend that participants in a collaborative process voice disagreement in the following manner:

- Be clear and direct about the disagreement;
- Focus on the problem, not the people;

- Frame the disagreement, when appropriate, in a way that ties it to one's own interests, acknowledging that other parties' interests may be different;
- Openly express a willingness to work out the disagreement with the group or the other parties.

Disagreeing, we should note, is one of the categories in Bales' scale for groups (see Figure 10.1). When done constructively, it is indeed a useful leadership tool.

Leadership Tool 9: Under-promise and Over-perform

It is often repeated that it is better to under-promise and over-perform, and as in many circumstances, that practice is a powerful trust-building tool in a collaborative governance process, particularly when contrasted with its opposite of over-promising and then under-performing. Particularly when there may be a lack of trust, there is an understandable impulse to show good faith, to appear as collaborative as possible. In these circumstances, we observe participants succumbing to the temptation to make promises or commitments that sound impressive in the moment, but which may not be realistic. The intentions are laudable. The results, unfortunately, are not.

This problem is sometimes compounded by representatives to the process who get too far ahead of their own organization or constituency. They lose sight of what we sometimes refer to as the "table behind the table." These representatives to the collaborative governance process have a responsibility to keep their constituents up to date on the group's progress to ensure members of the broad constituencies do not oppose the direction of the collaborative group. Sometimes, however, a representative will fail in that responsibility. When that happens, they may make a commitment that seems reasonable in the milieu of the collaborative governance group, but their own organization or constituency will not support it. When they have to backtrack, trust, and credibility decline.

We saw this play out in a collaborative process to develop plans for agricultural water quality management. It was a controversial topic, with a history of distrust among some of the parties. The representatives at the collaborative governance table worked hard together to overcome these obstacles, and after many months, came up with a consensus plan. When one of the key parties brought the plan back to his organization, however, he met a response along the lines of, what were you thinking? He had to return to the group with the message that the deal was off. The trust level of the group never quite recovered.

Sometimes it is the little things that leave an impression, such as promising a response to a question within weeks, but delivering it in months; committing to attend a meeting and not showing up; promising to review materials prior to a discussion, but coming unprepared. Especially when there are low levels of trust, others will see these behaviors as cues that a party cannot be trusted to cooperate on more important matters, to reciprocate an olive-branch if offered, or to follow up on larger commitments. And when there is an absence of trust to begin with, what psychologists call "confirmation bias" leads people to gather evidence that confirms preexisting expectations. Regardless of any other behavior, some will see these actions as evidence that distrust was justified all along.

Trust is built slowly over time. That trust-building begins with participants meeting or exceeding commitments, which is much easier to do when people do not over-promise in the first place. There is a balance to be had, of course. Expectations or commitments should not be set so low that participants seem uncooperative or uninterested in collaborating. The right balance was illustrated in a project we worked on that was highly time-sensitive and required extensive regulatory review and approval from a federal agency before the project could begin in earnest. As part of the collaborative governance team, the agency was aware of the time constraints, and was under tremendous pressure to complete the review in what the agency viewed as an unreasonable timeframe. In response to the pressure from the other parties, the federal representative at the table acknowledged the time constraints, said the agency would do what it could to help the project go forward, but did not make any promises. This was an act of courage and leadership, as the agency representative explained that cutting corners on the review might only jeopardize the project, subjecting it to legal challenges. Some of the collaborative partners were disappointed, but the agency held to its position. In the closing days before the deadline, however, the agency staff worked around the clock to get the review and approval done within the necessary timeline. On the morning the project was to begin, with crew and equipment waiting, the federal agency approved the project. The other collaborative partners were very much aware of the agency's extraordinary effort to meet the deadline, and the tremendous social capital the agency earned as a result was instrumental in the later success of the project.

Leadership Tool 10: Finding Mutual Affiliation

We have a tendency to define others in a collaborative process through the binary lens of the issue being discussed, that is, people at the table are either private-sector or public-sector, pro-environment or pro-business, and so on. We then ascribe a whole range of attributes to them based upon those categorizations. More importantly, we place higher trust in those who share our category and reserve less for those in another category (Moore et al. 25).

But human beings are not one-dimensional. Everyone has multiple facets, multiple ways by which to identify themselves, which, when explored, can create stronger interpersonal bonds and trust. This, in turn, creates greater opportunities for collaboration (Enfield). Mutual affiliations are a particularly rich way of establishing relationships, which is why strangers meeting for the first time in many cultures tend to comment on the current weather, the one thing they know they have in common. It is also why two people on a first date, or the initial stages of a friendship, spend considerable time and energy looking for mutual affiliations as evidence of connection (You're into minor league baseball? Me, too!).

Those most skilled in collaboration intrinsically understand all of this, and will invest the time to listen more deeply to others' experiences and perhaps even find mutual affiliations. These affiliations become what Nicholas Enfield refers to as common ground, a foundation upon which trust and cooperation can be built. By finding mutual affiliations, we "invest in a resource that will be drawn on later, with interest," says Enfield, by creating a greater degree of trust, commitment, and intimacy (223). Mutual affiliations remind us of our human complexity, that we are more than our policy positions, and in turn help us to listen to one another.

We recall a recent course where students were asked to break into pairs and get to know one another. One student had been quiet and less engaged with his classmates. As he began sharing information, however, it came out that he and his assigned partner were both musicians. Once this mutual affiliation was established, it was like turning on a switch. He seemed to relax a bit, and he became much more engaged and talkative.

We will often structure time in the collaborative process itself for participants to get to know one another, to share these other dimensions of themselves. We also use field trips for this purpose. In addition to giving people time to make these informal connections, the shared experience of the field trip itself, the "joint attention," as Enfield describes it, becomes its own mutual affiliation, its own common ground (224).

Of course, there are limitations to how far mutual affiliation can go. The complexity of human identity has other implications, which sometimes result in compounded disadvantage. Participants, facilitators, and conveners should therefore be attentive to the intersectionality of identities that can sometimes exacerbate oppression (Crenshaw 14). For example, the experience of a Black lesbian is different and more complex than the experience of a white straight woman, a Black man, or a white lesbian. The dynamics of intersectionality are at play whenever collaborative governance participants seek to forge identity-based or other affiliations.

Conclusion

In a collaborative governance process, everyone has both the opportunity and responsibility for leadership, to change the course of the project for the better. The ten leadership tools listed above are useful in any group setting, but may be pivotal in setting and adjusting the course of a collaborative governance project.

References

Axelrod, Robert. *The Evolution of Cooperation*. New York Basic Books, 1984.

Covey, Stephen. *The 7 Habits of Highly Effective People*. Free Press, 1989.

Crenshaw, Kimberle. "Demarginalizing the Intersection of Race and Sex: A Black Feminist Critique of Antidiscrimination Doctrine, Feminist Theory, and Antiracist Politics." *Chicago Law Review*, vol. 1989, no. 1, 1989, pp. 139–167.

Enfield, Nicholas J. "Common Ground as a Resource for Social Affiliation." *Intention, Common Ground, and the Ego Centric Speaker-Hearer*, edited by I. Kecskes and J.L. Mey. Mouton de Gruyter, 2008.

Fisher, Roger, and Scott Brown. *Getting Together: Building a Relationship That Gets to Yes*. Houghton Mifflin, 1988.

Fisher, Roger, and Daniel Shapiro. *Beyond Reason: Using Emotions as You Negotiate*. Penguin Books, 2006.

Kruger, Justin, et al. "Egocentrism Over E-mail: Can We Communicate as Well as We Think?" *Journal of Personality and Social Psychology*, vol. 89, no. 6, 2005, pp. 925–936.

Mayer, Bernard. *The Dynamics of Conflict Resolution: A Practitioner's Guide*. John Wiley and Sons, 2000.

McCarthy, Robert E. *Navigating With Trust: Transform Your Organization With Energy, Direction and Joint Effort*. Rock Bench Publishing, 2012.

McCraty, R., and D. Childre. "The Grateful Heart: The Psychophysiology of Appreciation." *Series in Affective Science. The Psychology of Gratitude*, edited by R. A. Emmons and M. E. McCullough, Oxford UP, 2004, pp. 230–255.

Mehrabian, A., and S. R. Ferris. "Inference of Attitudes from Nonverbal Communication in Two Channels." *Journal of Consulting Psychology*, vol. 31, no. 3, 1967, pp. 248–252.

Moore, Don A., et al. "Long and Short Routes to Success in Electronically Mediated Negotiations: Group Affiliations and Good Vibrations." *Organizational Behavior and Human Decision Processes*, vol. 77, no. 1, 1999, pp. 22–43.

Nowak, Martin, and Roger Highfield. *Super Cooperators: Altruism, Evolution, and Why We Need Each Other to Succeed*. Free Press, 2012.

Okdie, B. M., et al. "Getting to Know You: Face-to-Face Versus Online Interactions." *Computers in Human Behavior*, 2011.

Ostrom, Elinor. "A Behavioral Approach to the Rational Choice Theory of Collective Action: Presidential Address, American Political Science 1997." *American Political Review*, vol. 92, no. 1, March 1998, pp. 1–22.

Thrimm, Caja. "Technically-Mediated Interpersonal Communication." *Handbook of Personal Communication*, edited by Gerd Antos et al., Mouton de Gruyter, 2008.

CONCLUSION

In this book, we sought to explore the crossroads where theory and practice meet, or at least the intersection where they touch and move on. In our experience, theory and practice meet and diverge and meet again, each one testing and strengthening the other. Because collaborative governance is a comparatively new field of practice and study, there are many directions a book like this could have taken. We opted to situate it in the practical, the place where students and practitioners and public managers might apply theory—and especially lessons learned—to the real-life issues they encounter in their communities.

Throughout this book, we have highlighted not only the instances where collaborative governance has succeeded—which are numerous—but also the instances where it has not or has not as of yet. We have grappled with times where the practice gets ahead of the theory. And vice versa. And, we have written about the places where collaborative governance still has not entirely lived up to its democratic promise, particularly in the area of racial justice.

In the incredibly dynamic political and social context in which collaborative governance operates, there are bound to be new questions to explore, as well as old ones that are still not entirely resolved. For example, questions surrounding the authority and legitimacy of collaborative governance processes are evergreen. Whenever actual power is at stake, there will be a challenge to the legitimacy of the process. More than anything, those challenges are a sign that collaborative governance provides a platform where real influence is exerted. And yet, questions of authority and legitimacy cannot be glibly dismissed. In order to ensure that collaborative governance groups are operating with due authority—as well as with integrity—they should tack as close as possible to the definitional norms set forth in chapter 1, and they should cultivate the sense of democratic stewardship discussed in chapter 2.

Questions of legitimacy and authority are closely related to another perennial question—the question of whether and how to institutionalize the practice of collaborative governance. With regard to the legitimacy question, specific authorizing legislation at the state or even the local level can create sustainability for collaborative governance platforms and can provide clarity both for parties directly involved in collaborative governance processes and for members of the public who might otherwise be watching suspiciously from the sidelines.

A word of caution is in order here. Part of what has made collaborative governance so successful in addressing otherwise intractable problems has been its flexibility. At the conceptual level, collaborative governance has its roots in political science and public administration, yes, but also in human development and game theory and dispute resolution, as well as in other disciplines. The interdisciplinary nature[1] of collaborative governance gives its adherents a broad range of ideas and practices from which to draw, and formal institutionalization might well narrow some of those options. Similarly, because individual collaborative governance processes are fully conceived only after a thorough assessment, each process is designed to meet the particular needs of the community at hand. If the practices and protocols of collaborative governance become too institutionalized, that institutionalization has the potential to suffocate some of the flexibility and creativity that made collaborative governance successful in the first place. It will continue to be important for theoreticians, practitioners, and advocates for collaborative governance to manage the tension between the tempting solidity of explicit authorization and the creative responsiveness of a flexible system.

Because the context in which collaborative governance operates is so dynamic, scholars and practitioners also must attend to the line between ongoing adaptation and abandonment of principles. We know that collaboration is practiced in many different ways in our communities. Sometimes it is called cooperation or mediation or even neighborliness. Sometimes it is called nothing at all, but it bears many of the characteristics that we describe throughout this book. Those of us who are regular practitioners of collaborative governance cannot be so arrogant as to believe that our vocabulary is the pinnacle of what collaborative governance is and can become.

That said, however, "collaboration" is an easy word to toss around, and it can be used so frequently and in so many contexts that it ends up meaning nothing at all. It seems as if, everywhere we turn, there is someone else staking a claim to collaboration. Some of these self-described collaborations are robust and rigorous, and we can and should learn from them. In other instances, however, calling something "collaboration" is an attempt to prop-up a milquetoast exchange of information or the parallel play discussed at length in chapter 9. This is where we turn back to the definitional norms for guidance. As we learn to adapt collaborative governance to be more culturally responsive, and as we become more adept at recognizing forms of collaborative governance in unexpected contexts, the definitional norms of public purpose, cross-boundary participation, representativeness, inclusiveness and belonging, shared authority and power-balancing, and deliberativeness, can help separate the wheat from the chaff.

Similarly, we are also deeply curious about how collaborative governance or its close cousins show up in countries other than our own. In recent years, we have had contact with an increasing number of scholars and practitioners from outside the United States. We have developed a mutually enriching learning network with scholars and practitioners in Finland, Vietnam, the United Kingdom, and elsewhere. From those conversations and partnerships, we have become increasingly curious about the essential preconditions of collaborative governance. We devoted a good deal of this book to the legal, structural, social, cultural, and interpersonal preconditions for a successful collaborative governance process. We wonder what happens when those preconditions are different. For example, we wonder whether or how collaborative governance might work in a non-democratic regime or in a culture in which the citizens are unpracticed in deliberation in their day-to-day lives. We wonder how the practices—and even the norms—that seem so unassailable here in the United States might differ in contexts around the world. We wonder whether the dynamics of human interaction that we have presented as universal—or at least typical—might be at least somewhat culturally constructed, and how those dynamics might play out in a different context. All that is to say that we are eager to further explore collaborative governance's place in a diverse and ever-changing world.

That humility extends to our work here in the United States, as well. As we have discussed throughout this book, we—both as active participants in the American system of governance and as individual citizens—are in the midst of an existential struggle that requires us to look directly at the legacy of white supremacy, racism, and xenophobia that is baked into our culture and our institutions. Mere looking, however, is not enough. It is incumbent on us, as students and practitioners of collaborative governance, to disrupt racism and dismantle other patterns of oppression when they show up in our processes. For us, that is the learning edge. We have been working along that edge for several years, and we have learned a great deal. But we have also gotten it wrong sometimes. And we have undoubtedly made mistakes and missed things in this book, too. But that is also part of the work—staying alert to racism and other oppressions, interrupting them where we can, and then continuing to interrogate where we could have done better.

But even in that humility, we leave you on an evangelical note. If practiced well and with integrity, collaborative governance works. We have seen these practices help pull communities through decades-old conflicts and harrowing disasters and persistent inertia. We have seen a community devastated by a changing economy transform itself into a creative hub with a bright future. We have seen a group of neighbors with a good idea attract millions of dollars to build a park in their otherwise paved-over neighborhood. We have seen former adversaries band together to protect their joint achievements from outside agitators and then work together on a series of new projects.

Meanwhile, we write this during one of the most challenging and inspiring summers of our lifetimes—the fissures of political polarization are as deep as they have ever been, wildfires have decimated communities and landscapes in our state and neighboring states, misinformation is blossoming faster than traditional news organizations can respond, a global pandemic still rages, white nationalism is on the rise, and yet demands for racial justice and a more democratic society are clear and persistent. So as we look into the future, no outcome is guaranteed. Democracy might be on the ascendency, or it might be on the decline. We need the principles and practices of collaborative governance more than we ever have. We need the theory and practice of collaborative governance to cross-pollinate. We need to build a table devoted to public purposes that is cross-boundary, representative, inclusive, power-sharing, and deliberative, and it is our fondest hope that this book might make a contribution to those efforts.

September 30, 2020
Stephen Greenwood
Laurel Singer
Wendy Willis

Note

1 Because collaborative governance is an interdisciplinary practice, there are lessons to be learned from still more disciplines. In particular, we are keen to learn more about how the tenets of popular education, mutual aid, and other forms of participatory democracy (such as sortition) might inform our work going forward.

INDEX